TO LIVE AND PLAY IN DIXIE

Pro Football's Entry into the Jim Crow South

ROBERT D. JACOBUS

Prometheus Books

Guilford, Connecticut

Prometheus Books

An imprint of The Rowman & Littlefield Publishing Group, Inc.
4501 Forbes Boulevard, Suite 200, Lanham, Maryland 20706
www.rowman.com

Distributed by NATIONAL BOOK NETWORK

British Library Cataloguing in Publication Information Available

Library of Congress Cataloging-in-Publication Data

Names: Jacobus, Robert, author.
Title: To live and play in Dixie : pro football's entry into the Jim Crow
    South / Robert D. Jacobus.
Description: Lanham, Maryland : Prometheus, 2021. | Includes
    bibliographical references and index. | Summary: "In post–World War II
    America, when professional football owners scheduled exhibition games in
    the South and later placed franchises, they simply overlooked Jim Crow
    conditions endured by African American players. To Live and Play in
    Dixie is an oral history from the players themselves on how they battled
    discrimination while playing and living in the still-segregated South"—
    Provided by publisher.
Identifiers: LCCN 2021013661 (print) | LCCN 2021013662 (ebook) | ISBN
    9781633886827 (cloth) | ISBN 9781633886834 (epub)
Subjects: LCSH: National Football League—History—20th century. | American
    Football League—History. | Football—Social aspects—Southern
    States—History—20th century. | African American football
    players—History—20th century. | African
    Americans—Segregation—Southern States—History—20th century. | Race
    discrimination—Southern States—History—20th century.
Classification: LCC GV955.5.N35 J34 2021 (print) | LCC GV955.5.N35
    (ebook) | DDC 796.330975/0904—dc23
LC record available at https://lccn.loc.gov/2021013661
LC ebook record available at https://lccn.loc.gov/2021013662

To Eva, my everything

CONTENTS

FOREWORD

It was 1965, and I was attempting to do the impossible—secure my spot on the roster of the Green Bay Packers. They were being called by many the greatest professional team of all time, even before they won three NFL championships in a row.

Still, making the team was by no means my biggest challenge.

I was coming from Georgia Tech, where Coach Bobby Dodd was the epitome of the southern gentleman. Coach Vince Lombardi of the Packers was the exact opposite of Coach Dodd in a lot of ways—by no means "southern" in any sense of the word. He was profane, Catholic, Italian, a Yankee, loud, demanding. Playing for him came as a bit of a culture shock, to say the least.

But playing for Coach Lombardi was still not my biggest challenge.

The biggest challenge I faced was that in all my years of playing in the late fifties through the mid-sixties, I had never been on a team with an African American person, aside from some all-star games. I was a naive twenty-two-year-old, southern white boy, and I found myself utterly unprepared and unsure of how to conduct myself in such a diverse setting. I found myself thrust into a situation I had never been in before. Everything was up in the air.

I walked into that locker room, looked around, and in my young mind reasoned that these African American guys would hear my southern accent, knock me out on the practice field, injure me, and send me home. I knew enough about the struggle for civil rights in the United States that I wouldn't have blamed them. It was a time of great change in our country, and tensions were high. I was acutely aware of all this as I made my first steps to joining the Packers squad.

To Live and Play in Dixie

Fortunately, I was able to find my footing soon enough, thanks to several factors. An overwhelming desire to compete burned inside of me. With every fiber of my being, I wanted to belong, to become a Packer. This passion still rings true for me today: If I'm trying to make your team, I will give you my heart, every day, every play. My fire was fueled by the careful mentorship and support of great leaders of all races and backgrounds on the Packers team. In addition to being incredibly talented, they were also wonderful human beings. I began to see way more similarities than differences, as my naivete, fears, and hesitancy faded. Soon enough, we began to press forward like a well-oiled machine, driven by our shared goal.

Indeed, the Green Bay Packers had the greatest team of all time up until that point. Nobody could beat us. Coach Lombardi was special for many reasons, but in my opinion, his best attribute was his zero-tolerance policy for racism. While other teams had no African American players—and even had the nerve to brag about it—Lombardi had ten black players on his forty-man roster. He cared about two things: Can you play? Are you a decent person? That's all.

Walking out of the team meeting one night, I was stopped by Willie Davis of Grambling State University, the future Hall of Fame defensive end and captain of the Packers defense. His manner exuded kindness as he looked me in the eye and said, "Bill, I have been watching you, and I think you can make our team. I'm going to help you." Willie told me that when I felt insecure, I could seek out his counsel. He assured me, "When Lombardi's screaming and you think you're going to pass out, come find me. I'll get you through it!"

Sure enough, he was true to his word. I should add that Marv Fleming, Elijah Pitts, and Herb Adderley were also especially helpful during my time with the Packers. I couldn't have asked for better mentors. Later on in my career, during my time with the Baltimore Colts, John Mackey became one of my closest friends and allies. We would spend hours sharing our stories, and he prodded me into succeeding him as president of the NFL Players Association.

In fact, since my early days as an outsider in the Packers locker room, the entirety of my time in the NFL has been filled with unexpected, undeserved, and often unrewarded acts of kindness from amazing men, great leaders, and great players. My life was never the same after I joined the Packers and pushed myself to live beyond the bounds and restrictions imposed in late-fifties and early sixties southern football. My young mind was rewired and reshaped anew by my time in the Packers locker room. Beyond and indeed more valuable than championship plays and scrimmages, there I learned that we are all human beings, made of the same stuff, fighting for the same goals in life. After my time with Coach Lombardi and his incredible roster and staff, I was never the same.

If you have ever wondered what truly makes a great team, look no further than leaders who transcend absurd racism and illogical hatred to become a constant source of unselfish deeds in the pursuit of shared victory. The cultures formed by such leaders inspire players who refuse to let each other down when it's crunch time. Such leaders can transform the lives of impressionable young people forever, which I know from firsthand experience. My entire career is a testament to this fact.

Robert Jacobus's book, which details the lives, stories, and fabled careers of such pioneering players and leaders, is nothing short of astonishing. The sheer number of hours required to complete the exhaustive research for such a manuscript would overwhelm most. Jacobus's ability to document and write about the stories herein with a lively and entertaining style is nothing short of a gift. Beyond this, *To Live and Play in Dixie* serves as an important historical document—it should be required reading for every person aiming for a career in professional sports.

Most importantly, this book memorializes the unsung heroes, both on and off the field, who bore the sting of cruel taunts, job loss, humiliation, forced segregation, and more. During the timeframe documented throughout these pages, some African American players even endured unthinkable intrusions into their relationships and marital choices. These stories deserve to be documented, honored, and remembered. Jacobus has seen to this in a unique and powerful way, ensuring that the stories are told—lest we forget the sacrifices and bravery of those who have gone before us and paved a way for our lives and traditions today.

When I showed up in the Packers' locker room in 1965, I missed by a scant couple of years the embarrassment, confusion, and divisiveness that must have loomed over my would-be teammates as they dealt with widespread institutional racism. Would those giants of the gridiron have welcomed and nurtured a clueless white boy if they were still enduring the horrors of such injustice?

I guess we'll never know, but this much I do know: If my teammates don't deserve to be treated like real human beings, then neither do I. Nor does any human being. We can all consider ourselves to be on the same team, pressing down the great field of life together, one yard at a time—a great lesson for all of humanity.

Bill Curry
April 7, 2021

PREFACE

While the story of the reintegration of professional football in 1946 after World War II is a topic that has been covered, there is a little-known aspect of this integration that has not been fully explored.

After World War II and up until the mid- to late 1960s, the All-America Football Conference (AAFC), the National Football League (NFL), and the American Football League (AFL) scheduled numerous preseason games in the South. Once African American players started dotting the rosters of these professional teams, they had to endure Jim Crow conditions while playing games in the South. Early on, players were barred from playing in some cities. Most encountered segregated accommodations when they stayed in southern cities. And when African American football fans came to see their favorite black players perform, they were relegated to segregated seating conditions.

To add to the challenges these African American players and fans endured, the AAFC, NFL, and AFL gradually started placing franchises in still-segregated cities as early as 1937 in Washington, DC; 1946 in Miami; 1950 in Baltimore; and 1952 in Dallas. Then, in 1960, the new AFL placed franchises in Dallas and Houston, and the NFL followed suit by placing a franchise in Dallas that year. Now, instead of just visiting a southern city for a day or so to play an exhibition game, African American players that were on the rosters of these southern teams had to live in these still-segregated cities. Many of these players, being from the North or West Coast, had never dealt with de jure or even de facto Jim Crow laws.

Team owners rarely took into account (or cared about) the challenges that black draft picks would face while playing in the South. Exhibition games were big moneymakers for the owners, and they cared little if at all about the Jim Crow conditions the African American players would endure. The same applied when pro football franchises were placed in the South.

Early on, if the African American players didn't toe the line or fought back (via contract disputes, openly engaging in interracial relationships, protesting living accommodations in the South, protesting segregated seating, etc.), they were traded, cut, and even blackballed from the league. Eventually, though, as the civil rights movement gained steam in the 1950s and 1960s, African American players were able to protest the conditions in the South with success. Much of what happened in professional football during this time period coincided with or mirrored major historical events in America and the civil rights movement.

Parallels can be drawn between key events in professional football in the Jim Crow South and the mobilization of the civil rights movement. For example, in August 1963, four black Oakland Raiders forced their exhibition game to be moved from Mobile, Alabama, because of segregated seating. Just four days later, Dr. Martin Luther King Jr. gave his "I Have a Dream" speech at the March on Washington. Then, ten days after King's speech, the Houston Oilers opened their home season at Jeppesen Stadium, which upheld a policy of segregated seating—the last professional sports franchise to practice this policy. August 31, 1957, marked the last time a black player was prohibited from playing in an exhibition game in the South, when John Henry Johnson of the Detroit Lions was banned in Birmingham. Just five days later, on September 4, 1957, the Little Rock Nine attempted to integrate Little Rock Central High School.

To Live and Play in Dixie is mainly an oral history—one that focuses on the experiences of the African American players who lived through these challenging times, told mostly in their own words. This book uses oral history and extensive interviews to tell the story of these athletes, using an approach that is similar to the one used for my first two books: *Houston Cougars in the 1960s: Death Threats, the Veer Offense, and the Game of the Century* (2015) and *Black Man in the Huddle: Stories from the Integration of Texas Football* (2019).

The idea (or story) for *To Live and Play in Dixie* rose out of the early manuscript for *Black Man in the Huddle*. The original intent for that book was to not only examine the integration of high school and college football in Texas but also look at when the professional franchises of the Dallas Cowboys, Dallas Texans, and Houston Oilers arrived on the professional football scene in 1960 while those two cities were still segregated. Those franchises all had African American players on their rosters as well as opposing teams with African American players who traveled to those cities for away games. I interviewed former Cowboys, Texans, and Oilers players from the early 1960s, as well as players who came to these two cities to play those franchises, and formulated a couple of chapters chronicling their experiences.

After these chapters were completed, much to my surprise, I discovered that the first version of the Dallas Texans, a 1952 NFL franchise, had two African American players on their roster: Buddy Young and George Taliaferro. I then created a chapter that discussed what the conditions in Dallas were like for these two Texans players and their families. Due to the length of these chapters and a limitation on the overall length of *Black Man in the Huddle*, I decided to cut the chapters on professional football from the final manuscript; however, those three chapters on the early Texas franchises weren't long enough to sustain a whole new book in and of themselves.

I decided to dig further and expand my research. I got to thinking: Were there other cities that were segregated when professional football reintegrated after World War II? How did African American players deal with those conditions in places like Baltimore and Washington, DC? I then discovered that pro football franchises from all three post–World War II leagues (the AAFC, the NFL, and the AFL) played a large number of exhibition games in the South in the first twenty years after reintegration. Once again, the question arose: How did African American players adapt to playing, staying, and traveling in the South? I decided to set out and interview as many of these former players as possible to capture their experiences before their words were lost forever to the tides of time and history. And I didn't restrict my interviews to just African American players from that time period; white players and coaches, some fans (black and white), and select office personnel were also consulted.

The players interviewed for this book are a virtual who's who of pro football rosters in the 1950s and 1960s. Included in the interviews are seven members of the Pro Football Hall of Fame: Dave Robinson, Jerry Kramer, Bud Grant, Gino Marchetti, Lenny Moore, Tom Flores, and Bobby Mitchell.

In addition, George Taliaferro, who in 1949 was the first black player to be drafted by the NFL (and ended up playing in the AAFC), and Wally Triplett, who was drafted the same year and became the first black draftee to play in the league, were interviewed before they both passed away in the fall of 2018. Sherman Howard was the oldest living African American player interviewed, at age ninety-four (before passing away in December

2019); Willie Irvin was the oldest surviving player to come from a historically black college and university (HBCU).

The players interviewed for this book combined for ninety-seven selections to the Pro Bowl and were collectively selected fifty-two times as a first-team all-pro. In 2019, Gino Marchetti was chosen number thirty-nine and Lenny Moore number ninety-four on the NFL's top one hundred players of all time. Marchetti, Moore, and Jerry Kramer were selected to the NFL fiftieth anniversary team in 1969, and Marchetti was also named to the NFL's seventy-fifth anniversary team in 1994. Six players interviewed were chosen as rookie of the year in their respective leagues. Eleven of the players interviewed had their jersey numbers retired by their teams.

Luckily, I was able to capture many of these players' thoughts before they passed away. As far as I can tell, the interviews that many of these players were kind enough to provide me were very possibly the last they ever gave before they passed. Unfortunately, numerous other players I interviewed for this book have since departed, including all of the members of the 1952 Dallas Texans (who I interviewed between the spring of 2016 and the spring of 2018): Zollie Toth, George Taliaferro, Gino Marchetti, Don Colo, Joe Reid, and Chuck Ortmann. There are now no surviving members of the Texans. The only person I interviewed who is still alive and connected with the Texans in some way is Geraldine Young, the widow of Buddy Young, who lived in Dallas while her husband was playing for the Texans and had to endure the Jim Crow South for a few torturous months.

Sadly, this book could have been even better. Numerous players were unable to provide interviews because of dementia, Parkinson's disease, or chronic traumatic encephalopathy (CTE), a brain disease caused by repeated head injuries. I will not mention any of the names of these players out of respect for them and their families; however, many of them were Pro Bowl–caliber players, and their stories would have enhanced the narrative even more if they had been healthy enough to be interviewed. Some players who were afflicted by these conditions were able to add to the narrative, but in many cases, the amount of information they could provide was very limited.

Unfortunately, to make matters more difficult for these former players, most of them received very little in the form of a pension, disability pay, or other benefits from the NFL, since their careers ended well before 1993, when the NFL Players Association signed a collective bargaining agreement that granted NFL players full free agency. Any player whose career ended before then ended up with greatly reduced benefits. A ten-year NFL veteran who retired before 1993 (around four thousand players total) receives somewhere between $24,000 and $43,560 a year before taxes at age fifty-five. In comparison, Major League Baseball players who retired after 1980 receive $200,000 per year at age sixty-two, and ten-year NBA veterans receive $215,000 a year at age sixty-two if they retired after 1965. It should be noted that playing ten years in the NFL is uncommon, since the physical demands of professional football often leave the players with shorter careers (3.3 years on average) than their professional counterparts in baseball and basketball. In addition, more NFL players have health issues to deal with after retirement, including dementia, Parkinson's, and CTE because of repeated head trauma. This is compounded by the fact that pre-1993 NFL players don't receive health insurance options after retirement like present-day players do. The early players are also excluded from the NFL's 401(k) plan and subsequent annuity, a health reimbursement account, and the option to continue on the NFL life insurance plan.

Without going into too much detail (again, out of respect for the players and their families), it should be noted that several individuals with whom I had face-to-face interviews at their residences are living in impoverished conditions, partially because of the way the present-day NFL has chosen to ignore them and their needs. These are men whose sacrifices helped create the modern NFL, and this should be duly noted, not just in print but in compensation. The NFL should take care of their own. Just as troubling and perhaps even far worse than the afflictions of dementia and CTE brought on by brain trauma on the field is the way the NFL has treated these players who helped make the organization the multibillion-dollar industry it is today.

This book is a tribute to these brave men, both living and passed on, who not only had to endure Jim Crow conditions in the South after World War II but also continue to rise from adversity long after their careers have ended. May their words be a source of inspiration for football fans and freedom fighters alike—and their legacy live on through the ages.

1

SLOW PROGRESS AND THE FACE OF CHANGE

The Post–World War II Integration of Pro Football

In 1949, Wally Triplett, a star running back from Penn State, became the first African American in the post–World War II era to be drafted and actually suit up for an NFL franchise. He joined the Detroit Lions as a nineteenth-round draft pick, a groundbreaking and controversial move for the Lions that ushered in a new, inclusive era for pro football in the United States. But the transition was far from smooth, as Triplett and his teammates faced the looming prejudices of not only mainstream America, but also the Jim Crow South. Obstacles posed by institutionalized racism and de jure segregation seemed to meet Triplett at every turn as he bravely pioneered a new dawn for what is today hailed as America's most popular major-league sport.

Triplett recalled the state of the nation at the time of his entry into pro football:

> America was not what it is today back in 1946 and 1947. It was a black-and-white situation. Negroes couldn't do certain things, and whites wouldn't let Negroes do certain things. There were unwritten rules. It was a lonely life—one you had to live carefully. People didn't think anything of not including you. That's what America was about back then—to no fault of a lot of people who you wanted to give fault to. It was just a different world. America as a whole was that way.

As far as football was concerned, Triplett added,

> In the postwar years, football became a game played by all [races] mainly in the East and the Midwest, but not so much in the South. Football in the South was played by white people for the pleasure of white people,

Wally Triplett, Detroit Lions. *Wally Triplet*

and they wanted to keep it that way. I myself was witness to that, first in college at Penn State and then as a member of the Lions.

When Triplett was added to the rosters of both Penn State and later the Lions, he and his teammates inevitably traveled South, where they faced fierce opposition both on and off the field. Sometimes African American players met defeat before they even entered the locker room. In the first of many incidents to come, while a sophomore at Penn State, Triplett (along with black teammate Dennie Hoggard) was denied the chance to play in a game against the University of Miami to open the 1946 season. Rather than not take Triplett and Hoggard to Miami, the Nittany Lions canceled the game.

Despite the institutionalized efforts of the Jim Crow South, racist re-strictions on black players did not withstand the test of time. After Triplett's junior season, Penn State traveled to Dallas on New Year's Day in 1948 to play in the Cotton Bowl against the Doak Walker–led Southern Methodist University Mustangs. Here, Triplett and Hoggard became the first African Americans to play in a college football game in the South. Triplett had broken down barriers for college football. Now, in the pros with the NFL's Detroit Lions, he faced a whole new ballgame.

After being drafted by the Lions, Triplett once again encountered situations in the South where he was denied the opportunity to play alongside his teammates. Early in his career, he was barred from preseason games in New Orleans and Birmingham. In the Jim Crow South, football was a sport exclusively for white people, and the same held true in other sports like Major League Baseball.

Then World War II happened and everything changed. White America began to adopt a different attitude toward African Americans in general after they helped defeat fascism in World War II. Approximately one million African Americans served in the military during the war. While they didn't fight alongside their white comrades, as troops were still segregated, they nonetheless fought and sacrificed their lives for their country. This helped jump-start the reintegration of professional football (and baseball) when the troops returned in 1945, while also adding steam to the fledgling post–World War II civil rights movement. To sum up the feelings of many after World War II, Major League Baseball Commissioner Albert "Happy" Chandler said, "Many people questioned that if blacks could die for their country to free the world of fascism, why were they not allowed to participate on the playing fields with whites?"

Like the military, the world of professional football was segregated up until 1946, as was Major League Baseball, which was by far the most popular sport. No African American had played pro football since 1933, and none had been signed by a Major League Baseball team in the twentieth century, due in large part to the previous commissioner of baseball, Kenesaw Mountain Landis, who served from 1920 to 1944. Although some maverick owners like Bill Veeck of the Cleveland Indians had expressed interest in signing black players, Landis, as commissioner, would not approve their contracts.

After Landis passed away in 1944, he was succeeded by Chandler in April 1945. Thanks to the newfound attitude toward African Americans held by many, Jackie Robinson's contract was ultimately approved by Chandler, enabling him to become the first African American Major League player since Moses "Fleetwood" Walker suited up for the Toledo Blue Stockings in 1884. Chandler supported Robinson's signing on October 23, 1945, with Branch Rickey and the Brooklyn Dodgers organization. As commissioner, he could have voided Robinson's contract, but chose not to. Chandler also didn't tolerate any backlash from teams or fans against Robinson.

Chandler reflected on Landis and the right of African Americans to play:

For twenty-four years, Landis would not let a black man play. I had his records and I read them, and for twenty-four years Landis consistently blocked any attempts to put blacks and whites together on a big-league field. I was named commissioner in April of 1945. Two black writers from the *Pittsburgh Courier* came to see me. They asked where I stood on the issue, and I said, "If a black man can fight at Iwo Jima or Okinawa, they should be able to play baseball."

Chandler later commented to Rickey, the man who signed Robinson to his contract:

Branch, I've done a lot of thinking about the racial situation in our country. As a member of the Senate Military Affairs Committee, I got to know a lot about our casualties in the war. Plenty of Negro boys were willing to go out and fight and die for this country. Is it right for me [to say] when they come back that they can't play the national pastime? You know, Branch, I'm going to have to meet my maker someday. If he asks me why I didn't let this boy play, and if I say it's because he's black, that might not be a satisfactory answer. If the Lord made some people white and some black and some red and some yellow, he must have had a pretty good reason. It isn't my job to decide which colors can play big-league baseball. It's my job to see that the game is played fairly and that everyone has a fair chance. I think if I do that, I can face my maker with a clear conscience.

In addition to the signing of Robinson by the Dodgers organization, another significant event that arose for the benefit of African American football players was the creation of a new professional football league in 1946—one that gave more African American players the opportunity to play where they previously did not have the chance.

The All-America Football Conference started after World War II as a rival to the NFL. The league lasted four seasons, with the Cleveland Browns dominating the league, winning all four championships while fashioning a 52–4–3 record over that time period. The league was dissolved at the conclusion of the 1949 season and three of its franchises—the Browns, the San Francisco 49ers, and the Baltimore Colts—were absorbed into the NFL for the 1950 season.

At first, some in the African American community had their doubts about a new professional football league helping to reintegrate the sport. On January 12, 1946, *Pittsburgh Courier* sports columnist Wendell Smith lamented the fact that the new AAFC would be segregated because a team was put in Miami:

Any hopes fans may have had for Negro players in the new All-American Conference . . . died recently when a franchise was awarded to a syndicate in Miami. The insertion of Miami into the new loop killed all chances for Negro players, for that city is one of the most Nazi-fied of all the cities in the world on the matter of racial equality. All-America Conference officials . . . will tell you that there will be no ban against Negro players. But you can bet that Sunday topper there'll be no such young men admitted into the league. We figured that the organization might be operated by more liberal men—men who wouldn't draw the color line as the NFL has been doing for years. But it's the same old story: Negroes won't be permitted to play.

Smith's fears, fortunately, were mostly unfounded. First of all, the Browns, coached by Paul Brown, were, along with the Rams, the first post–World War II pro football team to have African American players. In August 1946, Brown signed fullback Marion Motley, who had played college football at the University of Nevada and then later for Brown at the Great Lakes Naval Training Station football team, and defensive tackle Bill Willis, who played for Brown at Ohio State from 1942 to 1944.

The AAFC was more progressive than the NFL in signing black players. In the four years the AAFC existed (1946–1949), the league was a trendsetter in signing black players. During this four-year period, the NFL saw only seven African American players come into the league. By contrast, during the same time, the AAFC employed twenty-one African American players. Eventually, NFL owners—now that they were in competition with the AAFC for players, profits, and survival—didn't tend to look so much at skin color when signing new talent. This created more opportunities for black players in the NFL, with players being rightfully judged by their stats, not their skin color.

Coincidentally, on the same day that Wendell Smith expressed his doubts about the AAFC employing black players, another incident helped fuel the reintegration of professional football. The Los Angeles Coliseum Commission was a recently created organization whose meetings tended to concern typical administrative affairs, mostly dealing with entities that wanted to use the LA stadium. However, on January 12, 1946, the Cleveland Rams, who less than a month earlier had claimed the NFL title with a tense 15–14 decision over the Washington Redskins, decided they were going to move their franchise to Los Angeles, thus becoming the first professional sports franchise to be located on the West Coast. On January 15, Rams general manager Charles Walsh and other team executives flew to Los Angeles to negotiate a lease from the Coliseum Commission to allow the

Rams to play in the 100,000-plus-seat stadium. What Walsh didn't count
on running into at the meeting was a group of editors and sportswriters
from black newspapers in the Los Angeles area.

These newspapermen, led by *Los Angeles Tribune* sports editor Halley
Harding, came with the goal of persuading the Coliseum Commission to
deny the Rams the right to lease the stadium unless they agreed to sign
black players. This was not the first time Harding protested matters, and it
would not be the last. He was no stranger to controversy or standing up for
rights for blacks. A Chicago native, Harding had been a football, baseball,
and basketball star at Wiley College in Marshall, Texas. He played football
there for Melvin B. Tolson, who was also the college's legendary debate
team coach (later immortalized in the 2007 movie *The Great Debaters*, starring Denzel Washington as Tolson). After college, Harding had been an
actor and played basketball briefly for the Savoy Big Five, an all-black team
that was a precursor to the Harlem Globetrotters. He also played in the
Negro leagues for the Philadelphia Giants and Kansas City Monarchs, and
in later years, he served as manager for Satchel Paige's affairs.

A very outgoing and opinionated man, Harding often rubbed people
the wrong way. He wrote for black newspapers in Baltimore, Chicago, and
Pittsburgh, and used his pulpit as sports editor of the *Los Angeles Tribune*
to champion the causes of African Americans. Using just 1943 as an example—three years before he appeared before the Coliseum Commission
—Harding led pickets in the spring to force the Los Angeles Angels minor-
league team to integrate. That summer, he pressured the Pacific Coast
League, of which the Angels were a member, to integrate as well. Not
stopping with the PCL, in 1943 he enlisted the help of President Franklin
D. Roosevelt in his campaign to pressure Kenesaw Mountain Landis to
integrate Major League Baseball.

With the decision of Major League Baseball to allow African Americans to play, it seemed natural that the other U.S. professional sport at the
time, the National Football League (the NBA did not begin play until
the 1946–1947 season), would follow suit by signing black players. Like
Kenesaw Mountain Landis and his crusade to keep African Americans
off the same field as white players, the NFL had a gentleman's agreement
among the owners not to let blacks play. It appears the catalyst behind this
agreement was Washington Redskins owner George Preston Marshall.
Thus, by his influence (along with many others), from 1933 to 1945, African American football players were denied the chance to compete in the
NFL. But all that was about to change.

After Charles Walsh spoke to the commission at their January 15 meeting about items such as length of the lease; how gate receipts, television revenue, and concessions would be split; and dates for home games, Halley Harding got up to speak. He proceeded to launch into a four-minute speech that caught the commission completely off guard. Because of his defiant words and harsh criticisms of the institution of segregation, Harding, who is little remembered today, turned out to be a key player in the reintegration of the NFL. He refused to allow the men in the room to overlook the NFL's self-imposed ban on African American players from 1933 to 1945. His speech had a ripple effect that carries on to this day.

During his remarks, Harding laid the origins of the ban on black players since 1933 at the feet of Marshall. He traced the Jim Crow policy directly to Marshall's influence from the 1932 inception of the Braves franchise in Boston, of which Marshall was the owner. In 1937, Marshall moved the Braves to Washington, DC, which was still segregated, and renamed the team the Redskins. Harding then argued that permitting a league that barred black players from using the Los Angeles Coliseum was nothing less than a retreat from democracy. He talked about how it was strange that Kenny Washington of UCLA, who just a few years earlier had been the top player on the West Coast—and, in all likelihood, the nation as well—had received nary a look from the NFL. He also lamented the poor treatment and lack of recognition of pioneering black players like Fritz Pollard and Joe Lillard.

After Harding's speech, Herman Hill of the *Pittsburgh Courier*, who was also in attendance, said, "Walsh was really shook up." Abe Robinson, a reporter for the *California Eagle*, another black newspaper, said that Walsh "turned pale and started to stutter." According to Hill, Coliseum Commission member Roger W. Jessup then said, "I just want you to know that if our Kenny Washington can't play, there will be no pro football in the Los Angeles Coliseum." Walsh, obviously feeling the pressure from all sides and faced with the potential impending loss of the use of the Los Angeles Coliseum if he didn't sign a black player, got up before the Coliseum Commission and said that "Kenny Washington or any other Negro football player is invited by me at this moment to try out for the Los Angeles Rams."

A week after the Coliseum Commission meeting, Harding met with some of the Rams' executives in a follow-up meeting at the Last Word, a black Los Angeles jazz club on South Central Avenue. Aided by a group of black newspaper writers, including ones from the *Los Angeles Sentinel* and *California Eagle*, along with Hill from the *Pittsburgh Courier*, he pressured

Charles Walsh and Rams PR director Maxwell Stiles into agreeing to sign former UCLA star Kenny Washington.

Walsh made good on his word when, on March 21, 1946, the Los Angeles Rams did indeed sign Washington, paving the way to his becoming the first African American to play in the NFL since Ray Kemp of the Pittsburgh Pirates and Joe Lillard of the Chicago Cardinals suited up for their respective teams in 1933. Washington was given a one-year, no-cut contract to show that his signing wasn't just a publicity stunt. It was also believed that since Washington was a local product, his signing would boost gate receipts and attract black fans. Rams assistant coach Bob Snyder said of signing Washington, "I doubt [we] would have been interested in Washington if we had stayed in Cleveland." After he signed with the Rams, Washington—who could not room with a white teammate on the road—needed a roommate for road games, and in May the Rams signed his former UCLA teammate Woody Strode to a contract.

Many felt Washington's signing had come too late, after he was past his prime. On March 22, 1946, *Los Angeles Times* columnist Dick Hyland wrote,

> I am most tempted to predict, flatly, that either Kenny will not make the grade or the class of ball played in the National League during 1946 is not going to be what most people will think it will be. Washington's "break" is coming five or six years too late. . . . Had Kenny Washington been signed by a National League team in 1940, he would undoubtedly have been . . . one of the greatest of professional backs and a drawing card from one end of the league to the other.

He added,

> But that was six years ago. In the meantime, Washington has become a beaten-up ballplayer who is neither so strong nor so quick in his reactions as he was before the war. He has a trick leg . . . and he has lost just enough speed . . . to enable tacklers to nail him with punishing tackles. Kenny Washington will work his head off to prove this prediction wrong, and I hope he does.

As it turned out, Hyland was somewhat correct in his prediction about Washington. Beset by knee injuries, he lasted only three seasons with the Rams, 1946–1948, and while he showed flashes of his former brilliance, only played in only twenty-seven games and never rushed for more than 444 yards in a season.

After Washington's signing by the Rams, Halley Harding was not finished fighting for the rights of African Americans to play pro football. In September 1946, Harding led a group of four black sportswriters in filing a lawsuit against the Los Angeles Dons, the new team in the inaugural AAFC season. The Dons secured a lease with the LA Coliseum by saying that they, too, would sign black players. By the time the 1946 season rolled around, however, the Dons had no African American players on their roster. The suit filed by the sportswriters requested a restraining order against the Dons since they did not have any African Americans on their team, which was a violation of the team's agreement with the Coliseum Commission to employ black players, just like the Rams had agreed. In the end, a California superior judge refused to carry out the restraining order, which allowed the Dons to use the LA Coliseum for the 1946 season despite not having any black players on their roster. However, less than a year later, in 1947, perhaps caving under Harding's pressure amid changing times, the Dons made up for their breach of contract by signing three black players to the team.

African American football players now had opportunities that never before existed, thanks to the brave efforts of black soldiers during World War II, the creation of the AAFC, and consistent pressure and activism by Harding and others pushing for the reintegration of the NFL. But after numerous African American players were signed to both NFL and AAFC franchises, there were still several roadblocks that stood in the way of these players and their African American fans.

By the late 1940s, many pro football teams had gotten in the habit of playing some of their exhibition games in the South. The powers that be in pro football never really took into account (or cared about) the problems black players might face in the South, insofar as being barred from playing in some Southern cities, not being able to eat or stay with their white teammates when visiting the South, or contending with ill-mannered treatment from fans.

Then, to make matters even more challenging, after World War II professional football started placing franchises in still-segregated cities in the Deep South, like Miami in the AAFC and Dallas and Houston in the NFL and AFL. In addition to visiting African Americans having to play regular-season games in these cities, these franchises in the South (with the exception of the Redskins) eventually integrated. This meant black players on teams like the Dallas Texans (both the 1952 and 1960 versions), Dallas Cowboys, and Houston Oilers now had to live, practice, and play in segregated cities. Some of these black players, not being originally from the South, faced conditions they had never before experienced.

Once black players started appearing and living in southern cities, African American football fans in the South wanted to get a glimpse of their black gridiron heroes finally having the opportunity to play pro football. However, in most southern cities, black fans who attended games were subjected to segregated seating at numerous venues. This practice of segregated seating eventually became a lightning rod of controversy and protest as the civil rights movement gathered steam in the late 1950s and 1960s.

This book is not specifically about the integration of pro football; it is more about how these early integration pioneers and their fans dealt with the conditions that were prevalent in the South when the NFL reintegrated in 1946. It's also about how, just like the civil rights movement, black players, fans, and allies gradually started resisting segregation in the South and started fighting back with some success. Change came slowly in both professional football and the civil rights movement.

As mentioned earlier, in the inaugural AAFC season of 1946, there was a franchise in Miami called the Seahawks. In their only year in Miami (they moved to Baltimore after one season to become the first version of the Colts), the Seahawks stumbled to a 3–11 record, including a 44–0 rout by the Browns in the September 6 season-opening game in Cleveland. Marion Motley and Bill Willis played in that game, with Motley scoring one touchdown on a 35-yard pass reception and becoming the first African Americans to play in a professional football game since 1933. (Kenny Washington and Woody Strode did not play in their first regular-season game with the Rams until September 29.)

Earlier, Wendell Smith had voiced concern about African Americans having the opportunity to play in the AAFC because there was a franchise in Miami and that might prevent other AAFC teams from signing black players. The Browns did sign Motley and Willis to contracts, but a controversy still arose when it became time to go to Miami.

The Browns and Seahawks were scheduled to play a return game on December 3 in Miami. However, Motley and Willis did not get the historic chance to integrate professional football in the South. The two players were left at home. Miami, like most cities in Florida, had an ordinance prohibiting black and white players from performing on the same field together. The ordinance was similar to those that many towns in Florida had used in 1946 to prohibit Jackie Robinson from playing in spring training games for the Brooklyn Dodgers.

Partially because of this law, and in spite of criticism by black newspapers and civil rights groups, head coach Paul Brown decided to leave his two star players at home. The *Cleveland Call and Post*, an African American newspaper, wanted Brown to take his two black players to Miami and force the hands of Miami officials. An editorial in the *Call and Post* said, "Let them be shown up as a group of contemptable so-and-so's when they send the local gendarmes to take Willis and Motley off the football field; every newspaper in the country will take up the hue and cry, which will be heard around the world." In the end, Brown didn't relent to the pressure. He claimed to be a football coach, nothing more. He was not a civil rights pioneer.

Marion Motley, Cleveland Browns. *University of Nevada Athletics*

What also helped Brown's decision was the fact that the Browns had already clinched their division, so it wasn't crucial that Motley and Willis play. In addition, Motley had received a death threat a few weeks prior to the game, which made Brown's decision easier. To help save face for everyone involved, Brown made a statement three weeks prior to the game in Miami: "When I signed the boys last summer, I made an agreement with the league that I wouldn't use them in Florida. I wouldn't do anything that might embarrass the boys."

Yet, Brown appeared to be worried about missing his two black stars. A couple of days before the rematch with the Seahawks, he said, "Our squad is not in the best condition because we had to leave Motley and Willis at home. The loss of those boys is bound to hinder us." It didn't. The Browns rolled to a 34–0 victory over the Seahawks before nine thousand fans.

After Miami missed their opportunity to play an integrated professional football game in 1946, the integration of pro football in the South made no headway in 1947. There were no preseason games scheduled for the AAFC in the Deep South in 1947. In addition, only one NFL game was played in the South that year—a preseason game on September 19 at the Cotton Bowl in Dallas, with the Boston Yanks taking on the Chicago Cardinals. Neither team had a black player on their roster.

The Miami Seahawks went on to relocate to Baltimore in 1947. The franchise cited financial concerns as their reason for the moving, having been bought out by a group of Baltimore businessmen. The move provided no reprieve for black players. Although not the Deep South, Baltimore was a segregated city nonetheless. While African American players were allowed to play in Baltimore, they had to find separate accommodations from their white teammates when they stayed there.

African American players on opposing teams started playing in Baltimore in 1947. Elmore "Pepper" Harris, who had been a football and track star at Morgan State (located in Baltimore) played in Baltimore for the Brooklyn Dodgers football team on September 7, 1947, a 16–7 Dodgers loss. Harris was the first black to play a regular season post–World War II pro football game in a segregated city.

After Harris broke the color barrier in Baltimore, numerous other African American players on opposing teams made the trek to Baltimore between 1947 and 1949. Later in the 1947 season, Bill Willis and Marion Motley of the Cleveland Browns; Buddy Young of the New York Yanks; Bill Bass of the Chicago Rockets; and John Brown, Ezzret Anderson, and Bert Piggott of the Los Angeles Dons also played in Baltimore.

In 1948, African American players in the AAFC that played in Baltimore were Willis, Motley, and newcomer Horace Gillom of the Browns; Young and Tom Casey with the Yanks; and Brown, Lin Sexton, and Len Ford of the Los Angeles Dons. The San Francisco 49ers also brought to Baltimore their first-ever black players, Joe Perry and Robert Mike.

The 1949 group of African American players to play in Baltimore expanded to include Paul Patterson and James Bailey of the Chicago Hornets; Gillom, Motley, and Willis with the Browns; and Perry and Mike for the 49ers. The Dons were up to five black players who went to Baltimore: Brown, Ford, George Taliaferro, Ben Whaley, and Ollie Fletcher.

On August 16, 1949, Buddy Young and Sherman Howard of the Brooklyn/New York Yanks played in an exhibition game in Baltimore, then made a return visit during the regular season two months later, on October 16, for a 24–21 Yank victory. Young and Howard's return visit to Baltimore was significant because it marked the first time the issue of segregated accommodations for black and white players was dealt with directly by team management. Howard, who at ninety-four is the oldest living African American professional football player, explained:

> It was my rookie year, 1949, and the last year of the AAFC. My first preseason game I ever played was in Baltimore. Buddy Young and I couldn't stay at the Belvedere Hotel with the white players. When Buddy and I went back a few weeks later for our regular season game in Baltimore, this time the Yanks sent Buddy and I down by train in a private rail car the morning of the game. Our general manager met us at the train station and took us to the stadium. After the game, we took the train back to New York. We didn't have to deal with staying at some run-down motel or having to eat apart from our white team-mates. That was nice.

Even after Baltimore desegregated in the early 1950s, de facto segregation was very much still part of the southern city's culture. There were places in Baltimore throughout the 1950s and into the early 1960s where African American players were not welcome.

After failing as an AAFC franchise in 1947 and as an NFL franchise in 1950, the city of Baltimore got one more version of the Colts in 1953, when the Dallas Texans went bankrupt in 1952 and moved to Baltimore. George Taliaferro, Buddy Young, and Mel Embree were black players for the Colts. In their last preseason game on September 20, the Colts defeated the Washington Redskins, 9–3, at Memorial Stadium in Baltimore. After the game, the players went to the Lord Baltimore Hotel to celebrate. The *Pittsburgh Courier* reported in its October 3 edition that

> Buddy Young, George Taliaferro, and Mel Embree, Negro members of the Baltimore Colts professional football team, were denied service at the Lord Baltimore Hotel last Sunday. The Negro players walked out of

the hotel, it is claimed, after they had been denied service at the cocktail bar. A short while later, white teammates who heard of the hotel's action followed the three Negro players and withdrew from the banquet.

Taliaferro, one of the black players at the Lord Baltimore Hotel that evening, recalled,

> I had just come to Baltimore to play from another segregated city, Dallas. It's hard to compare the two cities segregation-wise. Dallas was a bit more rigid. Everything was segregated there—movies and other entertainment, housing, and so on. Baltimore, not quite as much. It was still the South, but not the Deep South like Dallas. I remember the incident at the Lord Baltimore Hotel. We had beaten the Redskins, and I showed up to celebrate and be with my teammates. Buddy Young was already at the party because he was from the area and knew a lot of people. He was trying to make some business contacts. When I arrived, Buddy met me at the hotel entrance, so I never really went into the party. At the door, Buddy told me, "Come here, I have something to tell you. We were not served alcohol at the bar. I'm leaving. You can come with us if you like." Well, I left with Buddy, so I was not personally denied drinks at the bar. I believed what Buddy told me, so that's why I left.

Taliaferro concluded,

> I have to give our owner, Carol Rosenbloom, credit. When he found out about what happened, he put a stop to us not being able to be served at the Lord Baltimore Hotel. The part about the white guys walking out of the hotel that night in support of us? That's the first I've heard of it. I'm not saying it didn't happen—it could have. I think there were a number of white guys who would have taken that position and supported us. For example, Gino Marchetti I know would have been one of the first white guys to walk out, if they in fact had.

This was not the only incidence of de facto discrimination at the Lord Baltimore Hotel. One of the Pittsburgh Steelers' early African American players, Henry Ford, told of an incident in 1956 where he experienced racism even after the city had "officially" desegregated:

> We went to go play the Colts in preseason. We weren't able to stay at the Lord Baltimore Hotel with our white teammates. You have to remember, Baltimore was still the South. The club told us on the plane

George Taliaferro, Baltimore Colts. *Indiana University Athletics*

we had someone who would be meeting us. Luckily for me, it was one of my old track teammates from Pitt, Herb Douglass, who lived in Baltimore, and he picked up myself and our other black players, Willie McClung, Jack McClairen, and Lowell Perry, at the airport. Herb and I were friends, and he knew the area since he was from there. We had a good time. We just made the most of it.

In 1956, future Pro Football Hall of Fame running back Lenny Moore came to play for the Colts out of Penn State. He described Baltimore in the 1950s:

> Pretty much through all of the 1950s, black Colts players couldn't go downtown. There were places we just weren't welcome. I couldn't go to the movie theaters; I couldn't eat in a restaurant down there. It just wasn't worth the hassle. I was an All-Pro and I couldn't even go downtown? Segregation was reality.

In addition to Baltimore in the AAFC, Washington, DC—home of the NFL's Redskins since 1937 and just a few miles down the road from Baltimore—was also segregated. The nation's capital allowed black players to play in contests against the hometown Redskins, but, like Baltimore, wouldn't allow them to stay with their white teammates. African American players started playing games in Washington against the Redskins in 1948, the year after black players started playing in Baltimore.

The first African American player on a visiting team to suit up against the Redskins in Washington was rookie Emlen Tunnell of the New York Giants, who played in Washington on October 3, 1948, in a 41–10 Giants loss. This was the first time in NFL history an African American played a regular-season game in a segregated city. Later that season, on November 14, the Lions lost to the Redskins in Washington, 46–21. Mel Groomes and Bob Mann were African Americans who played for the Lions, with Mann catching 5 passes for 147 yards in the loss. The Los Angeles Rams played in Washington on December 5, in a 41–13 victory over the Redskins. Kenny Washington contributed to the Rams victory by hauling in a 26-yard touchdown reception from Jim Hardy in the second quarter to give the Rams a 20–0 lead.

Several black players from this time period recalled their experiences in Washington. Eddie Bell, who traveled to Washington in the 1950s when he was a member of the Philadelphia Eagles, said,

> When we went to Washington, DC, to play the Redskins, the Redskins at that time were the only NFL team without an African American player, and that's the only time I ever heard anything coming from the stands. You'd hear the n-word, but it wasn't any kind of massive demonstration of racism where a whole group would holler or something like that. You might hear a smattering here or there—from the stands, not from other players. The other thing about the Redskins is that their band would come onto the field playing Dixie, and although the uni-

forms the band wore were the Redskins colors rather than white, they were like the Klan uniforms with the big hooded cap and everything like that. It was George Preston Marshall's team of the South. I am sure the Redskins and other teams scheduled exhibition games in the South because they were trying to increase interest in the NFL and make a profit. Of course, any time we went into the South, we went into a segregated situation: hotels, restaurants, and the like. Even Washington was segregated.

Sherman Howard said about Washington,

> When, in 1950, the Yanks in the NFL acquired eighteen players, myself included, from the AAFC Yanks once the league folded, we were placed in a different conference than the Redskins, so we never played there. I do know other black players who weren't allowed to stay with their white teammates when they went to Washington. As far as going to Washington, DC, when I was with the Browns in 1951 and 1952, I was injured both years and didn't make the trip. I do know for a fact, though, that the whole team did stay together, because that's what the Browns and coach Paul Brown insisted on back then.

Another African American Browns player, Emerson Cole, who also played for the Browns from 1950 to 1952, acknowledged that the Browns did stay together as a team. This was because Paul Brown insisted on his team staying together. Other NFL teams didn't follow Brown's policy, however. Although he got to stay with his white teammates, Cole faced other problems when he went to Washington. He faced some of the same de facto segregation that Lenny Moore did in Baltimore.

Cole said about playing in Washington, DC,

> Sometimes on the road it was kind of rough. I went in a restaurant in Washington, DC, and they acted like I wasn't even there. I never was a hell-raiser or complainer, so I just sat there. After about an hour, someone I knew from Ohio, Mike DiSalle, came up to me. He had been mayor of my hometown of Toledo and governor of Ohio. He was now working for the federal government. He went to this restaurant all the time and was well known there. He came over to me and said, "Hi, how you doing, Em? Do you mind if I have breakfast with you?" I said, "I would be delighted." And boy they came running. It looked like a mob had come to serve us after I had been sitting there for an hour and they had pretended I wasn't even there. What I'm saying is, there are a lot of psychological scars. But you know, if you can live through that kind of thing, you can live through anything.

The dream of playing an integrated football game in the Deep South finally came to fruition when that honor was bestowed on Dallas in 1948. Professional football was finally integrated in the South when Kenny Washington of the Rams played in an exhibition game in Dallas against the NFL champion Philadelphia Eagles on September 15, 1948. The contest was played at Dal-Hi Stadium, a twenty-two-thousand-seat high school stadium. Not that there wasn't some apprehension on Washington's part about going to Dallas—a September 26, 1948, article in the *Pittsburgh Courier* titled "Washington Balked at Texas Trip" said,

> The *Courier* learned from an authentic source that Kenny Washington, ace Los Angeles Rams halfback, was reluctant to go to Dallas, Texas, with the Rams to play an exhibition game with the Philadelphia Eagles last week. Washington . . . balked at going South assertedly because of possible race bias. Washington finally agreed to play after he was assured that he would receive a royal welcome.

There were no incidents reported at the game, a 21–7 Eagles victory, and Washington ran for 60 yards in the contest, including a 25-yard first-quarter run. Eighteen thousand fans made their way into Dal-Hi Stadium, including five hundred black fans, who were forced to sit in segregated seating in the end zone.

Although he had been an integration pioneer in college at Penn State, segregation reared its ugly head when Wally Triplett turned pro with the Lions in 1949. In 1948, the team had signed their first two African American players: receiver Bob Mann from the University of Michigan and halfback Mel Groomes from Indiana University.

On September 3, 1949, Triplett, Mann, and Groomes were the first known African American players being denied the chance to play an NFL exhibition game in a southern city, when the three Lions were not able to suit up for a game against the NFL champion Philadelphia Eagles at City Park Stadium in New Orleans.

There were no laws on the books in Louisiana against blacks and whites playing against each other. Just a year earlier, at Pelican Baseball Park in New Orleans, Jackie Robinson and Roy Campanella of the Brooklyn Dodgers were allowed to play in an exhibition game there. That game was a financial success, drawing fourteen thousand black fans, with room for just a few hundred white fans. When Groomes, Mann, and Triplett were held out of the exhibition game at City Park Stadium and word got out ahead of time, blacks in New Orleans boycotted the game. It was estimated that about five thousand did not attend the game, costing the promotors around $75,000.

Some were surprised Triplett, Groomes, and Mann were held out of the game, because their coach was Bo McMillin. McMillin was born in Prairie Hill, Texas, and played high school ball in Fort Worth at Northside High School. He eventually coached at Centenary College in Shreveport from 1922 to 1924, so his roots ran deep in Texas, Louisiana, and the South. McMillin eventually became the head coach at Indiana University and coached African American players there, including George Taliaferro and Mel Groomes, who was one of the players caught up in the controversy in New Orleans. After his stint at Indiana, McMillin took over as head coach of the Detroit Lions in 1947. Although he was from the South, McMillin was seen as very progressive and liberal toward black players, as he had coached black players at Indiana and had a hand in signing Mann, Groomes, and Triplett to contracts with the Lions. However, there is some dispute over whether or not he denied his players the chance to play in New Orleans.

By some accounts, the players apparently knew they were not going to play as far back as July. They were informed that Lions officials, along with Eagles officials, decided they would honor an unwritten agreement "not to break southern tradition." They were not denied the privilege of playing by the game's promoter, Sports, Inc. of New Orleans. Sports Inc. apparently had originally decided to let them play and had allocated five thousand tickets for the black fans. It was to be the first time in a decade black fans were admitted to a sporting event at City Park.

When Groomes, Mann, and Triplett supposedly asked McMillin why they weren't making the trip, the coach claimed there had been an agreement made by Vincent McNally, business manager for the Eagles, who said that when the contract for the game was signed, it was stipulated that neither team would break southern tradition concerning the color line.

However, when W. Rollo Wilson, Philadelphia correspondent of the *Pittsburgh Courier*, got hold of the contract entered into by the Eagles, Lions, and Sports, Inc., he found no mention of the black Lions players being barred from the game. McNally, who had been designated by most as the scapegoat for the ban on the black players, also told the *Courier* that he had not entered into any contract or agreement, either oral or written, whereby the "traditions of the South" would be respected. Since McNally of the Eagles, McMillin of the Lions, and Sports, Inc. all denied their role in the black players not being able to participate, the question was, who was to blame?

Once the Lions and Eagles were in New Orleans, an attempt was made to get officials for the two teams and Sports Inc. together to reveal the reason the trio were not going to be able to play. McMillin related that he would not have time to attend the meeting, but he sent the following statement: "I know that I am going to be condemned by the Negro press, but you cannot lay the blame on me. If it were up to me, the boys would play, but I am going by the terms of the agreement, and I can't change it—only the officials can do that."

Sports, Inc., officials quickly absolved themselves, reiterating that they had no objections to Groomes, Mann, and Triplett playing. Once again, there was no law in Louisiana at the time that prohibited black and white players from participating against each other in sporting events. Just a few months earlier, Larry Doby of the Cleveland Indians appeared in an exhibition baseball game against white players in Shreveport, like Jackie Robinson and Roy Campanella in New Orleans the year before.

In his version of the story, Bob Mann laid the blame on Bo McMillin. Before the Lions departed for Crescent City, according to Mann, McMillin met in his office with Mann, Triplett, and Groomes. McMillin told the three that the sponsors of the game had left the decision to him as to whether the black Lions could play. While McMillin would sign and draft black players in Detroit, some people, like Mann, felt McMillin didn't want to betray his Texas roots by making history in New Orleans. The three would not be able to play in the game or stay with the team in the same hotel.

"Bo told us he didn't think he should be the one to break it," a still-angry Mann said in 2005.

> I thought to myself, "Fine, that's his decision." Bo could have ended all that. He was supposed to be Mr. Great Liberal. But he didn't do it. He just passed it by. He could have been a big guy, a big fellow, but he didn't do it. I've never forgotten that. Don't tell me how liberal Bo was; he wasn't. He had a chance to be a hero, step up to the plate, but he didn't do it.

Wally Triplett, by 2018 the only surviving member of the trio, said in an interview,

> I'm not sure who was to blame. All I know is we got caught up in the middle of it and in the end didn't get to suit up. I thought I was past all of that after Dennie Hoggard and I integrated the Cotton Bowl. Then

the next year in Birmingham, I didn't get to play again. That was rough too—humiliating, as a matter of fact.

All was not lost, however. Progress, however small, was made by the end of the decade. Ironically, on the same September day in 1949 that Triplett, Groomes, and Mann of the Detroit Lions were denied the chance to play in an exhibition game in New Orleans, Sherman Howard and Buddy Young of the Brooklyn/New York Yankees played in an exhibition game in Charlotte, North Carolina, against the Charlotte Clippers, a local semipro team, and won, 24–7. Howard and Young thus became the first black players in an AAFC exhibition game in the South.

At the end of 1949, further progress was made when the first fully integrated pro football game in the South was played in Houston on December 17. The Cleveland Browns, champions once again of the AAFC, took on an all-star team from the rest of the league. Both squads had African American players on their rosters. However, out of this perceived progress in Houston, problems arose.

2

NO RECOURSE

The NFL's Blackballing of "Troublemaker" Players

Moving into the new decade of the fifties, there was some progress made, integration-wise, for black players in the South. For the first time, black players were allowed to play in a city in the Deep South—Houston, the largest segregated city in the South.

After the Cleveland Browns won the last-ever All-America Football Conference championship on December 11, 1949—defeating the San Francisco 49ers, 21–7—the Browns traveled to Houston the next week to play an all-star team made up of the remainder of the AAFC teams. It was the final game in AAFC history. After the game and season were completed, the AAFC folded and three AAFC teams were merged into the NFL the following year: the Browns, the San Francisco 49ers, and the Baltimore Colts.

Since there were black players on both squads, the Shamrock Bowl was the first fully integrated football game in Texas and in the former Confederate states. The African American players consisted of fullback Marion Motley, defensive tackle Bill Willis, and punter Horace Gillom for the Browns, while the all-star team had running back Joe Perry of the San Francisco 49ers and running back Claude "Buddy" Young of the Brooklyn/New York Yankees on their roster.

But the talent of the African American players present in Houston didn't matter when it came to lodging accommodations. The black players on both teams had to stay in the homes of prominent black Houston citizens, since they couldn't stay at the Shamrock Hotel, which was segregated by law.

Buddy Young's widow, Geraldine Young, spoke decades later of her husband's experience in Houston:

Buddy went down to Houston to play in the All-Star Game in Houston against the Browns. I stayed with our first child in Chicago. Buddy said he didn't experience any real problems in Houston. He didn't get to stay with the rest of the team. He had also found out ahead of time where things like the black restaurants were so he wouldn't have any trouble. For whatever reason, Glenn McCarthy, the man who put the game on, liked Buddy and gave him five hundred dollars.

The Shamrock Bowl was organized by McCarthy, a Houston oilman who earlier in 1949 had opened the Shamrock Hotel, the largest hotel built in America in the 1940s. McCarthy supposedly inspired the character Jett Rink in the 1956 movie *Giant*, starring Rock Hudson, Elizabeth Taylor, and James Dean. The event combined football with show business. Freddie Martin's orchestra played in a covered area before the game, and there were appearances by comedians Phil Harris and Jack Benny, along with singer Dinah Shore.

The price for the game and entertainment was a steep fifteen dollars. In comparison, twenty-five years later, in 1974, when Super Bowl VIII between the Miami Dolphins and Minnesota Vikings was played at Rice Stadium, tickets were also fifteen dollars. The steep price, along with a heavy rainstorm that lasted the whole game, limited the turnout to only ten thousand fans. McCarthy figured he needed twenty thousand fans to break even.

One would think the high price of a ticket to the Shamrock Bowl would have kept the African American fans away. However, that was not the reason black fans did not attend the game. According to the *Pittsburgh Courier*, "Negro stars from the All-American Football Conference are being asked to participate in the Shamrock Charity Bowl in Houston, TX, on December 17th—notwithstanding the fact that Negro spectators will be barred from attending the game at Rice Institute Stadium."

The *Courier* added,

John H. Murphy, Houston newspaper publisher, admitted, "that no tickets are being offered to Negroes for the Shamrock Charity Bowl game. This is not due, however, to racial animosity. It is due entirely to the fact that Rice Institute's charter prohibits the attendance of students of the Negro race, and this same rule applies to its football stadium. The stadium was loaned to us with the very explicit provisions that Negro fans could not, by both school laws and state laws, be allowed to attend."

The article also indicated, "Murphy and others interested in the game have not to date been able to explain how the several Negro football players can play and still not be using the stadium, its facilities, or breaking a state law."

Barring African American spectators from attending a sporting event was rare. For games in the South, segregated seating was usually set up for black spectators—most commonly in one of the end zones. Down the road, by the time the civil rights movement was gaining momentum, segregated seating eventually became a lightning rod for protests by black players, the NAACP, and sportswriters like Lloyd Wells of the *Houston Informer.*

Thus the victory was marred: What should have been a landmark occasion for civil rights and integration in the South, with the first fully integrated football game in Texas and the old Confederate states, ended up leaving a bad taste in everyone's mouth. While African American players suited up on both sides of the field, the stands lay noticeably vacant— African American fans had been barred from attending the game.

At the end of the day, the all-stars won the game over the AAFC champion Browns, 12–7, in a torrential downpour. It was later discovered that Marion Motley had been denied entrance to the stadium before the game and had to wait in the pouring rain to be admitted. Buddy Young was the leading rusher, with 75 yards on 12 carries.

McCarthy lost thousands on the game. What little money he raised was slated to benefit several charities: the Holly Hall home for the aged, the Damon Runyon Cancer Fund, and National Kids Day. Later in his stint in football, McCarthy tried to acquire a franchise in the AAFC for the 1950 season, but the league folded. Within three years of the Shamrock Bowl, McCarthy's financial empire began to crumble. In the end, though, fully integrated professional football had come to the Old South. However, in spite of the fully integrated AAFC football game in Houston, African American players were still barred from NFL exhibition games in some southern cities.

The very next year, in the 1950 preseason, Wally Triplett was held out of the Lions' September 9 exhibition game in Birmingham with the Chicago Cards. Mel Groomes, who had been cut, and Bob Mann, who had been traded, were no longer with the Lions. Triplett made the trip to Birmingham thinking he was going to get to play. He went through the pregame warm-ups with his team but was then informed he would not be able to participate in the contest.

Once word got out that Triplett would not be playing in the contest, black fans stayed away from the game, costing the promoters thousands of dollars in revenue in ticket and concession sales. The *Pittsburgh Courier* reported, "Hundreds of Negro fans stayed away from the game after hearing whispers of the plan to keep Triplett on the bench."

Triplett said years later, in 2016,

> I thought I was past that not letting me play mess. In 1946 Penn State cancelled our game in Miami, but then Dennie Hoggard and I integrated the Cotton Bowl in 1948 when we played SMU. I just didn't think it would happen again after New Orleans, but it did again in Birmingham in 1950. When I got to the pros, it seemed like things were going backwards, not being able to play in New Orleans or Birmingham.
>
> With Birmingham, I actually did make the trip there. I went there with the intention of playing, and I thought I was going to play. I even got to warm up with the team before the game. Someone, though, pulled me aside and told me I couldn't play. I don't remember who it was who actually told me, whether it was Coach McMillin or whoever. Talk about taking the wind out of your sails. It was embarrassing and humiliating.
>
> The funny thing was, I actually got to play the two previous weeks in the South. I played in Dallas and then in Little Rock before we went to Birmingham. I remember in Little Rock having a nice kickoff return against the Eagles, even though we lost to them.

On September 19, 1950, just ten days after Triplett had come to Birmingham with the intention of playing against the Cardinals, the city of Birmingham adopted a city sports segregation law, likely in hopes of preventing any controversy in the future. The law forbade whites and blacks from appearing together on the same field or court of play.

The law was used in Birmingham the very next year in 1951 against New York Giants Hall of Fame defensive back Emlen Tunnell and fullback Bob Jackson. Tunnell and Jackson were denied the chance to play in a preseason game against the Washington Redskins in Birmingham on September 8, 1951. Sadly, it was not the first time they had been prohibited from playing in a southern city.

Although Tunnell joined the Giants in 1948 and Jackson became his teammate in 1950, the Giants did not play any exhibition games in the South until 1951. That year, however, the Giants played three of their four exhibition games in the South. Their first game in the South was a preseason game against the Detroit Lions on August 24 at the Cotton Bowl in Dallas. Tunnell and Jackson were allowed to play, as had other black players since Kenny Washington of the Rams first played there in 1948.

Although the Giants lost, 21–7, according to Associated Press accounts, Tunnell "stood out brilliantly on defense. Tunnell intercepted one pass and was batting down throws all night."

Nine days later, on September 2, Tunnell and Jackson were not allowed to play in Memphis against the Chicago Bears, a 14–0 Giants win before 10,822 fans. The *Chicago Tribune* said about the absence of Tunnell and Jackson in a summary of the game, "The Giants umbrella pass defense proved too rugged . . . even with Emlen Tunnell, the pivotman in the defense, sitting out the contest. Tunnell and his teammate, Bob Jackson, were unable to play due to a rule that prohibits Negro athletes from competing with whites in Memphis."

On September 8, just days after being held out of their game in Memphis, Tunnell and Jackson were not allowed to play in Birmingham, just like Wally Triplett the previous preseason. A week before the game, the *Pittsburgh Courier* said about the incident,

> A year after Wally Triplett was not allowed to play in Birmingham, it appears New York Giants Emlen Tunnell and William Jackson will be held out of the game with the Washington Redskins. Publicity before the game and local newspapers omitted the names of these two players despite the large number of black fans in Birmingham. Negroes promoting the sale of tickets to the game were told that the matter of Tunnell and Jackson playing in the game was being considered. Last year Wally Triplett of the Lions did not know he would be held out of the game. He went through pre-game warmups but was then informed he would not be playing in the contest.

The Birmingham NAACP took action, adopting a resolution that protested the barring of the two black players. The resolution was directed at Birmingham municipal officials, including Mayor Cooper Green and Police Commissioner T. Eugene "Bull" Connor. A copy of the resolution was sent to the Giants head coach Steve Owen, to no avail.

Owen had already informed Tunnell and Jackson that they would be benched because of their skin color. They were, however, able to work out with their teammates in practices at Rickwood Field at night under the lights. Fans both black and white came out to watch the Giants practice. The next morning, however, Tunnell and Jackson were not allowed to attend team meetings at the Shamrock Motel, where their white teammates were staying. At the game, a 12–10 Giants loss, Tunnell and Jackson sat in the segregated seating section of the stadium in their street clothes.

Birmingham also holds the dubious distinction of being the last city where a black player was not allowed to play in an exhibition game in the South. After Tunnell and Jackson were denied the chance to play there in 1951, there was not another preseason game played in Birmingham until August 31, 1957. The Detroit Lions played the Washington Redskins, and future Pro Football Hall of Fame fullback John Henry Johnson of the Lions was not allowed to play in the contest.

Johnson had been acquired from the San Francisco 49ers in a trade hoped to help propel the Lions to the NFL title. It worked—Johnson was a key player in the Lions' drive to the 1957 NFL title, with a 59–14 win over the Cleveland Browns. He led the Lions in yards rushing and in total yards from scrimmage. However, that did not prevent him from being denied the opportunity to play in Birmingham.

On August 28, the *Detroit Free Press* acknowledged that Johnson was barred from play in Birmingham: "Detroit's attack will no doubt be slowed by the loss of John Henry Johnson for the game. Because of State law and local ordinance, which prohibits the Negro from competing with whites in Birmingham, Johnson will stay home this weekend."

With Johnson prohibited from playing in Birmingham, Lions coach George Wilson was left shorthanded. Because of injuries to two other fullbacks, Wilson had no fullbacks. He said, "We'll have plenty of regular running backs, but no regular fullback. We'll have to move Gene Gedman over to the fullback spot."

Wilson also used halfback Dick Kercher at fullback to fill in for Johnson. Kercher was trying to make it back to the Lions roster; after playing for them in 1954, he was drafted into the army and missed the 1955 and 1956 seasons.

Kercher said of Johnson not being able to make the trip to Birmingham, "I felt kind of sorry for John Henry, and not just for having to miss the game in Birmingham. He was our only black on the team. I used to hang around him in training camp to keep him company and also because he was a nice guy. It couldn't have been easy for black players back then."

Unfortunately for Kercher, the Lions game in Birmingham was his last in the NFL, as he was cut a couple of days after the game. Detroit in turn did not appear to miss Johnson as the Lions rolled to a 31–14 win. This was also the last time an African American player was held out of an exhibition game in the South.

Although the NFL reintegrated in 1946 and the AAFC had signed black players since its infancy, black players had no recourse when they tried to play exhibition games in the South just after World War II. They had no choice or input, for fear of repercussions.

Sherman Howard reflected on how he and other African American players had no say in matters early on. When Howard and Buddy Young took the train down from New York to play in Baltimore during the regular season in 1949, it was not arranged directly by the players. The Yanks front office did it so the players would not have to face discrimination when they traveled there during the preseason.

Howard said,

> Buddy and I didn't like that we didn't get to stay at the Belvedere Hotel with our white teammates when we played there in August, but we

Sherman Howard. *University of Nevada Athletics*

knew better than complain about it. That may have gotten us released. You had to be really careful about speaking out about anything. It was the front office of the Yanks that arranged for us to take the train down the morning of the game there in October. Buddy and I knew better than to make waves.

What Howard said held true in the early days of the reintegration of the NFL—that protesting segregated accommodations in the South for white and black players, going to play for a rival league like the CFL, a contract dispute, or a personal life that was considered unsavory (interracial marriage) could cost you your job. There were many examples of this happening all the way into the early to mid-1960s.

In the post–World War II era, when players were held out of preseason games in the South, they had no say or recourse. Later, when some black players complained about their treatment down South, they were traded, released, and in some cases blackballed out of the league. In early days of reintegration, even your stature as a player or value to your team couldn't save your job. There were several reasons teams would cut a player loose.

Bob Mann was one of the first African American players on record to take a stand and protest perceived mistreatment. (He was also one of the African American Detroit Lions players held out of an exhibition game in New Orleans in 1949.) During the 1949 regular season, Mann had an All-Pro-type season, finishing second in the NFL in catches, with 66, to Tom Fears of the Rams at 77, and led the NFL in receiving yards, with 1,014, to Fears's 1,013. One would think this would land him a handsome contract. After the season, when Mann asked for more money for the upcoming 1950 campaign, he was drummed out of the league.

Mann explained what happened after the 1949 season:

> In 1949 I led the league in yards receiving and I was second in catches. The way I left Detroit was interesting. I was working for Goebel Brewery, whose president was Edwin Anderson, who also happened to be president of the Lions. They didn't have any black drivers at the company, and I got into a strong discussion, not an argument, with Anderson over that fact. Well, all of this crept over into my contract. I said I would just quit working for the brewery, and they said they wanted to cut my salary, which didn't seem fair to me. The next thing I knew, I was cut from the Lions.

Salaries were dropping after the 1949 season because the AAFC merged with the NFL, so there were no bidding wars to drive player salaries up. Anderson insisted that Mann take a pay cut from $7,500 to $6,000 per year. Goebel was accused of discriminatory hiring practices and was boycotted by African Americans. Mann got caught in the middle and was traded to the Yanks for quarterback Bobby Layne, who ended up having a Hall of Fame career with Detroit. Mann lost his offseason job at Goebel, was traded and released by the Yanks before the regular season, and became the first African American to play for the Packers, finally signing a contract in late November.

When asked about being let go by the Lions and subsequently cut by the Yanks, with no other teams picking him up, Mann claimed he was being blackballed out of the league. In response, Anderson said that all the other teams in the NFL "want something more from an end than pass-catching ability." Anderson was also quoted as saying that Mann did not make the team due to his "inability to block."

Mann said he was "railroaded out of the league" because he refused to take a salary cut. "I must have been blackballed," he said. "It just doesn't make sense that I'm suddenly not good enough to make a single team in the league." Mann contended in 1950 that the NFL had adopted a "hands-off" policy toward him ever since he objected to a $1,500 pay cut from the Lions. Mann said, "Detroit sent me to the New York Yanks in payment for Bobby Layne, but I think the cards were already stacked against my continuing in pro football." Mann also claimed that the NFL owners observed a gentleman's agreement not to sign any player deemed as an "undesirable."

NFL Commissioner Bert Bell shot back, saying that he had never heard Mann described as "undesirable" by any of the NFL owners and that there was nothing preventing him from "catching on" with any other NFL team. After he was cut by the Yanks in 1950, Bell said, "When the Yanks asked waivers on Mann, twelve other teams could have picked him up, or he could have sold himself to any one of the twelve just as many other players have done."

Eventually, Mann did catch on with the Green Bay Packers at the end of the 1950 season. Mann enjoyed three more productive seasons for the Packers from 1951 to 1953, never quite performing at the level he was at with the Lions, before a knee injury ended his career.

Another player in the early 1950s that aroused the anger of his franchise was running back Eddie Macon, who in 1952 became the first black player for the Chicago Bears. However, Macon ended up on the wrong side of a salary dispute with Bears owner and head coach George Halas, which led to his blackballing by the NFL.

Macon, who played at the University of the Pacific from 1949 to 1951, was the first African American to play for the Tigers, and on New Year's Day 1952 he became the first African American to play in the Sun Bowl in El Paso. Macon was drafted in the second round of the 1952 NFL draft by Halas, who told Macon, "I want you to be my Jackie Robinson." Halas also informed Macon that he wanted him to be "just a football player and a gentleman." Like Robinson five years earlier, Macon faced racism on and off the field, including in the locker room.

In 1954, Macon incurred the wrath of Halas when he decided to play in Canada, where his college coach, Larry Siemering, was currently working and where the pay was higher. When Macon tried to return to the NFL, Halas used his considerable influence to have Macon blacklisted. In addition, Halas and the Bears sued Macon for $100,000. Macon spent a couple of years as a longshoreman before returning to Canada in 1957 to play with the Hamilton Tiger-Cats, where he remained until 1959. He ended up with the AFL Oakland Raiders in 1960 in their inaugural season and played defensive back, recording nine interceptions. After the season, at age thirty-four, he retired.

Macon told his story:

> After I had played with the Bears for a couple of years, I had the chance to go to Canada to play for the Calgary Stampeders and my old college coach Larry Siemering. In the end, it cost me a lot of money. At first, I got more money in Calgary than I made playing with the Bears, but George Halas thought I was a traitor. He sued me and the Stampeders, and I basically was blackballed out of the NFL.
>
> To show you Halas's power, I also didn't play for two years in Canada because the Hamilton Tiger-Cats were trying to contact me back here in the states and the Bears wouldn't furnish them with contact information. They finally got a hold of me in 1957, and I played in Canada for three more years. There were other players that had gone to Canada, like my old college teammate Eddie LeBaron. However, Eddie was white, as were the other former NFL players who went to Canada, and they were allowed to return to the NFL and play. I contacted every team in the league, and none of them got back to me.
>
> Even though I was the first black Chicago Bear, I have never received any type of invitation to any Bears reunions, so to me the blackball is still in place. I thought about suing the Bears and the NFL back in 1955, but the civil rights movement was just getting into full swing and I could never get anybody to really represent me. We did pretty well in Hamilton and played for three Grey Cup titles, winning one.

In 1960, the new AFL was looking for players and the Raiders came to Stockton, my hometown, worked me out, and signed me. I'm proud to have been an original AFLer. I played defensive back, and I intercepted nine passes and made some All-Pro teams. After that first season, though, I had had enough. When the Raiders wanted to go with some younger players and try and help me catch on with another team, that was enough. I was thirty-four years old, so I went back to Stockton.

As noted by Macon, the civil rights movement was just starting to build momentum in 1955, with the backlash from the murder of Emmett Till in August and Rosa Parks's refusal to give up her seat on a Montgomery, Alabama, bus in December. Before these key events that helped push the civil rights movement forward, black players really didn't have much recourse in matters like being blackballed from the NFL. Players could be blackballed for any reason, from daring to protest segregated conditions to contract disputes to even their personal lives. Ranked high among the list of punishable offences that could cost them their career was the social taboo of being associated with a white woman. Such is the case of Milt Campbell.

In the mid- to late 1950s, Campbell was one of the best-known athletes in the world. At age twenty-two, he won the decathlon at the 1956 Olympics in Melbourne—the first African American to do so. Campbell had played football in addition to running track while in college at Ohio State, so he tried out for the Cleveland Browns in 1957 as a fullback. Unfortunately for Campbell, that was the same year Jim Brown arrived from Syracuse to play fullback. Campbell made the squad but played sparingly, rushing just 7 times for 23 yards on the season. Optimistically, Campbell was looking forward to better times in 1958.

However, in September 1958, Campbell was called into the office of Paul Brown just before the team's opening game. During the meeting, Brown demanded to know why Campbell had married a white woman, Barbara Mount, on the eve of his second season with the Browns. Campbell informed Brown it was none of his business and was cut by the Browns the next day. Effectively blackballed by the NFL, Campbell went to play football in Canada, where he remained until 1964.

Decades later Campbell recalled,

> Paul Brown called me into his office and said, "What did you get married for?" I looked him in the eye and said, "Two reasons. Number one, I got married for the same reason you got married, I presume. And number two, that's not a question you want to be asking." The next day, I got a notice to come to the office, where they handed me a let-

ter saying my services would no longer be needed. When I got there, I waited a half day in Paul Brown's office to talk with him, but he didn't have the courage to come see me. And just like that, I was blackballed out of the league.

Campbell tried to catch on with the New York Giants, who had previously expressed interest in him, but they wouldn't return his calls. Neither would any other NFL team. Campbell said, "Here I was, the greatest athlete in the world in 1956, and in 1958, I couldn't get a job in America. With all of the things I could do? I got my ass kicked because I fell in love. But you know what? In America, nobody is going to dictate to me who I can love and who I can't love." Campbell concluded, "An idiot like Paul Brown, he changed my history. I'm sure I would have been a hall of famer in football if I'd stayed with it."

That season Henry Ford, a former star at the University of Pittsburgh, was also blackballed out of the NFL for similar reasons. Ford told his story in a 2017 interview:

My wife, Rochelle, is Syrian. We've been married fifty-nine years. I thought she was a colored girl when I first spotted her. A teammate of mine, Joe Moore, and I were going through the town of Ligonier, Pennsylvania, when I spotted her. I was playing football at Schenley High School in Pittsburgh, and my senior year we were headed to Ligonier for a preseason football camp.

I was a co-captain for Schenley. I was sitting next to the other co-captain, Roy Moore, when I first spotted Rochelle in town. When I saw her, I asked the bus driver to stop. I went up to her and said, "Oops, sorry." "Sorry for what?" Rochelle responded. "I thought you were colored." I thought she was black—light-skinned, but black.

Rochelle and I ended up seeing other occasionally starting around 1950, and we ended up dating for about four years; then we went to Pittsburgh together. We didn't get married until 1960, though.

In 1955, Ford, who had been the first black quarterback in Pitt history, went to play professionally for the Cleveland Browns. In Cleveland, he thought he would get a chance to play quarterback. "Since the Browns and Paul Brown were considered progressive," said Ford, "I thought I might get a chance to play quarterback. I ended up being a halfback and defensive back."

Ford was eventually cut by the Browns and ended up in Canada for the remainder of the 1955 season. He eventually caught on with the Steelers in 1956 and started at defensive back. A promising career was derailed, however, when the Steelers found about his relationship with Rochelle.

"I was happy about going to the Steelers because I thought I would be there a long time," Ford explained. "I was one of their better defensive backs, and I felt like I had a career ahead of me. What got in the way was they didn't like that I had a white girlfriend. They were eavesdropping on our phone conversations."

The Steelers ordered Ford to stop dating Rochelle, and he informed them, "I have two lives, one professional and one personal, and the two are separate." Ford continued,

> I had been having a really good preseason in 1957. I played really well when we beat the Eagles in preseason. I got in on offense, and I led the team in rushing. I played well against the Lions the following week, playing both offense and defense. I thought I had a helluva day. The next week at Tuesday's practice, I wasn't put on offense, defense, or special teams. The rest of the week wasn't any different.
>
> On Saturday, the day before game day, I was packing for our game against the Bears. I got a call from one of our local news reporters, who informed me that I had been cut. The reporter called me and said to me, "That's it." I said, "What do you mean, 'That's it?'" The reporter said, "They told me to tell you that's it, and they'll take care of you when we get back from the game." So just a week after playing two great games back-to-back, I was cut by the Steelers. Nobody on the coaching staff or front office had the courage to tell me.

Ford concluded,

> I know why I was cut. It was because of my relationship with Rochelle. No question about it, I was blackballed. I never played in the NFL again, even though I knew I had the ability. After I got cut, it was rough. I thought my world was coming to an end. No one called me, and no one wanted me. The one positive that came out of all of it is that what happened to me was over sixty years ago, and I'm still married to Rochelle.

Besides having a relationship with a white woman, another way to be blackballed from the NFL was to protest against discrimination when traveling south for an exhibition game. In two separate cases, Art Powell and Walter Beach found themselves unemployed in 1960 and 1962, respectively, because they stood up for themselves and their African American teammates.

Al Davis, who in 1963 was the coach and later became owner of the Oakland Raiders, said of Art Powell, "I wish I could take you back to 1963. I had one of the greatest players who had ever played this game and he was tough to handle. He was the T.O. of his time. And he was great. His first year for me, he carried us. His name was Art Powell."

In 1960, however, Powell was cut by the Philadelphia Eagles just before they began their trek to that year's NFL title. Powell, like Terrell Owens, was a headstrong nonconformist who was not afraid to take a stand. And that is exactly what he did in 1960, when his bold actions cost him his job.

Bill Walsh, who eventually won three Super Bowls in the 1980s as head coach of the San Francisco 49ers and coached Powell with the Raiders in 1966, said, "Art was his own man and fiercely independent. He was not afraid to voice his opinions and take a stand."

Powell refused to bow to the societal norms of the Jim Crow South, reflecting on his efforts: "The challenges before me were social challenges. I chose to challenge them, while others chose not to. I made a lot of people angry. All I wanted to do was be a football player. The rest of this stuff was dumped in my lap."

Powell was cut following a promising rookie season with the Eagles in which he played defensive back and returned kicks. In August 1960, the Eagles headed to Norfolk, Virginia, to play an exhibition game against the Redskins. Powell said, "We were told that colored players would not be allowed to stay with the rest of the team at the hotel. I chose not to play. The other African American players [Tim Brown, Ted Dean, and Clarence Peaks] said they weren't going to play either—but they did. I was the one that ended up being cut."

The Eagles tried to explain Powell's sudden exit from the squad, reporting that Powell was overweight and that his play against the Rams and 49ers in preseason games was something less than inspired. Eagles coach Buck Shaw also stated he made his decision based on performance, not promise.

Some newspaper reports questioned Powell's sudden departure. Bill Wallace of the *New York Times* wrote, "Just how or why this fellow, who ran a kickoff back 95 yards against the Giants last year, was waived out of the National League and no other club made a claim on his services is mysterious." Harold Rosenthal of the *New York Herald Tribune* said of Powell, "A lot of eyebrows went up when [Powell] was waived out of the National Football League." Newspaper accounts from 1959 said Powell "was the most exciting rookie to come along in some time." Bob Brozman, his former coach at San Jose State, said of Powell, "This fellow can't miss being a star in your league."

After he was let go by the Eagles, Powell was fortunate enough to catch on with the New York Titans of the new AFL and became an All-Pro. But his protest in Norfolk in 1959 was not the end of his militant ways. Later, while a member of the Titans and then the Raiders, Powell became involved in other protests. He was able to participate in these protests without reprisal because he had become the best wide receiver in the AFL in the early 1960s. Given his uncontested success on the field, in addition to the momentum of the burgeoning civil rights movement, Powell could now let his feelings be known without fear of repercussion.

Like Art Powell, Walter Beach also found himself without a job when he protested the accommodations provided for him and his Boston Patriots teammates. Beach, a defensive back from Pontiac, Michigan, played at Central Michigan from 1956 to 1959 after a two-year stint in the army. In 1960, Beach was drafted in the fifteenth round by both the New York Giants and the Oakland Raiders, but he opted to sign with the Giants. Beach did not stick with the Giants and ended up in Boston, playing six games for the Patriots in their inaugural season. Beach, a cornerback, played twelve games with the Patriots in 1961 and looked to have a promising career ahead of him.

Never one to back down from discrimination, Beach's career with the Patriots ended abruptly in August 1962. As Beach explained,

> Even though the AFL was considered the more liberal of the two pro football leagues, they still practiced Jim Crow segregation when we went to the South as far as hotel accommodations were concerned. Well, I questioned this policy. If we could play together on the field, why couldn't we stay together off of it? Military barracks had integrated by then, but in pro football in the 1950s and 1960s, whenever we played in the South, the white players would stay in the luxury hotels and most of the time we would stay with local families.
>
> In August of 1962, the Patriots were scheduled to play an exhibition game in New Orleans against the Oilers. When our coach, Mike Holovak, posted the separate itineraries at our practice facility in Boston early in the week, I noticed the white players were staying at a nice hotel not far from the practice facility in New Orleans, while the black players were sent to an out-of-the-way hotel in the black part of the city. To me, I thought it was unfair to the black players to stay at an inferior hotel and also to be inconvenienced by the additional travel time to the practice facility.

Beach continued,

> I presented my views on this to Coach Holovak, but it fell on deaf ears.
> We then had a meeting of the black players on the Patriots: Rommie
> Loudd, Ron Burton, Houston Antwine, LeRoy Moore, Clyde Wash-
> ington, Larry Garron, and me. I was elected spokesperson for the group.
> What we suggested was that the black players fly down the day of the
> game and fly back to Boston when the game was over. When I went to
> speak to management, I got a plane ticket all right. A plane ticket back
> to Michigan. I was cut by the Patriots and labeled a "troublemaker."
>
> I sat out the 1962 season, not by choice. In 1963 I decided to write a
> letter to the Cleveland Browns asking for a tryout. They were known as
> one of the more accommodating teams in the NFL with regard to hav-
> ing blacks on their roster. To my amazement, they sent me a contract
> and I ended up with the Browns, winning a championship with them
> in 1964. I've always been a black with attitude. I was never ashamed
> of anything. I never had to be validated by a racist system. It's just who
> I am.

When Beach was with the Browns, he struck up a friendship with Hall
of Fame Browns fullback Jim Brown that has lasted to this day. In 1964,
Brown showed that his pull as a star could influence the choices made
within the organization. From day one of Beach's stint with the Browns,
a watchful eye was set on him for any signs of "trouble." Art Modell had
explicitly told Beach when he signed, "We took a chance with you when
no one else would."

"That stuff follows you around," Beach said.

> I knew racism was involved. I eventually was blackballed by the Browns
> too, but it took them a while. The only reason I stuck around so long
> was I had Jim Brown on my side. Art Modell may still have been angry
> with me about the plane ride the season before. On a flight home in
> 1963 at the end of the season, I was reading a book titled *Message to the
> Black Man*, by Elijah Mohammed. Art Modell saw me reading, and he
> said, "I don't want you reading that book." I pretty much ignored him
> and kept on reading. When he passed by again a while later, Modell
> repeated, "I thought I told you, I don't want you reading that book." I
> told him, "I thought you were joking. A man cannot tell another man
> what to read. I play football. I am under contract to play football, but
> no one can tell me what to read."

During training camp in 1964, Beach was called into a meeting with Modell and the Browns coaches, who informed Beach he was being released. Later in the day, Brown came by the dormitory to get Beach for practice, only to be told by Beach that he had been cut. Brown asked Beach to wait there and then returned a few minutes later and said, "Let's go to practice." Beach was back on the team, but he never received an explanation or an apology from the Browns for his release. Brown had informed Modell that Beach was one of the best cornerbacks on the team and that Beach gave them a chance to have a better team. Brown informed the Browns coaches that if they weren't going to do all that they could to have the best team possible, then he might not be able to do all that he could to help the Browns win.

When Brown left the Browns after the 1965 season, Beach knew that his days were numbered. Sure enough, in 1966 Beach played five games with the Browns and was cut. Beach then said the Browns more or less placed him in limbo for the next few years. He was placed on waivers, which would allow another team to sign him. However, the Browns would retract the waivers whenever another team tried made an offer. Beach was convinced this was done to blackball him. "I was a threat to them," he said. "I was one of those who stood up against racism, and they blackballed me." Beach ended up suing the NFL, claiming that if he had been allowed to sign with another team, he could have played longer. He won, receiving years of service added to his career, which in turn helped his pension.

The individual stories of Bob Mann, Eddie Macon, Milt Campbell, Henry Ford, Art Powell, and Walter Beach are living proof that if you were black and did not conform to your team's wishes—whether it be over money, interracial marriage, or accommodations for black players in the Jim Crow South—it could cost you your job and end your career.

Eventually, though, individuals like Dr. Martin Luther King Jr., spearheading the civil rights movement in the 1950s and 1960s, and events like the 1960 lunch counter sit-ins in Greensboro, North Carolina, the Freedom Riders going down south in 1961 and 1962, and the March on Washington in 1963 brought to the attention of the nation the struggles of African Americans—and black pro football players found themselves being able to speak out at last.

3

PIONEERS OF INTEGRATION

The Rise and Fall of the 1952 Dallas Texans

The year was 1960. The civil rights movement was gaining momentum with the Greensboro lunch counter sit-ins and the resounding voices of brave leaders like Dr. Martin Luther King Jr. In the world of professional sports, the Dallas Cowboys of the NFL and the Houston Oilers and Dallas Texans of the AFL joined their respective leagues, which was a monumental occasion for civil rights and integration advocates. Most were under the impression that these three teams were the first professional teams in history to have African Americans on their rosters while playing in a segregated city. And while this indeed marked a major transition for Houston, Dallas, and professional football, it wasn't the first of its kind. The groundwork for such a major transition away from the traditional customs of the segregated South had already been laid eight years before the Cowboys, Oilers, and Texans came into existence. As the civil rights movement was in its infancy, the 1952 Dallas Texans were among the first to pave the way for integration in professional sports.

The 1952 Texans carried two African American players on their roster: running back Buddy Young, from Chicago and the University of Illinois, and halfback/quarterback George Taliaferro, from Gary, Indiana, and Indiana University. Although they were not native Texans and were transplanted from their northern home states, Young and Taliaferro were the first two African Americans to live and play pro football in the segregated South. Their stories, and the story of the team that dared to carry them on its roster, stand as a cornerstone of the legacy of integrated professional football in the Deep South—long-lost innovators and unsung heroes laying the groundwork for the changes to come.

The 1952 version of the Dallas Texans came to be when the New York Yanks football franchise was sold to investors in Dallas. Originally

known as the Rangers, the team's name was quickly changed to the Texans. (And when the 1960 Dallas Texans of the AFL came into the new
league, they also strongly considered becoming the Rangers before settling
on the Texans.) Giles Miller, a thirty-one-year-old textile magnate, was
president of the combined sixteen investors who purchased the Yanks.
Miller and the other investors bought the franchise for a steep $300,000.
Regarding the investment, Miller mused, "Money means nothing to us.
We have so many millions behind us we don't know which millions to accept. We can make pro football pay—just as we do oil and cotton."

"Right now, I would like an all-star Texas team but above all else
I want a winner," Miller said, "and I don't care if the players are white,
black, green, or pink. Places on our team are open strictly on the basis of
ability without regard to race or creed." Miller and his fellow investors
chose Texas for their new venture—and for good reason. George Halas,
owner and coach of the Chicago Bears, once said of the Lone Star State,
"They have everything in Texas to make our venture a huge success—
football interest, a big stadium, a source of tremendous native material, and
an enthusiastic group of owners who love the game and are willing to go
along if they never make a dollar out of it."

Jim Phelan was chosen as coach of the Texans. He carried with him a
history of success as a college coach, with a compiled record of 137–87–14
from 1920 to 1947 with Missouri, Purdue, Washington, and St. Mary's.
Phelan would be elected to the College Football Hall of Fame in 1973.
In 1948, Phelan then gave pro football a try when he took over the Los
Angeles Dons of the AAFC in 1948 and 1949. He coached the New York
Yanks in 1951 before they were moved to Dallas. Prior to coaching in Dal-
las, his pro record was 11–15.

Miller and his other investors then negotiated to use the seventy-
five-thousand-seat Cotton Bowl for their home games. J. Curtis Sanford,
founder of the Cotton Bowl and the secretary of the Texans, was very
optimistic about the upcoming season. He said, "It was a Dallas crowd
that caused the league to locate a club here. . . . Dallas was the only
place outside of the league that drew over fifty thousand for an exhibition game." Sanford was referring to an exhibition game that took place
in 1951 at the Cotton Bowl between the Giants and the Lions, drawing
fifty-six thousand fans.

Sanford also believed the addition of African Americans Buddy Young
and George Taliaferro to the team would make them an attraction. He
pointed to the fact that the Dallas baseball team in the Texas League had
a black pitcher, Dave Hoskins, and they had had a very successful year at

the gate. The Texans hoped that with a roster including Taliaferro, Young, and possibly Sherman Howard (who later refused), they could replicate the success of Hoskins and the Eagles in Dallas. They couldn't have been more wrong.

The news media picked up on the fact that there could potentially be three African Americans on the Texans roster in a segregated city and re-layed their concerns. On January 21, 1952, the *Cumberland News* addressed the race issue:

> The Yanks roster lists three Negro players—Buddy Young, Sherman Howard, and George Taliaferro, all backs—and their status in the new Jim Crow surroundings became a question. Unless traded, Young and his mates are expected to play as usual. The Cotton Bowl has no rule against Negro players. Wally Triplett of Penn State played in a bowl game there a few seasons ago, and there have been Negro participants in games there since.

Wendell Smith, sports columnist for the *Pittsburgh Courier*, reported in a February 18, 1952, column that

> Buddy Young, as they sometimes refer to as the "Mr. Zip" of pro football, surveyed the situation carefully and said, "Football is football wherever you play it. If they don't draw the color line in Texas, I'd just as soon play for Dallas as any other city. All I want is the salary I've been getting down through the years. . . . I'm sure we will be okay down in Dallas. If Mr. Miller wants me to play for him, I'll go down there and do my very best for his club."

Smith continued,

> A couple of years ago, Buddy played in an all-star pro game in Hous-ton. The memory of that event is still fresh in Buddy's mind. He said, "I played in that game and the people treated us fine. The people in Texas are football crazy. Bill Willis and Marion Motley of the Cleveland Browns were down there with me and we all had a wonderful time. We never had a bit of trouble. We were there for about two weeks and enjoyed every moment of it. That's why I say I won't mind playing in Dallas if the club wants me. Insofar as the players are concerned, I have no worries. . . . We had a large number of Southerners on the Yanks and we got along just fine. They are no different from payers from any other part of the country. All they want you to do is produce. If you play good ball, that's all they ask."

Sharing Young's sentiments, Miller scoffed at the idea that his African American players would be snubbed by the fans, asserting, "In Texas, Negroes and whites get along very well. They sit in their own sections, but we are reserving just as good seats for our Negro fans as we do our white fans."

Yet, despite Young's and Miller's protestations, there was indeed cause for concern. Out of the three African American players, only two of them, Young and Taliaferro, eventually came to Texas to play for Dallas. Howard did not. More than six decades later, he discussed his reasons:

> Going to Dallas was a bad experience. I went down there with Buddy and George to talk with Mr. Miller, the new owner. I remember him discussing our relationship with him, among other things.
>
> When it became time for lunch, Mr. Miller had his chauffeur pick us up. Well, the chauffeur took us to downtown Dallas, and we went behind the railroad tracks to what I guess was the black part of town. Once there, he took us to this little hot dog stand to get us lunch. After that, I knew I didn't want to go to Dallas. I just didn't want to be part of that situation.
>
> What I did was get traded to the Cleveland Browns. I knew the trainer there, and he let Paul Brown know that I didn't want to go to Dallas. So, the Browns traded for me, and I didn't have to endure what Buddy and George did in Dallas.

When interviewed about the segregated conditions faced by blacks, white teammates of African American players seemed to downplay the issue at hand. Center Joe Reid said,

> As for our black players in Dallas, I was fond of Buddy Young. He had a great sense of humor. He worked really hard. George Taliaferro, though, he was kind of sour. To me, the segregation for the blacks in Dallas wasn't that bad. I'm from Mississippi and played college ball at LSU. Compared to those two places, segregation in Dallas wasn't that bad.

Pro Football Hall of Fame member Gino Marchetti was a rookie defensive end with the Dallas Texans in 1952. He echoed Reid's complacency:

> As far as how Buddy and George were treated by the people of Dallas, I thought they were treated fairly well. They were both nice guys who played by the rules. Sometimes they couldn't stay at our hotel or eat with us. There was nothing we could do about it. I do remember one time when we went to Houston to play an exhibition game. A car

picked up Buddy and George when we got to Houston. I didn't see them again until we saw them at the practice field. Then I didn't see them again until right before the game. They told us they had a great time in Houston. They had no bed check and got to go to a bunch of parties, while the rest of us were stuck in our hotel.

Segregation was strange for me, though. I had grown up in California, and things were relaxed there. I had always played with and against blacks. When I got to Dallas, I was kind of upset how things were there.

In reality, Young and Taliaferro, along with their families, experienced racism, bigotry, and hardships in segregated Dallas. Geraldine Young, Buddy's widow, described life in Dallas in 1952:

We weren't in Dallas that long before the team folded. When we got there, Giles Miller's maid and chauffeur were a big help to Buddy and me. There was also a black sportswriter in Dallas who was a big help to us. The maid and chauffeur told me that if I ever got into trouble, I should just say I was "Giles Miller's nigger." Sure enough, not long after that, I was taking my seven-year-old to school one morning, and I was downtown and made an illegal U-turn. I got pulled over, and I said to the white cop, "I'm Giles Miller's nigger." The officer said, "Well, why didn't you say that in the first place?" and he let me go. The whole experience, though, was very belittling to me. Although I was born in Alabama, I was raised in Chicago. I didn't know these kinds of things went on in Dallas.

We found a place in Dallas on Peabody Street. It was a mixed-race neighborhood. Every other house had a white person living there. When the local kids found out Buddy Young lived in their neighborhood, some of them came over and cut our grass. Some of the people were nice as pie. Some said they didn't mind the black kids in the neighborhood going to the local white high school. There were some classrooms that weren't being used there that the blacks could have used. But the school district wouldn't let us go there, so the black kids had to go all the way across town to the black high school by Love Field.

There was one incident where we lived when Buddy's eight-year-old sister came to visit us. I really didn't know anybody in the neighborhood yet. She rode her bike down to the corner, and some white lady told her, "Don't no niggers ride around here! Don't come back!" However, a white man came down from upstairs from where that woman was and said to Buddy's sister, "Little girl, you did the right thing and you can ride that bike anywhere you want." That one incident showed me that there were good white people and bad white people.

Once the games started, we found out there was segregated seating in Dallas. My seven-year-old asked why we had to sit where we did. Rather than cloud his mind and explain to him about segregated seating, I just told him our seats were closer to the field, so that's why we got to sit where we did. We had to go through the mud at the "colored" entrance, and we had a section that was roped off. After a while, some of the whites would come over to the ropes, and they got into a conversation with my son. They couldn't believe that a seven-year-old could know so much about football.

One of Young's teammates who helped ease his transition in segregated Dallas was fullback Zollie Toth. Toth and Young had played together on the New York Yanks, and Toth followed Young to Dallas. When the two roomed together in the early 1950s on the Yanks, it marked the first time white and black players had roomed together in professional sports.

Buddy Young. *University of Illinois Athletics*

Toth, a fullback who played his college football at LSU, spoke of his time with the Dallas Texans and his relationship with Buddy Young:

> We only lasted four or five games in Dallas. After that, we moved to Hershey, Pennsylvania. We practiced right across the street from the Hershey chocolate factory. They had no idea in Texas how to run a ball club.

Zollie Toth. *LSU Athletics*

I met Buddy up in New York when we played with the Yanks. Buddy asked me one day if I wanted to room with him. I said, "I would love to room with you," and that was it. It was no big deal to us. Buddy was a fine gentleman. We got along great. When we got to Dallas, we stayed roommates. I would go over to his place in Dallas to eat. His being black didn't bother me one bit. It did bother several people I knew back in Louisiana. They couldn't figure out why I would room with a black man. When Buddy and Geraldine named their son after me, it was quite an honor.

Geraldine Young discussed her husband's relationship with Toth:

We named our son after Zollie Toth. He was quite a character. He used to spend the night with us when we went to Baltimore. He was from Virginia but played at LSU. He used to tell Buddy and me, "I can't take you to my parents' house in Virginia—they wouldn't understand." He and Buddy were the best of friends. They roomed together on the road. When we were in Dallas, Zollie used to go to the black restaurants with us. If there was a raid on the place, he had to sneak out the back door.

Geraldine Young told more stories about their short stay in Dallas:

After the few home games we had in Dallas, Buddy and I would have parties after the game. Almost everyone came—whites, blacks, and prominent people from Dallas. People like judges and lawyers. To them, "nigger" was a word that was common. They used it matter-of-factly in their everyday language. I remember a judge asking us one night, "What was the name of that nigger that played for the Rams?" He meant Woody Strode.

In another instance, Bob Celari, our quarterback, invited this girl he was dating to one of our after-game parties. When she got there, Bob didn't answer the door; I did. She said, "Excuse me, I must have the wrong address." She left but came back about ten minutes later and said, "I'm looking for Bob Celari." Her face was beet red when she found out she had been invited to a black person's house.

There was another incident occurred where the word "nigger" was thrown around. One day I took Buddy to practice and I was waiting for him. A white fellow came up to the car and said, "Ma'am, I'm waiting for a nigger named Buddy Young." This man knew everything athletically about Buddy—all of his accomplishments and all. This other man who was with him came up and said, "I want to apologize for my friend here. He's waiting for a nigger football player. I'm an opera buff, and I don't care too much about football. We're drunk, though, and I hope he's not annoying you." That incident turned it around for me. I can't explain it, but after that, I wasn't scared anymore about being in Dallas.

In the end, though, I was glad to get away from Dallas. It was not a good experience. It was a rude awakening getting to Dallas and seeing segregation. For example, one night, Buddy and I were invited to go to a minor-league baseball game in Dallas. We had to go in the "colored" entrance. Seeing that "colored" sign does something to you if you haven't seen it before and you're not used to it. It was kind of unsettling. Then, to make it worse, there wasn't a big crowd that night, and they let the white fans move down to get closer to the action. We had to stay in our seats in the "colored" section, though.

Another event or incident was when we went to the Texas State Fair at the fairgrounds there in Dallas where the Cotton Bowl stadium is. Since we were black, there was a day set aside for us. It was known as "Negro Achievement Day."

2ND BIG
NEGRO ACHIEVEMENT DAY
OCT. 13
PLAN NOW TO ATTEND
SENIOR DAY OCT. 13

PRIZES
* 4-H CLUB AND FUTURE FARMERS' AWARDS
* 115,000 NEGROES ATTENDED IN '46

IT'S
A
WHALE
OF
A
SHOW!

* PARADE 9:30 A. M.
* TWINS' CONTEST
* BEAUTY CONTEST
  Beautiful girls from all ove Texas
* CHORAL CLUB CONTES
  20 clubs will participate
* FOOTBALL GAMES
  Lincoln High School vs. Bool er T. Washington High Schoc 2:30 P. M.
  Prairie View College vs. Wile College 8:00 P. M.

THE STATE FAIR OF TEXAS
THE SHOW WINDOW OF THE SOUTHWEST

NOW THRU OCT. 19   DALLAS

Negro Achievement Day Poster, 1947. *Robert Jacobus*

Negro Achievement Day dated back to 1889, when it was called "Colored People's Day." Colored People's Day was discontinued in 1910 and was brought back as Negro Achievement Day in 1936. Negro Achievement Day was touted as a way recognize the progress and accomplishments of African Americans in Texas. The day would start with a parade and then the crowning of the Negro Achievement Day Queen. Later in the day was the presentation of the Most Distinguished Negro Citizen Award. In the afternoon, there was a high school football game between rival black high schools at the Cotton Bowl, and in the evening, two black colleges would square off under the Cotton Bowl lights.

Opinion was mixed among the black community back then. Some thought it was not a form of segregation, but others felt that the money spent on Negro Achievement Day contributed to segregation more than fighting it. In 1955, the NAACP led the first large-scale protest against Negro Achievement Day, and by 1957, the word "Negro" had been dropped from the name. The specified day for blacks ended in 1961, and in 1967, the State Fair of Texas fully integrated.

"For whatever reason," Geraldine Young concluded, "I remember the 'colored' restrooms there at 'Negro Achievement Day.' Even when we had our own day there, we still had to use the segregated restrooms."

George Taliaferro was the other African American who came from the New York Yanks to Dallas. A halfback, quarterback, and punter, Taliaferro had led Indiana to their only Big Ten title in 1945 with a 9–0–1 record and a number four national ranking. When he left Indiana, he was their all-time leader in rushing, passing, and punting.

In 1949 Taliaferro became the first African American ever drafted by the NFL when the Bears chose him in the thirteenth round. Taliaferro did not play for the Bears, however, because he had already signed a contract with the Los Angeles Dons of the AAFC, and he chose to honor that contract. After the AAFC folded in 1949, Taliaferro played for the New York Yanks in 1950 and 1951 before heading to Dallas. He made the Pro Bowl squad with the New York Yanks in 1951, the Dallas Texans in 1952 (their only Pro Bowl selection), and the Baltimore Colts in 1953.

Always outspoken, Taliaferro stood up for himself and other African Americans back at Indiana University. In 1947 he did his part in breaking down racial barriers in Bloomington, Indiana, the home of the Indiana Hoosiers. African Americans could only attend the local movie theater on weekends, and when they did, they had to sit in the balcony. Taliaferro, who had just returned from a stint in the army, took matters into his own hands. Taliaferro went to the theater on a Tuesday and went up to the sign that said "colored." Taliaferro said, "I took a screwdriver, took down that sign, and went and sat downstairs. I think that ended segregation in that movie theater." Taliaferro still has the sign in his home today.

Decades later, Taliaferro discussed his experience in Dallas, along with other events:

> We only stayed in Dallas for part of the 1952 season. We stayed in the home of an African American schoolteacher named Jewell Price. My wife, Viola, and I rented a room from her. We came in July and left Dallas after our last game there.
>
> In Dallas, nothing was integrated yet. No hotels or restaurants. Now Buddy and Geraldine Young did have a house in Dallas, and we would go over there and have parties. We got to know other black citizens in Dallas. I really didn't go out much during the season, though. I was pretty strict about my training.
>
> At the Cotton Bowl, Viola and Geraldine Young could not sit with the other wives; they had to sit in the end zone, which is the only place African Americans were allowed. Somehow this was made known to the owners, and they said they could sit with the other wives, but Vi and Geraldine refused as long as no other African Americans would be allowed to anywhere but the end zone. It was their way of making a statement.

Viola Taliaferro added, "Things in Virginia where I came from were bad segregation-wise but not as bad as it was in Texas. One thing that happened was that we were unable to integrate the Cotton Bowl. They wanted Geraldine Young and me to sit in the end zone with the other blacks. We didn't stay; we left."

George Taliaferro remarked,

> Back then in Texas and the South you couldn't get too bent out of shape about discrimination. It was everywhere. You had to be careful. I remember when we went to Houston to play the Cardinals in an exhibition game. We weren't allowed to stay at the Shamrock Hotel with our white teammates. We stayed with a local black businessman and his family. We ended up having a ball, going to all of the parties.
>
> You know, being discriminated against and the way we were treated helped us African Americans playing in the NFL to play harder. We wanted to show those honkies that we could play.

Before the Texans headed to Dallas to begin their season on September 28 at home in the Cotton Bowl against the New York Giants, they held their training camp at Schreiner Institute, a small college in the Texas Hill Country town of Kerrville. In August 1952, Texas was in the midst of a drought that lasted through most of the 1950s.

Rhett Miller, grandson of Giles Miller, talked about the conditions in Kerrville:

> The team was brought to a ramshackle training facility in Kerrville where there were so many rattlesnakes that if the ball wound up in the tall grass surrounding the field, the Texans sent equipment manager Willie Garcia to retrieve it. The thinking was that since Willie had a wooden leg, he only stood a 50 percent chance of being bitten.

Texans center Joseph Reid said,

> The Texans were kind of a hodge-podge of coaches and players. The whole thing was disjointed. Some wealthy people in Dallas decided they wanted a pro football team. They were big talkers. They weren't really committed and didn't spend their money wisely. It was kind of a fun year, though.
>
> We went to training camp in Kerrville at Schreiner College. I remember it was hot and dry—it didn't rain much. Our coach was Jim Phelan. He was a nice guy, mostly a college coach. He didn't believe in "down and mean" and working your butt off. Who knows—maybe if he had worked us harder in Kerrville, we would have won more than one game.

Hall of Fame defensive tackle Art Donovan, who also played for the 1952 Texans, said about Jim Phelan and his methods, "We had a good time in spite of everything, mostly because of Phelan. He was one of the greatest men I ever met, but he didn't know a thing about football. At practice we used to bat the ball back and forth over the goalposts like we were playing volleyball."

Phelan was also popular with the players mostly because he had a disdain for practice. "Once," Donovan recalled, "we ran a couple of plays without fouling up. Phelan stopped practice, loaded everybody on a bus, and took us to the racetrack. Jimmy loved the races."

Don Colo was another Texans player. When the Texans folded after the 1952 season, Colo went to the Cleveland Browns in a fifteen-player trade. At Cleveland, Colo became a Pro Bowl defensive tackle and played on the Browns' 1954 and 1955 championship teams.

Colo reminisced about his experience with the Texans:

Dallas was quite an experience. So was Kerrville, where we trained. Hell yes, I remember it. It was hot as hell. All in all, Kerrville wasn't a bad place. Schreiner College where we trained was nice. I'm Catholic, and I remember a church there where the priest would deliver these forty-five-minute sermons in an un-air-conditioned building. That was rough, let me tell you.

Our coach, Jim Phelan, was a nice guy, but things were a mess. Once we got to Dallas to play the season, things were okay there. When we couldn't finish out the season in Dallas and had to leave and go to Pennsylvania, we didn't want to leave Texas. If the owners just could have put in a little more money to keep it going. . . . It's too bad because, in a lot of ways, we had some good players in Dallas, like Gino Marchetti and Art Donovan. When they went to Baltimore, they added some players and ended up winning a couple of championships.

As far as my black teammates, Buddy Young and George Taliaferro, Buddy was an exceptional young guy. His wife Geraldine was wonderful too. George was a little hard-headed, but he was okay. We did have a third black, Sherman Howard, who was with us for just a little while. He ended up with me on the Browns. I wasn't aware of the segregated seating at the Cotton Bowl. Being from the North, I didn't know about things like that or I didn't realize that's how things were down South. One incident I do remember with Buddy and George was before the season we had a banquet at either the Baker or Adolphus Hotel in Dallas. Buddy and George were able to attend, and that was the first time the hotel had served black people in their dining room.

Gino Marchetti said about joining the NFL and the Dallas Texans in 1952,

I was so excited about going to play professional football. When I got drafted by the Texans, everybody was telling me how lucky I was, that I would have a great life in Texas, and the Millers had all this money. That's a laugh! I ended up going to the most disorganized camp in the world. The equipment manager burned all of the ankle wraps. He didn't know what they were. We didn't practice for six or seven weeks. When Coach Phelan called practice, we really didn't practice.

George Taliaferro also spoke of the conditions in Kerrville:

I had never seen weather as hot as it was in Kerrville. It was like 105 degrees every day, and it was arid. The coaches warned us not to go out of dorms at night out on to the campus grounds. There were these huge cracks in the ground from the lack of rain. The coaches were afraid

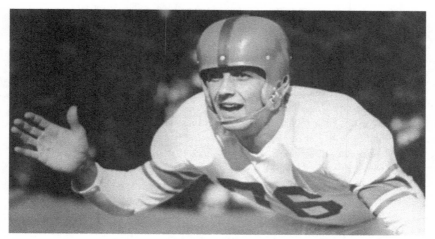

Gino Marchetti, Dallas Texans. *University of San Francisco Athletics*

we might fall into one and mess up an ankle or leg. I never went out at night. I never saw the town of Kerrville. I couldn't tell you if the people there were bad or indifferent towards blacks.

Chuck Ortmann played quarterback for the 1952 Texans. He had previously played quarterback and punted at the University of Michigan. He went to the Steelers with the twentieth pick of the 1951 NFL Draft and was their leading passer his rookie season. He then went to Dallas for 1952, severely injuring his ankle in the fourth game of the season, effectively ending his NFL career.

Ortmann talked about his time in Dallas and playing with Buddy Young and George Taliaferro:

I was put on waivers by the Steelers on September 24 and then signed by the Texans on October 1. I started that Sunday the 5th against the 49ers. I lasted three games with the Texans before I got hurt. I found out quickly things were sort of a laugh in Dallas. It was pathetic there. There was supposed to be a lot of fan support. That didn't happen. The stands were empty.

We had an all–Big Ten backfield in the short time I was in Dallas, with me, Buddy Young, George Taliaferro, and Dick Hoerner. Buddy Young was fast. He was also calm and casual. Not much bothered him. He could roll up in a blanket and fall asleep in a moment's notice. He was a great teammate.

As far as race in Dallas, I didn't realize there was segregated seating at the Cotton Bowl. I'm sorry to hear that. I never really thought about where Buddy or George lived, or where they went after practice. They went their way, and the whites went theirs. Now that I think about it, living in Dallas back when it was segregated couldn't have been easy. Once again, though, you just didn't think about it. Your main concern was sticking with the team. You know, Buddy and George's color didn't mean much to me. . . . They were my teammates. George was terrific. The color of his skin didn't matter to me. I had black teammates at Michigan and never gave it a second thought.

Ortmann concluded, "We could have had a good team in Dallas, but the coaches never really got us to work together. Things were unorganized under Coach Phelan. We had Buddy and George there, Zollie Toth, Art Donovan, Gino Marchetti, and Don Colo, among others. We just never got it together."

When the exhibition season started for the Dallas Texans, things went well at first. The first exhibition game was August 16 at Antler Stadium, the local high school venue in Kerrville. The Texans played the Brooke Army Medical Center Comets of San Antonio. A large crowd was expected, many of them coming up from San Antonio, seventy miles southeast from Kerrville. The Texans won, 34–7. About five thousand people packed Antler Stadium, and according to the *Kerrville Mountain Sun*, "Great numbers of the spectators were from Dallas, Houston, Austin, and San Antonio." Buddy Young scored three touchdowns, including a 78-yard dash. Young also caught a 33-yard touchdown pass from George Taliaferro. No mention was made of the fact that Young and Taliaferro were the first African Americans to play against white players in Kerrville.

On Saturday, August 23, the Texans played their second exhibition game in Corpus Christi against Carswell AFB. Again, Young and Taliaferro were the first African Americans to integrate football in Corpus Christi. Six thousand fans came to Buccaneer Stadium to see the Texans triumph, 27–0. Taliaferro had 88 yards rushing in 15 carries to lead the Texans. There was a well-known segregated seating policy at Buccaneer Stadium, and an ad in the August 21, 1952, *Corpus Christi Caller Times* said that black fans "will be assured of 150 end zone seats in a special section for Negroes."

On Friday, August 29, Young and Taliaferro integrated Broncho Stadium in Odessa, Texas, along with Ralph Goldston and Don Stevens of the Eagles, as the Dallas Texans played the Philadelphia Eagles in an exhibition game before sixteen thousand fans. The Eagles romped to a 24–7 win in the Texans' first game against NFL competition. Bud Grant scored on an 8-yard touchdown reception for the Eagles. Later in the regular season, on

December 7, Grant burned the Texans for eleven catches for 203 yards and 2 touchdowns in a 38–21 Eagles win.

Notable in the preseason game in Odessa was the performance of Grant, the Eagles wide receiver and future Minnesota Vikings Pro Football Hall of Fame head coach. Grant said about playing in Odessa and the South in general,

> I played against Buddy and George in the Big Ten. I remember it was hot in Odessa. I played almost the whole game. I bet I lost eight to ten pounds. I remember one fella on our team got overheated. For whatever reason, we were always playing exhibition games in the South back then, in places like Shreveport and Little Rock. It was the hottest part of the year; we should have played those game in the North.
>
> I don't recall any problems, race-wise, at the game. I know Dallas had George and Buddy on their team, and we had a couple of black players on our team—Ralph Goldston and Don Stevens. They were just a couple of rookies trying to make the team, which they did. I don't remember any kind of incidents with them either. They were a couple of Big Ten guys too—Goldston from Indiana and Stevens from Illinois.

On Friday night, September 5, the Texans played their fourth exhibition game and defeated the Washington Redskins, 27–14, in San Antonio. The last Texan score came on an 8-yard touchdown pass from Taliaferro to Young. As with their first three exhibition games, Taliaferro and Young integrated their venue.

September 20 was the Texans' last exhibition game in Houston—the Shamrock Bowl charity exhibition game. Twelve thousand fans showed up in a rainstorm at the new Rice Stadium. The Texans lost, 10–0, to the Chicago Cardinals, who were led by rookie sensation Ollie Matson, an African American running back who had lived in Houston as a youth and who led the University of San Francisco to an undefeated season in 1951.

The Texans' first regular-season game was on September 28 against the New York Giants. The pregame festivities and the start of the game at the Cotton Bowl went well. Before the game, Barbara Gentry of Dallas, who was chosen as Miss Dallas Texans, was brought to the game by a helicopter that landed on the fifty-yard line, where she was greeted by Texas governor Allan Shivers.

The Texans season then started on a positive note when they capitalized on a fumbled punt by a Giant defensive back by the name of Tom Landry and turned it into a touchdown two plays later when Taliaferro passed to Young for a 6–0 lead. This was basically the high point of the

1952 season. The Texans promptly missed the extra point, and things went downhill from there. The Giants dominated the Texans after that and won, 24–6.

Despite the positive start to the season, attendance went steadily downhill from the opening game. A total of 17,499 attended the game at the Cotton Bowl. By their last home game, a 27–6 loss to the Los Angeles Rams on November 9, dropping the Texans' record to a dismal 0–7, attendance was well under 10,000 fans a game. Actually, attendance was a problem from the start. Giles Miller believed his team would have to average 20,000 per game just to break even. They averaged about 12,000.

The statistics show that the Dallas Texans were the worst team in the NFL, not just for the 1952 season, but possibly for all time. Frank Tripucka was the leading passer for the Texans, with 3 touchdown passes and 17 interceptions in six starts. For the season, Texan quarterbacks threw for 12 touchdowns and 30 interceptions. George Taliaferro was the leading rusher for the Texans with just 419 yards. As a team, the Texans scored only 15.2 points a game and turned the ball over 55 times in twelve games.

On defense, the Texans were also pitiful. Their defense gave 30 or more points eight times in twelve games, and more than 40 points five times. The fewest points any team scored that season was 23, which was the only game the Texans won. They allowed almost 400 yards of offense a game, including more than 200 per game on the ground. The Texans gave up an average of 35.6 points per game and 5.7 yards per play.

Eventually the Texans' owners turned the team back over to the league. Giles Miller and the other owners lost more than $225,000 in a little more than half a season. It was estimated they would need an additional $250,000 and the sale of fifteen thousand season tickets for the next season to keep the team afloat. In early November 1952, Miller and the other investors gave up the franchise. The team was run by the NFL for the rest of the season.

A couple of weeks later, a new group of Dallas businessmen offered to come up with $750,000 to keep the franchise in Dallas, but Commissioner Bert Bell said no: "The club owners would rather continue to operate the team themselves" than have it remain in Dallas. The Dallas Texans thus have the dubious distinction of becoming the last franchise in NFL history to fail. After the season, the majority of the Texans players' contracts were purchased by the brand-new Baltimore Colts franchise.

The Texans practiced in Hershey, Pennsylvania, the rest of the season. Their last two home games were played not at the Cotton Bowl, but in other cities. Their first "home" game away from Dallas was at the Rubber

Bowl Stadium in Akron on Thanksgiving Day, November 27, when they played the Chicago Bears. The game was to be played in Chicago but was moved to Akron so as not to conflict with the game between the Chicago Cardinals and Philadelphia Eagles in Chicago on November 30.

The game in Akron was actually part of a Thanksgiving Day double-header, with a local high school game being played in the morning and the Texans and Bears playing in the afternoon. The high school game drew more fans than the Texans game, which had only about three thousand fans in attendance. There were so few fans at the game Coach Jim Phelan recommended that instead of introducing the players before the game, they should "go into the stands and shake hands with each fan."

What those scant three thousand fans witnessed in Akron on that Thanksgiving Day was the Texans' only victory of the season. George Halas, coach of the Bears, was so sure of a win that he started his second stringers. The Texans jumped out to a 20–2 lead and held on for a 27–23 win, in spite of four Texans turnovers. It helped the Texans' cause that the Bears turned the ball over eight times.

What should have been the Texans' final regular-season game at the Cotton Bowl was their season finale with the Detroit Lions. The game was played at Briggs Stadium in Detroit, and the Texans were blasted by the Lions, 41–6. The Lions would go on to win the NFL title in 1952 with a 17–7 Championship Game victory over the Cleveland Browns.

Several former players and others associated with the 1952 Dallas Texans gave their opinions as to why the franchise failed. Art Donovan said, "The presence of black players did not help the team's popularity, and neither did the fact that the Cotton Bowl had segregated seating, which turned off most black fans."

Gino Marchetti gave his take as to why the Texans failed in Dallas:

> I think one reason the Texans failed was because they didn't publicize us at all. Before the season, I made a couple of personal appearances. I went into this one store and I said, "I'm Gino with the Dallas Texans and I'm here for my 2 p.m. personal appearance." The people at the store said, "Who are the Dallas Texans?" They had no idea who I was or who the Texans were. The people of Dallas just didn't accept us. Part of it was most of us weren't native Texans.

Rhett Miller discussed what he thought was his grandfather's biggest mistake with the Dallas Texans:

Despite initial enthusiasm within Dallas' African American community for the team's two black stars, very few black fans were on hand to see Young score. Cotton Bowl officials had coerced Pop into denying black fans access to the $3.60 grandstand seats, allowing them access to only the $1.80 end zone areas. The first preseason game was marred by overcrowding in these sections, and much of the local black community boycotted subsequent games.

He had many regrets about the 1952 Texans, but I believe the segregation of fans topped the list. He was, in fact, a pretty progressive dude. Pop established a charitable foundation called the Goins Foundation, named after Earl Goins, a black war-hero chauffeur who'd all but raised Pop. By going along with the racist ticket policy, Pop went against his own beliefs.

George Taliaferro echoed Rhett Miller's thoughts on the segregated seating at the Cotton Bowl. He recalled,

> The city of Dallas was not receptive to us. We were second-class citizens both in the city and in the Cotton Bowl. In the Cotton Bowl, SMU football was king in the early 1950s. I also think we failed in Dallas for a couple of other reasons. One was the team discriminated against African Americans. They had segregated seating at the Cotton Bowl. For that reason, the blacks in Dallas didn't support us. I also felt a lot of whites stayed away, too, because we had an integrated team.

Yet, amid the failure of the franchise, there was still victory—the silver lining of a dark cloud. Although the fiasco in Dallas in 1952 was a complete loss in many regards, the groundwork for desegregation had been laid and set a precedent that would inspire future teams to continue to make changes. Eight years later, in 1960, the NFL and AFL would return to Dallas with the birth of the NFL Cowboys and the AFL Texans. In addition, in Houston the Oilers became part of the inaugural AFL season that same year. When these integrated teams came to Texas and the South, they continued the legacy of the mostly forgotten 1952 team who, albeit imperfectly, began the long and arduous process of desegregation in Dallas. They are unsung and unknown heroes of desegregation in Texas, at a time when black players faced harsh conditions on and off the field in the Deep South.

4

HEADED DOWN SOUTH
Segregation during Exhibition Games

With the exception of John Henry Johnson being denied the chance to play in an exhibition game in Birmingham in 1957, by the early 1950s African American NFL players were allowed to play in southern cities. However, stretching into the mid-1960s, black professional football players faced many challenges when they traveled to the Jim Crow South. Whether it be travel arrangements, lodging accommodations, or other issues, these players were often subjected to humiliation and hardships both on and off the field.

Surprisingly, when interviewed about their experience during exhibition games during the fifties and sixties, players rarely mention unruly fans or facing racial epithets. Instead, they generally allude to staying apart from their white teammates and describe situations in which they were denied service, relegated to segregated areas, or made to feel inferior by bureaucratic, de jure policies enforcing segregation. The systematic racism posed by Jim Crow reared its ugly head during this time period, with players enduring harsh conditions in order to participate. For these brave players, pro football required strength and perseverance in more ways than one—especially when traveling to the Deep South.

George Taliaferro of the 1952 Dallas Texans shared his experience in early 1950s preseason games in Houston and Tulsa. The year before the New York Yanks were sold and moved to Dallas, they played an exhibition game in Houston against the Detroit Lions on September 21, 1951. The Lions took a 28–14 victory over the Yanks before forty-eight thousand fans at Rice Stadium. Sherman Howard, Buddy Young, and Taliaferro, the latter of whom both scored touchdowns in the losing effort, were the black players for the Yanks.

Taliaferro looked back on his Houston trip:

We went to play the Lions in Houston in 1951 when I was with the New York Yanks. Houston was pretty segregated at that time. It was Sherman Howard, Buddy Young, and myself. We could not stay at the Shamrock Hilton with the white players. The Shamrock was just down the street from Rice Stadium, where we played the Lions. We ended up staying at the home of a wealthy black businessman. What he did was invite members of the African American community in Houston to come over to his house so they could meet us. We had a good time and partied until early in the morning.

The next day after we had been fed at the businessman's house, we went over to the Shamrock Hilton to practice. At the Shamrock, someone reported us, and management excused us from the hotel. They wouldn't even let us attend team meetings there.

Taliaferro also recalled a trip to Tulsa as a member of the Colts on September 10, 1954, along with Young and Charley Robinson. Taliaferro tallied two touchdowns for the Colts in a 21–16 loss to the Steelers:

When we went to Tulsa with the Colts in 1954, I remember it vividly. When I went to college at Indiana, I met and knew a black student from Tulsa. I can't remember his name. He ended up going to law school at Indiana. When we got to the Tulsa airport, we were taken to a local high school, where we practiced.

After practice, Sam Banks, our road manager for the Colts, told me, "George, you guys aren't going to the hotel with the rest of the team." I told Sam, "You might as well count me out. I'm not playing!" The other black guys on the team, Buddy Young and Charley Robinson, weren't outspoken like I was, so they really didn't say anything. I complained to Sam Banks and Weeb Ewbank, our coach, "How are we going to get there, and once we do get there, how can we possibly go anywhere else? We have no money!" "Well," Weeb said, "I have some money," and pulled out some cash from his pocket. I snatched the money out of Weeb's hand, and we got a cab to the black hotel.

When we get there, who was the owner of that hotel? That black guy from Tulsa I went to college with at Indiana! We got to stay there for free. All of the blacks in Tulsa wanted to meet us, so they all came over to the hotel and we partied until two or three in the morning. We still beat the Steelers the next night, even though we were exhausted. The whole thing cost the Colts about three hundred dollars for our one night there in Tulsa. Segregation is expensive. I wrote a check that the Colts gave me to pay for the hotel for three hundred dollars, and the owner cashed it and gave us the money. The Colts supposedly looked into it, but we never really got into any hot water over it.

Starting in 1955, Jacksonville became the site of numerous exhibition games. African American players faced a variety of challenges when they went there. Many of players share stories of discrimination in Jacksonville during the preseason, both on and off the field.

The first exhibition game that ever took place in Jacksonville occurred on August 20, 1955, when the Chicago Cardinals beat the Chicago Bears, 21–6. This was also the first time an integrated game was ever played there. Black players for the Cardinals were Dave Mann and future hall of famers Ollie Matson and Dick "Night Train" Lane. Matson led the Cards with 145 yards on 13 carries, while Mann chipped in 68 yards on 10 attempts, with 2 touchdowns. Bobby Watkins and Henry Mosley were two African American players on the Bears' roster. Mosley was cut before the regular season, but Watkins, a rookie halfback who played his college ball at Ohio State, led the Bears that night, with 43 yards on 10 carries. He ended the 1955 season second in rushing for the Bears, with 553 yards from scrimmage.

A newcomer to Jim Crow, like many of the black players who went South to play in exhibitions, Bobby Watkins spoke of his Jacksonville experience:

> The first NFL game I ever played in was an exhibition game against the Chicago Cardinals in Jacksonville, Florida. It was the first time I had ever been in the South, but not the last. It was a big deal to the people in Jacksonville because I think it was the first time the NFL had been there.
>
> We were met at the airport with convertibles, and a couple of players would get into the back with a pretty girl, and we went downtown for a big parade. Henry Mosley and I were the only two blacks on the Bears at the time. As we were getting ready to get into one of the cars to go to the parade, an official with the parade ushered us to a "special car." When Henry and I were the last ones there, an old car pulls up with a black driver, and we brought up the rear of the parade. And, of course, there was no pretty girl in our car.
>
> After the parade, we stayed in a crummy hotel in the black part of Jacksonville. We stayed there with the black players on the Cards. At the time, Ollie Matson and Night Train Lane were playing for them, so we got to know them fairly well.
>
> We didn't stay with the team in other towns too, like Memphis, Dallas, and Little Rock. I complained to Coach Halas, but he didn't really care. I think Halas considered the Bears to be really popular in the South, so he scheduled games there.

Watkins summed up how many black players felt about the mindsets of their white owners:

> Of course, worrying about what his black players would have to deal with down South was the furthest thing from [Halas's] mind. We stayed in lousy hotels or with black families, while the white players stayed in first-class hotels. We usually had to take black taxis over to the white hotel for meetings, which took up a lot of our time. One time in one of those southern cities, I can't remember which, we got tired of standing outside in the middle of summer waiting for a cab after we had been to a team meeting at the white hotel. Me and a couple of other black players decided to wait in the lobby of the hotel where it was air-conditioned.
>
> Like I said, I went to George Halas and complained about our treatment. He more or less brushed me off with the usual, "That's just that way it is down here, Bobby." I did finally convince him to let us rent a car, rather than use a taxi. We ended up getting a car that was air-conditioned, which cost more. Halas wasn't too happy about that.
>
> A couple of weeks after we played in Jacksonville, we went to Memphis to play the Redskins. Of course, the Redskins didn't have any black players—Henry Mosley had been cut from our team, so I was the only black playing. I remember standing on the sidelines, and I looked up into the stands and noticed all of the black fans were sitting in the end zones, where there were hardly any lights. It was pretty dark. The other part of the stadium, the playing field where the whites sat, was all lit up. I've always remembered the contrast of the light and dark of those bleachers, both with the lights and the fans.

Watkins concluded:

> Then the next week we go to Little Rock. We beat the Giants and I scored the only touchdown. The game was pretty boring, and when I was taken out of the game, a fan starts hollering, "Hey, Halas, put the nigger back in! He's the only ball player you've got!"
>
> So, my rookie year, my most vivid memories of my first time in the South were the parade in Jacksonville, the stadium in Memphis, and that fan yelling at Coach Halas to put me back in the game.

The Bears played again in Jacksonville on August 17, 1957. This time their opponent was the Pittsburgh Steelers, who the Bears defeated, 24–7. Henry Ford, who would be cut from the Steelers less than a month after this game because of his relationship with his future wife Rochelle, a white woman, told a story about his parade experience in Jacksonville:

They had a parade in Jacksonville to help promote the game. The black players found out that we could not participate in the parade. The white players got to ride in convertibles with a pretty young lady sitting next to them. We got to watch from the crowd. When we got to the stadium a little later to play the game, the white players asked, "Hey, where were you guys in the parade?" We explained that we couldn't participate. After that, it wasn't really discussed again.

Jack McClairen was entering his third season with the Steelers in 1957. The wide receiver had his best year in 1957, with 46 catches for 630 yards. A Florida native, he knew what to expect when he went to play in Jacksonville in that 1957 preseason game against the Bears.

"We didn't get word that we couldn't stay together with our white teammates in Jacksonville until we got there," McClairen reminisced.

The front office didn't bother to tell the coaches. My black teammates, Willie McClung and John Nisby, had to stay at a black motel. The white guys got picked up and went to Jacksonville Beach. I remember they took a bus to the stadium while we took taxi cabs. When we went to Jacksonville, I didn't have it too bad. I'm from Daytona Beach, which isn't too far from there, and I stayed with family in the area, not with Willie McClung and John Nisby at the black motel. I also knew what to expect in Jacksonville, since I was from that general area. I knew where we could and couldn't go.

Other African American players who went to play preseason games in Jacksonville mentioned dealing with some of the same issues as Bobby Watkins. Like Watkins, Proverb Jacobs was a rookie when he went to Jacksonville in September 1958 with the Philadelphia Eagles. The offensive tackle from Oakland who played football at Cal-Berkley was traveling to the South for the first time.

Jacobs talked about his Jacksonville experience:

We went to Jacksonville, Florida, my rookie year to play an exhibition game against the Redskins in the Deep South. It was my first experience down there, since I was from California. I know the Redskins didn't have any blacks on their roster and that was by owner George Preston Marshall's choice. He didn't integrate the Redskins until four years later, and it wasn't by choice. I think he thought of the Redskins as the South's team.

When we landed at the Jacksonville airport, it was hot and humid. I could feel a tension in the air I hadn't felt before. I felt uneasy on the bus ride to the Sheraton Hotel. Vince McNally, our general manager, started handing out room keys. I noticed the bellboys, who were all Negroes, acted nervous. I had the distinct feeling it was because of the black players being at the hotel. They were scared for us. Then we found out why. When Vince McNally finished giving out all of the keys, only the Negro players remained in the lobby. Vince called us over and told us that they didn't allow blacks to stay in the hotel and we couldn't stay with the rest of the team. He then gave us cab fare for the ride over to the Negro section of town, where he had made arrangements for us to stay.

When we drove up to the motel, there was a guy standing outside leaning on a fancy gold Cadillac. As we approached, the guy introduced himself, saying, "Hi, my name is James Brown." James Brown and the Famous Flames were staying there also! Even *he* couldn't stay in the white hotels. All of the Negro players had a great time because there was no bed check. We stayed out all night.

The night of the game, I got another lesson on the Deep South. When we went onto the field for pregame warm-ups, I saw for the second time what segregation meant. The end of the stadium where the team entered was where the Negroes sat. They all sat in the end zone seats. As the Negro players entered the field, they all cheered for us. I'll never forget the empty feeling that I had in my stomach. People were crowded into one end of the stadium, just because they were black. They couldn't sit in another part of the stadium, even if they could pay to do so. I have never forgotten that.

Even as late as 1962, African Americans still were facing problems in Jacksonville. The St. Louis Cardinals and Green Bay Packers opened their preseason on August 18, with the Packers taking a 41–14 victory at the Gator Bowl.

Garland Boyette was a rookie with the Cardinals in 1962. A linebacker who came to the Cards as a free agent out of Grambling, Boyette later that season became the first African American middle linebacker in NFL history. Boyette said about Jacksonville:

I was a rookie, and this was going to be my first time going to Jacksonville. I grew up in Texas, so I knew all about segregation. The veterans on the Cardinals had played in Jacksonville before—guys like Luke Owens and Jimmy Hill. They explained what we were going to face to us rookies like myself and Bill Triplett before we went down there. We had to stay at our own hotel while the whites stayed at their own hotel downtown. We were picked up by buses, and the hotel we were taken to wasn't that bad. The local black professionals, like doctors and lawyers, gave us a nice party, a luau.

I do remember our defensive coordinator, Chuck Drulis, was supposed to give us a bed check. I called Chuck that evening and asked him if he was going to come for bed check. He said, "Hell no, I'm not coming across the tracks!" So we had a real good time that night because we basically didn't have a curfew.

Garland Boyette, Houston Oilers, circa 1966. *Garland Boyette*

Wilburn Hollis was also in training camp with the 1962 Cardinals but was cut before the regular season. Hollis made the trip to Jacksonville, his first journey into the Jim Crow South since he was from the North and played from 1959 to 1961 at the University of Iowa, where he was their first African American quarterback.

Hollis recalled in a 2017 interview,

> We landed at the airport in Jacksonville, and there were buses waiting for us—one for the white players and one for the black players. The white players stayed at a nice hotel downtown. We were taken to a black neighborhood to a hotel there. We, of course, had to eat our meals there too. Practice really wasn't a problem because we really didn't have one while we were there. We just flew in, spent the night, played the game the next day, and flew back out.
>
> Before we went down there . . . we met with the black veterans on the team: Prentice Gautt, Ernie McMillan, Ted Bates, Jimmy Hill, and Luke Owens. They had been to Jacksonville to play the year before. They knew what to expect down there, so when they met with us, they asked us rookies—myself, Bill Triplett, and Garland Boyette—if we wanted to go down there. The veterans were willing to stay at Lake Forest [the college where the training camp was] if we didn't want to go to Jacksonville. They were going to stick their neck out for us. Of course, they were established veterans, so they could somewhat afford to. We were rookies; we had no leverage, so we couldn't really protest. Being the idiots we were, we decided to go ahead and play.
>
> I was not really aware of the segregation down South. I was from the North, I had played in the Big Ten, where we never encountered anything on the road. . . . This was all new to us. I said, "Let's go to Jacksonville." Heck, I was just trying to make the team—that was pretty much my only focus. (I did make it, but I hurt my wrist and couldn't play.) I wasn't that aware of all the protests just really getting going in the South, like the Freedom Riders and Martin Luther King Jr. Things were just heating up. Now that I look back, we were right in the middle of the civil rights movement, but I didn't do anything about it. I was oblivious to it.

Little Rock was another southern city where exhibition games were played over the years.

Defensive lineman Willie Irvin came to the Philadelphia Eagles in 1953, as a fifteenth-round draft choice out of Florida A&M University. As of 2020, he was the oldest surviving player to come from an HBCU. Irvin got to play in three games for the Eagles in the regular season before being drafted into the army.

Irvin recalled his visit with the Eagles to Little Rock in the preseason on September 12, when they beat the Los Angeles Rams, 28–17. He said,

> We stayed across town at a black hotel. I had two black teammates, Ralph Goldston and Don Stevens. We stayed there with the Rams' black players. I got to know some of the black Rams, like Deacon Dan Towler. They came and got us on a bus to go to practice.
>
> Going into the South was no big deal to me. The team told us we didn't have to go if we didn't want to. I was born and raised there, so I knew what to expect. You go in one door and out the other. I knew the ways of the world. Goldston and Stevens, they were from the North, so this was new to them.
>
> One other thing I do remember about that trip was that we stopped in Memphis on the way and we couldn't sit with our white teammates. The restaurant put a big white sheet around us in the back, so the white patrons couldn't see us. What I really remember, though, about that was when one of our assistant coaches, Frank Reagan, went back there and ate with us. That meant a lot to us.

When the AFL came into existence in 1960, they played several preseason games in Little Rock. The first was when the Dallas Texans went to Little Rock to play the Denver Broncos on August 27. The Texans blasted the Broncos in a 48–0 rout.

Sometimes staying in a black hotel away from their white teammates worked to the black players' benefit.

The Texans' Chris Burford was a white rookie wide receiver out of Stanford in 1960. A first-round draft pick, Burford had led the NCAA in receptions as a senior in 1959, with 61 catches. He said about the African American Texans staying in Little Rock,

> I do remember when we went to Little Rock to play an exhibition game, the black players couldn't stay with us. This was new to me. I went to high school in Oakland, and we used to play against blacks from other high schools. McClymonds High School was one of them. That's the high school Frank Robinson and Bill Russell went to. I was upset. We're supposed to be a team, and we should stay together.
>
> It turns out, though, my friends like Abner Haynes and Clem Daniels ended up having a good time in Little Rock. They even got to go see Ray Charles there. We had no black assistant coaches, so there was no bed check or curfew for the blacks. They would go out every night

partying and get in about 4 or 5 a.m. They really struggled at practice the next day.

Halfback Abner Haynes backed up what Burford said. Haynes came out of nearby North Texas State University and signed with the Texans in 1960. The first black player at a four-year college in the South when he suited up for North Texas State College from 1956 to 1959, Haynes became the AFL's marquee player in the league's early years, winning the inaugural MVP award in 1960.

Haynes told of the pleasant surprise he and his other black teammates encountered in Little Rock:

> We didn't have a curfew. Clem and I and the other guys had a good time in Little Rock. We made the most of a bad situation. One night after practice, Clem and I were sitting around in our hotel room and we kept hearing what we thought was music. We went to investigate, and we found a nightclub. Everybody in there seemed to be having a good time and was drinking and dancing. We looked up on the stage, and we saw a guy at a piano wearing sunglasses. It was Ray Charles! We ended up staying, and we didn't get in until the next morning. Practice was rough the next day, let me tell you.

"Clem" was Clem Daniels, a running back from Prairie View A&M University. After spending his rookie year in 1960 with the Texans, Daniels went to the Raiders in 1961 and eventually became the AFL's all-time leading rusher, with 5,101 yards.

Daniels confirmed Haynes's Ray Charles story:

> It's true, we ran into Ray Charles in Little Rock. This was the first time I had ever seen him perform. I got to know him later. He and Bobby "Blue" Bland used to play a show in the Bay Area around New Year's for about four or five years in the 1960s. He was a great person, very conscious of the civil rights movement.
>
> When we saw Ray in 1960, he was well known in the black community because he hadn't started playing to mixed audiences yet. When he came out with his album in 1962, *Modern Sounds in Country and Western Music*, was when he became a mainstream music star. His popularity shot through the roof. You couldn't get a ticket to one of his shows. The first time I saw Ray in a mixed setting was in Dallas, when he played at SMU's Moody Coliseum.

Gene Mingo was one of the African American Denver Broncos who traveled to Little Rock to take on the Texans. Mingo, a return specialist, halfback, and placekicker, is widely regarded as the first black placekicker in pro football history. He led the AFL in scoring in 1960 and 1962.

Mingo did not get to see Ray Charles in Little Rock, like Haynes and Daniels. He did, however, recall his experience there:

> In Little Rock, we stayed at a black hotel. The Broncos dropped us off and gave us a per diem. We ended up going to nightclubs and staying out late partying. I do remember the Texans killed us when we played them. I also remember at the stadium there were some old white farmers perched at the top of the stadium. They kept yelling things like, "Nigger, you better not hit any white boys!" at us.

Gene Mingo, Denver Broncos. *Robert Jacobus*

When the Houston Oilers joined the AFL in 1960, the black players not only had to endure playing and living in Houston, they also encountered discriminatory treatment when they played exhibition games in the South.

One incident both black and white Oilers recalled was when they defeated the Denver Broncos, 42–10, in Mobile, Alabama, on September 1, 1961.

Bill Groman was an All-Pro receiver for the Houston Oilers during their two AFL championship seasons of 1960 and 1961. Groman, who is white, spoke about what his black teammates experienced when they went to play an exhibition in Mobile in September 1961:

> We played in Mobile our second year. John White, Julian Spence, Bob Kelly, and I think another black [player] who didn't make the team went down there with us. The white players stayed at a motel that was around fifteen to twenty years old—nothing fancy but clean.
>
> They picked us up for the game in a school bus. Just as we were getting off the bus at the stadium, this limo pulls up with a black guy driving. John, Julian, and Bob get out and strut past us. Turns out they had stayed at some black businessman's home. We kidded them. I told them, "We have to ride in an old school bus and you guys get to come up in style!"

However, as is sometimes the case, during interviews, white and black players present different versions of the same story. Bob Kelly, one of the three black players who rode up in the limousine, said,

> There were eight black players at that time in Mobile. When we got there, the team officials directed us to a limousine. When we got in, we noticed that two of the limousine's doors were missing!
>
> We stayed in an old black hotel next to a graveyard. I'll never forget that. The motel itself was filthy and mice infested. Rodent droppings were everywhere. They gave us meal money, but we didn't even practice with the team the day before the game. In fact, we were the last ones allowed on the field for pregame warm-ups. That was strange for me, because I always liked being the first one on and the last one off the field.

Some of the white Oilers sympathized with what their black teammates experienced, however. Former Oiler defensive end Dalva Allen commented, "Guys today don't know what discrimination was. It just made me sick that things were the way they were."

The Oilers played an exhibition game in Mobile the year before in their inaugural 1960 season, beating the Titans on August 26, 30–14. Julian Spence and John White made the trip for the Oilers. When the Oilers' chartered plane landed, Spence and White were pulled aside by team officials while the white players were taken to a white hotel in downtown Mobile. Charlie Milstead said, "The thought never occurred to me where John and Julian were going to stay. And it was kept quiet, because I didn't learn until years later that they didn't stay in the same hotel as the rest of the team."

This was common practice with the Oilers and with other teams. Black players were routinely ushered off to separate facilities quietly whenever they went into a segregated city. After Mobile, defensive end Dan Lanphear told Coach Rymkus, "Lou, if that's the way things have to be, let's not play here again."

Receiver Al Witcher, one of White and Spence's white teammates in 1960, recalled a somewhat humorous anecdote about a time the Oilers stopped in Dallas:

> We were flying in from a game on the West Coast and we had to stop at Love Field in Dallas. Our owner, Bud Adams, decided not to put us up at the Ramada Inn, which was a nice, fancy hotel next to the airport and one that would let Julian Spence, who at the time was our only black player on the roster since John White had been placed on waivers, stay with us. Rather, he found us an old, shabby, hotel miles away from Love Field. The white players slept two to a bed. Julian, on the other hand, got to stay in the luxurious bridal suite by himself. Talk about a turn of events!

Witcher then recalled a more somber moment when the Oilers traveled again to the South for an exhibition game in the 1960 preseason:

> I also remember one of our first exhibition games in Georgia or Alabama when we checked into our hotel. Julian and John White checked into the white hotel with us without their management knowing. They didn't pick up on the fact that we had black players. Well, when Julian and John came down for the team dinner that night, management saw them and made them check out of the hotel. They said, "They can't eat here." Bud Adams had to send them over to a black restaurant and then a black hotel. I remember me and some of the other players said to each other, "Well, crap, they're members of our team. They should be able to eat with us." We didn't approve of it, but we didn't protest. We more or less accepted it. Looking back, we shouldn't have accepted it.

Blanche Martin out of Michigan State was playing running back for the New York Titans on the Oilers' opposing sideline in Mobile that evening in August 1960. What he remembered about Mobile was the seating accommodations: "I remember playing the Oilers at Ladd Stadium in Mobile in 1960. I remember the end zones were packed where the black fans had to sit. The rest of the stands were virtually empty."

Martin then added a story about when the Titans were traveling to Mobile by train to play the Oilers. Sometimes African American players had to make light of their situation in the South to help them cope with it. Martin said,

> We had gone from playing the Raiders in Sacramento to playing the Texans in Abilene, Texas. From there, we took the train to Mobile to meet up with the Oilers. On the way to Abilene from Sacramento, we flew into Dallas first.
>
> My teammates played a trick on me in Dallas. Since I'm from the North, I hadn't experienced discrimination and segregation yet. We stopped for lunch and I went to the bathroom. When I came out, I couldn't find my black teammates. They were hiding in a corner of the restaurant where they served blacks. I went up to the white lunch counter and sat with my white teammates while I waited for my black teammates. The waitress proceeded to ignore me and waited on all of the other customers. I eventually asked her why she hadn't waited on me. She said, "I don't make the rules! You'll have to go sit with the other colored players!" That's when I realized I had to go to the black part of the restaurant. When I got back there, all of my black teammates were cracking up laughing.

After barely getting a look as a wide receiver free agent out of New Mexico Highlands by the 1959 Chicago Bears, Lionel Taylor became an All-Pro when he hooked up with the Denver Broncos of the new AFL in 1960. Taylor led the AFL in receptions five times during the 1960s, including catching 100 balls in 1961—the first professional player to do so.

Taylor spoke about a couple of his exhibition game experiences when he went to Texas. The Broncos lost a 31–13 decision to the Dallas Texans in Midland on August 12, 1961.

Taylor said,

> The biggest problem I had was in Midland. We came into the airport, and we all got on the bus. The bus takes the white players to their hotel and then takes us to our hotel. Well, I complained. I felt we should have

had our own bus instead of having to go all the way to the white hotel and then go to ours. What a waste of time.

When we practiced in Midland, they took us over to the white hotel because there was a practice field next to it. They said we could change in one of the hotel rooms there so we could practice. I spoke up and said, "If we can't stay here, we're not going to change clothes here." We made them take us back to the black hotel so we could change clothes, and then we went back to practice.

Taylor then spoke about what was a common situation when African American players stayed apart from their white teammates. Most of the time, no one from team management would head over to the black side of town to have a curfew check. The Broncos were in Fort Worth on August 28, 1964, to play the Chiefs. This time, someone from the Chiefs came to check up on the black players.

Taylor said,

One good thing about staying at a black hotel is that nobody from the team would come check on us for curfew. In 1964 we were staying in Fort Worth at a black hotel. I have no idea why we were there, since things were pretty much integrated in Fort Worth. Well, all the black players were hanging around the swimming pool drinking Lone Star Beer when our general manager Dean Griffing called and said he was coming over. Sure enough, he did come! That's the first time that ever happened. We really didn't get in trouble; Dean was pretty cool about it.

A first-round draft choice out of Penn State, Lenny Moore came to the Baltimore Colts in 1956. Moore, a halfback and flanker, played twelve seasons for the Colts and was a perennial All-Pro. Moore was elected to the Pro Football Hall of Fame in 1975.

Moore provided a wealth of information about what it was like for African American players traveling to the Jim Crow South to play in the preseason. Moore reminisced about his first experience traveling to the South for an exhibition game against the Chicago Cardinals in Austin, Texas, on August 23, 1958, during his third season with the Colts. The teams battled to a 31-all tie.

"I got my first real taste of racism in the South when we went to Austin in 1958 to play the Cardinals," Moore claimed.

NFL teams played a lot of exhibition games in the South back then. I think some of it was done to drum up interest, since there weren't any franchises down there at the time. I also think the NFL was trying to gauge the interest level in those southern cities to help them try and figure out where they could possibly put franchises in the South someday.

Well, the night before the game, we wanted to go out and grab some food and drinks. We planned to go to the black part of Austin so we wouldn't make any waves. Weeb Ewbank, our coach, decided to ask one of our white players, Ken Jackson, whether this was a good idea. Jackson was from Austin, and he told Ewbank that the Negro area was a rough part of town and we shouldn't go there. Weeb forbid us from going out.

We proceeded to question why Weeb would ask the opinion of someone who had never been to the Negro part of Austin about what it was like. I have to give Ewbank credit, though. . . . The black players went to him, and he decided to get some taxis to take us to the black part of town to have some fun. Weeb even went with us, and he actually got out and spoke to the owner of the black bar and had him [promise] we would be okay. That really was a nice gesture by Weeb; he didn't have to do that.

Moore then recalled an exhibition game trip to Dallas in 1959. Besides talking about his trip to Texas, he added some insight to the dynamics of the common practice of black and white players staying apart from each other when they played in the South:

We met the Giants in the preseason in Dallas in a rematch of the Championship Game the previous December. We beat them again, 28–3. When we got to the Love Field airport in Dallas, the plane wouldn't taxi to the gate because of the black players on the Colts. They sent a bus out to the tarmac, the black players got on, and then the plane went to the terminal.

After we left the airport, we had to stay, along with the black Giants players, in a black hotel called the Peter Lane Hotel. Peter Lane himself told us we would be taken care of, but the blacks on both teams were ticked. We voted on whether to boycott the game or not. Once we thought about what the great Jackie Robinson would have done in this situation, we decided to play.

When we walked into the locker room before the game, there was an uneasy silence. All of the white players had their heads down, trying to mind their own business. Raymond Berry, a Texas native, came up to each of the black players and apologized for the way we were being treated in his home state. Years later, Alan Ameche talked to me about Dallas and other injustices we endured, and how he wanted to complain to Colts management about it but never did. He said he felt ashamed about it. Berry and Ameche were the only two white teammates who ever said anything about the way we were treated.

When we played in the South, we were pre-prepared for what was going on. [This] one thing would [always] happen when the black players would arrive at the stadium after we had stayed apart from our white teammates. There was always the question of eye-to-eye contact with our white teammates. It was always a very awkward situation. Kind of like, "Here we go again; we're separated. Why is this happening again?" We had to mentally deal with it as a team. Both whites and blacks knew that we had been separated, and we would just look at each other sheepishly and kind of shrug our shoulders. How were we supposed to play together as a team? How could we come together? The white players didn't know how to respond to us. I think the separation thing was a big deal, and we had to overcome it as a team.

There [weren't] a lot of [internal discussions] with our white teammates about us being separate from them. They really didn't know what to say. Every time we would walk into the locker room, everything got quiet. You could hear a pin drop. They hesitated to look up at you. They didn't comfort or sympathize with us. Back then, the only guy who would come over to us was Raymond Berry. He would say, "We're together guys."

We just had to work through it the best we could. Whenever we had to stay separate from our white teammates, we were split, or divided, as a unit, and then we had to try and mold it back together. It made me and a lot of my black teammates feel inferior.

I used to talk to some of the guys who played here before me, like George Taliaferro. I would ask him how he dealt with it. He would tell me, "Relax, don't let it eat you up. Just try and get by it the best you can."

Whenever I was out on the banquet circuit, I would make it a point to talk to the guys who came before me. I met with people like Jackie Robinson and Fritz Pollard. I would ask them, "How did you do it?" Jackie would say, "I don't know, I just took it a day at a time. You just have to overcome it and be who you are."

Another thing Jackie said was, "Keep your mouth shut. Just like I opened the door for you, you have to open the door for those who will come along after you. You're going to be called 'nigger.' You have to expect it. Walk away from it."

A lot of racial incidents were going on back then that the Colts front office kept from us. If we had known about some of the things like staying separately or segregated seating, we may not have played in some of the games. Sometimes we didn't find out about things until after the fact. We were losers in the long run.

Going into the South, the owners didn't think of us. They knew that's where the money was. They didn't care if it was racist down there. It was all about the money. In spite of it all, we hung in there.

Early on in the days of the reintegration of the NFL, black players like Lenny Moore and numerous others had no choice but to hang in there, mostly for fear of retaliation by the management of and sometimes even the owners of NFL franchises. But, as we shall see, all that started to change around the start of the new decade of the 1960s.

5

ROOTING FOR THE HOME TEAM

The Cowboys and Texans Come to Dallas

The year was 1960, and much of the Lone Star State was still segregated. The city of Dallas was no exception. It was during this tense time that pro football collectively put three franchises in Texas. The Dallas Cowboys became an expansion franchise in the NFL, and the newly formed AFL placed the Texans in Dallas and the Oilers in Houston.

On the surface, it seemed like Texas would be prime real estate for pro football franchises in the South. Texas had led the way with integration in the southern states in both college and high school football. Just a few months after the 1952 version of the Dallas Texans went bankrupt and left for Baltimore, Ben Kelly of San Angelo College, at that time a two-year institution in San Angelo, integrated their football program in the fall of 1953. This occurred just nine months before the US Supreme Court struck down segregation in public education with *Brown v. Board of Education* on May 17, 1954. Kelly thus became the first black college football player in the South to play at a previously all-white institution.

Then, in the fall of 1955, Texas public high schools were the first in the Deep South to integrate their football programs when several African Americans, including future Buffalo Bills fullback Willie Jones of Robstown, Texas, suited up for the formerly all-white high schools in their hometowns.

However, the early integration of Texas college and high schools—and the general population, for that matter—was somewhat misleading. Early integration in Texas was mostly geographical in nature. In East Texas, closer to the former Confederate states and with a larger African American population, segregation was more rigid and lasted well into the 1960s. San Angelo, where Ben Kelly played, is in West Texas, where the African American population was relatively small. San Angelo is close to three hundred miles away from the eastern third of Texas. Robstown, where Willie Jones played, is close to Corpus Christi, in the Coastal Bend region of Texas; here the black population was also small, and it is two to three hundred miles away from East Texas.

However, Dallas and Houston are in the eastern third of Texas. Although the two cities were entering the last days of Jim Crow segregation when they were awarded franchises in 1960, this did not make things any easier for visiting African American players, let alone the black players on the rosters of these new franchises. These pioneer players now faced the challenge of trying to live in still-segregated cities.

Hotels and restaurants were still segregated in Dallas and Houston in 1960. Black passengers in both cities continued to go to the back of the bus. Although a 1950 federal law outlawed segregation on interstate carriers, this mostly applied to trains. Segregation on public transportation was still enforced in Texas.

Schools were also segregated in Dallas and Houston in 1960. Six years after *Brown v. Board of Education*, Dallas finally came up with a school integration plan—one that desegregated one grade at a time. That plan was struck down by the federal courts.

Finally, Dallas started the desegregation process. The city integrated its restaurants and cafeterias in 1961, more than a year after the Student Nonviolent Coordinating Committee (SNCC) at North Carolina A&T College integrated lunch counters in Greensboro, North Carolina. On July 27, a total of 159 black patrons dined at thirty-six previously all-white restaurants and cafeterias. This integration effort was organized in part by the Dallas Citizens Council, an all-white organization of business leaders in the city, which helped arrange this integration step.

In 1961, the Dallas Citizens Council also got involved with school desegregation. Dallas had been ordered by the court to desegregate, and to help with the process, the council produced a film narrated by Walter Cronkite, titled *Dallas at the Crossroads*, which encouraged cooperation from everyone involved with desegregation and also emphasized the importance of avoiding violence.

Like the city of Dallas, the Cotton Bowl had undergone changes since the first version of the Texans played there in 1952. Gone was the segregated seating for African American fans. Once segregated seating at the Cotton Bowl ended, the NFL started drawing thousands of black fans to their exhibition games in the late 1950s, and this continued when the Cowboys arrived in 1960 and in the years thereafter.

NFL teams with African American players on their rosters had been coming to Dallas to play in exhibition games since the Texans left in 1952. When black players on opposing NFL teams came to Dallas to play the Cowboys in the regular season in 1960, they found out that the city's racist tendencies really hadn't changed, despite the integrated franchises that called the city home. Several opposing NFL and AFL players who came to Dallas in the early 1960s, while the city was still segregated, shared their experiences.

Lenny Moore of the Baltimore Colts recalled that there was some progress made as far as visiting team accommodations:

> In 1960 we returned to Dallas to play the expansion Cowboys in the preseason. I had come to Dallas a couple of times before to play in preseason games. This time, I guess because the Cowboys were now part of the NFL, we got to stay with our white teammates instead of in a black hotel. We stayed at the Ramada Inn by Love Field.

The Ramada Inn at Love Field was the first and only hotel in 1960 that would let opposing teams, as well as the Cowboys and Texans, stay together as a team the night before their games. Cowboys general manager Tex Schramm negotiated the deal to desegregate the Ramada Inn. He realized that black Cowboys like Don Perkins and Frank Clarke needed to eat and sleep with their white teammates. Schramm quietly arranged for the Ramada Inn by Love Field to drop its all-white policy for visiting NFL teams, which had been busing their black players to a rundown black hotel in Fort Worth. For the Dallas Texans, owner Lamar Hunt made the same arrangement to use the Ramada Inn the night before home games. Hunt, however, did not make arrangements for visiting AFL teams to stay there.

Schramm described how he negotiated the use of the Ramada Inn:

> When we came to Dallas, there were no hotels that would accommodate our black players and any of the visiting teams' black players. There was a group of businessmen in Dallas I went to that had a lot of pull in the city. The Ramada Inn, at Love Field Airport, was the property of the airport. They said they would take the black players, but only if the other hotels in the Dallas area didn't retaliate. By retaliate, I meant back in 1960 if a hotel took in a black patron, other hotels would spread the word around town so whites would stop going there. The other hotels agreed to keep quiet, so that's how we got to use the Ramada Inn that first year. We would stay there the night before

games. We eventually moved to the Sheraton Hotel downtown, which desegregated hotels there.

The Cowboys' first regular-season contest was September 24, at the Cotton Bowl, against the Pittsburgh Steelers. The Cowboys jumped out to a 21–7 advantage over the Steelers in the second quarter, but the Steelers scored the last two touchdowns of the contest and took a 35–28 victory. Unfortunately for the Cowboys, the losses started to pile up after the loss to the Steelers. The Eagles, who would go on to win the NFL championship later that season when they defeated the Green Bay Packers, 17–13, in the title game on December 26, came to Dallas the following week and took a 27–25 win, in part because the Dallas kicker missed two extra points.

The rest of the 1960 season was an exercise in futility for the Cowboys. After the first two home losses, the Cowboys dropped their next eight games before tying the New York Giants, 31–31, in the next-to-last week of the season. The Cowboys lost their finale, 23–14, to the Detroit Lions, finishing their inaugural season 0–11–1.

When the Steelers came to Dallas for the first game of the 1960 season, they had five African American players on their roster. Two of the surviving five talked about their visit to still-segregated Dallas.

Jack "Cy" McClairen came to the Steelers as a twenty-sixth-round draft choice in 1953 out of Bethune-Cookman College in Florida. McClairen, an end, played six seasons with the Steelers, making the Pro Bowl in 1957. Although the Ramada Inn at Love Field in Dallas was integrated and much closer to the Cotton Bowl, for some reason Pittsburgh stayed at a hotel in Irving, fifteen miles away.

McClairen spoke about his visit to Dallas:

I remember when we went to Dallas, we stayed together but we had to stay in a hotel that would take the black players in too. The hotel was in Irving. We were told we couldn't stay in Dallas. Dallas was still segregated. I'm from Florida so the segregation thing wasn't that big a deal; I was used to it. Some of the blacks on our team hadn't experienced this before because they were from the North where things were integrated. Some of the northern black guys said, "Aw, we won't be segregated." They were surprised, but I wasn't.

The front office didn't tell us anything ahead of time either. That happened the year before when we went to Houston and Miami in preseason. We didn't get word until we got there that we couldn't stay together. We actually were taken to Miami Beach to the white hotel because nobody informed the coaches we couldn't go there. In Houston we had to stay at Texas Southern University. At the Dallas game there were no problems. That was the last game of my career. I caught one pass, and I injured my knee in practice the next week and couldn't play anymore.

Running back Tom Barnett came to the Steelers from Purdue in 1959. He said about playing in Dallas,

> Going into Dallas was not my first time going into the South. In 1958 Purdue played Rice in Houston. We had to stay at Texas Southern University. There were some challenges we faced in Houston; some things were said to the black players. I grew up in integration, and I thought the whole thing in Houston was silly. We practiced out front of the hotel the white players were staying in, the Shamrock Hilton, and we could hang around there until evening time, and then we had to go back over to Texas Southern.
>
> Now when we came to Dallas in 1960, I don't recall any challenges. We were all able to stay in the same hotel, but we stayed in Irving. Nothing really happened at the hotel or at practice. The game was no big deal either. Nothing racial was said.

The Cleveland Browns also came to Dallas during the 1960 season to play the Cowboys. The Browns delivered a 48–7 shellacking on the Cowboys on October 16, which ended up being the Cowboys' worst loss of the season.

Paul Brown was still head coach of the Browns. His policy in the 1950s was to not travel to the South for exhibition games. The only game Cleveland played in the South during this time was, coincidentally, in Dallas in 1954. Brown didn't schedule games in the South because he wanted his teams to stay together at hotels and eat together at restaurants. In 1960, however, the Cowboys were part of the NFL, and even though the city of Dallas was still segregated, Paul Brown and the Browns had no choice but to play there.

The Browns did stay together when they came to Texas. Browns halfback Jamie Caleb, who scored his only career touchdown in the rout of the Cowboys, said,

> I wasn't sure what was going to happen once we got to Dallas—it being segregated and all, and me being a rookie. I'm from the South and played at Grambling, so I kind of assumed we'd be staying apart from my white teammates. To my surprise, we ended up staying together at

the Ramada Inn at Love Field. Then again, we always stayed together, as I found out. Paul Brown made sure of that.

Browns guard John Wooten also spoke of the Browns' trip to Dallas. Ironically, after his playing career was over, Wooten became a scout and worked for the Cowboys from 1975 to 1991. He elaborated on what Caleb said:

The Cleveland Browns were different. We always stayed together. We stayed at the Ramada Inn at Love Field in Dallas. Paul Brown would not stand for segregating his team. That's why we never played exhibition games in the South. I remember when we came to Dallas that first year, it was during the state fair so we couldn't practice at the Cotton

John Wooten, Cleveland Browns. *University of Colorado Athletics*

Bowl; the area around it was where the fair was held. We practiced at
some park somewhere.

We always had a routine with the Browns, even for home games. In
Cleveland, we would stay at the Carter Hotel, have dinner together, and
then we would go to a movie together. In Dallas, because of segregation, we didn't go to the movies. If all of us couldn't go, none of us
would go. Back then, they had coin-operated televisions in hotel rooms.
What the Browns did was give us a stack of quarters so we could watch
TV in our rooms.

The San Francisco 49ers were another team with African American
players that came to Dallas, on November 20th, 1960, taking a 26–14 decision from the Cowboys that dropped Dallas's record to 0–9. The 49ers
carried eight African Americans on their roster, including Hall of Fame
running back Joe Perry. Two of the black players who still survive from
that 49ers team are offensive tackle John Thomas and running back C. R.
Roberts. They spoke about their Dallas experience.

Thomas was a twenty-third-round draft choice out of the University
of the Pacific in 1957. In a bit of irony, before the 1957 draft, Thomas
was invited to a tryout camp the Redskins held at Occidental College in
California. Because Redskins owner George Preston Marshall was opposed
to having African Americans on his roster, when the Redskins coaches
discovered that Thomas was black, they informed him they had no open-
ings. The Redskins thus missed out on another talented African American
athlete because of their owner's discriminatory beliefs. Thomas went on to
play ten seasons with the 49ers, eventually making the Pro Bowl.

Thomas recalled his trip to Dallas in 1960:

> Nothing special happened. We stayed at a hotel together by the airport.
> I know Dallas was segregated at that time. I had a black roommate.
> That's what they did back in those days—paired us together. We ate as
> a group, we rode the bus as a group, everything was done as a team. It
> was nothing special.

Roberts elaborated more about his 1960 experience in Dallas, which
was not his first time playing in Texas. In 1956, while playing running back
for USC, Roberts integrated the University of Texas home field, Memorial
Stadium. Roberts had a memorable day, racking up 251 yards rushing on
just 12 attempts and scoring 3 touchdowns on runs of 50, 73, and 74 yards.

Roberts talked about his trip to Austin in 1956 and then compared it
to playing in Dallas four years later:

Going to Dallas in 1960 was a picnic compared to Austin in 1956. It was a big hullabaloo for me to play UT. The USC coaching staff knew there might be problems. Jess Hill, our coach, a very religious and fair guy, met with me in the summer a couple of months before we went to Austin. He asked me, "How are you going to like Texas?" I didn't know what he meant. Turns out he was talking about the whole segregation thing, since I hadn't been exposed to that before, being from California. The coaches started making innuendoes about me staying in California and not going to Austin. Things like, "Maybe we can just use this as a practice game," alluding to the fact that I wouldn't have to go. I eventually said, "I'm the team captain; I'm going to Texas!"

A week before the game, Coach Hill said to me, "You know, there's a black family in Texas who would like for you to stay with them." That's when I found out things were segregated there. I informed Coach Hill, "I'm staying with my teammates!" My teammates came to my aid too. They said, "If C. R. doesn't go, we don't go!"

So we ended up going to Austin, and we tried to get into a hotel as a team. We got turned down twice when the owners saw me. I couldn't figure out why we kept going into hotels and then leaving them. Finally, we go to this one hotel—the owner must have been a USC fan or something. He broke the law and let us stay there as a team. The maids and servants at the hotel, when they saw me, said, "Hey, you can't be in here! They'll kill you guys!" All during the night, black labor help from all over Austin came to the hotel to see me and my roommate, Lou Byrd. They came to the back door of the hotel, and the staff gave them hotel uniforms to wear. Literally hundreds came. We didn't sleep all night. Somehow security didn't catch on.

At the game, I do remember there being segregated seating at their stadium. I had a great game both on offense and defense. I ran wild. I was taken out early in the third quarter, though. I found out later that we had gotten death threats, and they took me out of the game because of that. Supposedly, there were snipers out to get me. A couple of them were said to have camped out at our hotel waiting for us. After the game, however, we flew right out and back to California. Usually we stayed until the next day before we flew home.

So, Dallas, in 1960, was a paradise compared to what I faced in Austin. First of all, I was not going to stay away from my teammates. I made that very clear. We had some good white players on the 49ers. They stood by me. I had other black teammates: Joe Perry, J. D. Smith, R. C. Owens. They were old school; they wouldn't cause any trouble by protesting. We had another black player, Ray Norton, the track guy, but he was a rookie and wouldn't make any waves. So I made it clear. I was not going to play. Well, the 49ers always traveled first class. We got to stay together at the Ramada Inn at Love Field. We were a little concerned about the hotel being so far away from everything. The 49ers knew I was outspoken and I could be a problem. In Dallas, we really didn't have to be that careful about where we could and couldn't go in the city. We really didn't have any problems.

C. R. Roberts, San Francisco 49ers. *Robert Jacobus*

The AFL Texans were the more accomplished of the two Dallas franchises in the three years they shared Dallas. The team finished their inaugural 1960 season 8–6, and after a disappointing 6–8 record in their second year, they rang up an 11–3 record in 1962, which culminated in an AFL title when they beat the Oilers, 20–17, in a classic double-overtime tilt.

The first home game in Texans history took place on September 25, 1960, when they beat the Los Angeles Chargers, 17–0, before a crowd of forty-two thousand. One of the black Chargers, offensive tackle Ernie Wright, briefly recalled his trip to Dallas: "In Dallas we stayed at a godforsaken little country-ass prairie town full of crickets, called Grand Prairie. It was the only hotel in the area that would take blacks. We were on the third floor and had crickets in the room. I'll never forget that."

White Chargers all-star running back Keith Lincoln spoke about coming to Texas to play in the early 1960s:

> I went to school growing up in Los Angeles. I went to a high school with probably 40 to 50 percent minorities. Going down South was a shock to me. I had gone once in college at Washington State, when we went to Houston to play the Cougars. The black players had to stay in private homes.
>
> With the Chargers, we would traditionally go to a movie as a team the night before a game. When we went to Dallas to play the Texans, we all had to enter in the back of the theater because we had black players. After that, we had to go to a section of the balcony that no one else was in. One time we were up in the balcony, and this guy came up there with his date and they made us move from that part of the balcony. The African American players were not allowed to go to the concession stand either. I remember going down there and buying a bunch of popcorn and other stuff and bringing it back up. It was just ludicrous. It was unbelievable. It really was.

The Oakland Raiders visited Dallas on October 9 and lost a narrow 20–19 decision to the Texans. Tom Flores, who would later become a two-time Super Bowl champion coach with the Oakland/Los Angeles Raiders, was a rookie quarterback for the Raiders when they came to Dallas. He recalled,

> When we came into Dallas to play the Texans in 1960, we had to stay at a hotel a pretty good ways from Dallas so we could all stay together. I do remember that the hotel, although they let the black players stay there, didn't want to let them eat there. Our coach, Eddie Erdelatz, said, "We

all eat here or none of us eat here." The hotel relented. All of this was new to me. I didn't see any of this growing up in California.

On November 13, the Denver Broncos came to town and lost a 34–7 decision to the Texans. The Broncos' Gene Mingo, who was the first black placekicker in pro football history, said,

> With the Broncos in 1960, we stayed in Fort Worth when we went to play the Texans. We stayed at the Kings Inn, a black motel. We were basically left on our own. We couldn't go anywhere since we didn't have any transportation. The people at the motel were very inviting and accepted us. They treated us well. A bus picked us up to take us to the Cotton Bowl so we could play our game.
>
> In 1961 it was the same thing. We stayed at the Kings Inn, and the owners treated us great. We had a per diem from the team. In general, people both black and white treated us pretty well in Dallas and Fort Worth. We knew things were segregated and prejudiced there. We knew to watch our step. We did hear some words thrown out at us in Dallas at the Cotton Bowl. We just had to ignore it and play ball.

Broncos All-Pro receiver Lionel Taylor also recalled the Broncos' trip to Dallas:

> In Dallas, we stayed at some black hotel not too far from the airport. That was common practice back then. Now by 1962, we got to stay at the Hilton downtown. I remember when we stayed there, John Glenn's Mercury space capsule was on display in front of the hotel. I remember we went to a club downtown. We took a taxi there, and when I gave the driver a twenty-dollar bill, he was really slow to give my change back to me. He was waiting because he knew the club was segregated and we would need a ride somewhere else. We ended up getting into the club. Turns out on Sunday nights, the place was somewhat integrated because the band that played on Sundays was black. I honestly think that's why they let us in, because they thought we were in the band.

Like the African American players from visiting teams who experienced hardships in segregated Dallas, the black players on the early Cowboys and Texans rosters had to deal with living and playing in a city that, while evolving in the early 1960s, was nonetheless still segregated.

In their inaugural season, the Cowboys had four African Americans on their roster: defensive end Nate Borden, cornerback Don Bishop, receiver/

defensive back Woodley Lewis, and receiver Frank Clarke. A fifth black
player, fullback Don Perkins, was injured in training camp and was placed
on injured reserve for the season.

Perkins eventually became one of the Cowboys' early stars. In his
eight seasons with the Cowboys, Perkins made the Pro Bowl six times and
made first team All-Pro in 1962. Perkins came to the Cowboys from the
University of New Mexico. He led the Lobos in rushing from 1957 to
1959 and led the nation in kickoff returns his senior year.

Perkins had signed a personal-services contract with Clint Murchison
in 1959 for $10,000 a year with a $1,500 signing bonus. But he broke the
fifth metatarsal bone in his foot during training camp and sat out the 1960
season. Once he finally took the field for the 1961 Cowboys, he recorded
the first 100-yard rushing game for the team, averaged 4.1 yards per carry,
and earned NFL Rookie of the Year honors.

Perkins received less than a hero's welcome when he first arrived in
still-segregated Dallas. He landed at Love Field and hailed a cab to take
him to his temporary residence. The cabdriver informed him he'd flagged
down the wrong cab. It was against the law for a white cab driver to drive
a black fare from the airport. Perkins then waited for a colored cab, which
took him to his new home in South Dallas—Oak Cliff, to be exact—one
part of Dallas where African Americans could live, according to the segregation laws.

A few weeks later, after the 1960 College All-Star Game, which Perkins had been planning to play in until he broke his foot, Cowboys scout
Gil Brandt took quarterback Don Meredith and Perkins back to Dallas and
offered to treat them to dinner at the Highland Park Cafeteria.

Perkins said about the incident,

> After the College All-Star Game in 1960, I was traveling to San Antonio
> with Don Meredith where the Cowboys were practicing. We tried to
> stop on the way and eat in Dallas, but I was told I couldn't eat there.
> It was still that way in most of Texas back then. There were also white
> and colored bathrooms all over Texas and New Mexico.

It was not easy that first season—or in subsequent years. At the end of
every season, Perkins inevitably hightailed it back to Albuquerque, where
his football stardom at UNM guaranteed him a job better than driving
trucks, which was the best offer he could get in Dallas. Perkins's family remained in Albuquerque while he rented an apartment in South Dallas. He

could not see raising his family in a city that was divided by race. In Albuquerque, he could live wherever he wanted; that was not the case in Dallas.

For Frank Clarke, things were a little different. Clarke, who in his college days at the University of Colorado integrated their football program in 1954, came to the Cowboys from the Browns, where he had mostly languished on the bench for three seasons and caught just ten balls from 1957 to 1959.

Like Perkins, Clarke would become one of the early bright spots in the Cowboys' formative years. Clarke finished an eight-year Cowboys career with 281 catches for 5,214 yards and 51 touchdowns and made first team All-Pro in 1964.

Clarke said,

> Dallas was not like where I went to the University of Colorado. In fact, it wasn't even like Cleveland, my first NFL stop. It was in some respects like Beloit, Wisconsin, where I grew up, with some segregation. There it was covert. In Dallas, it was out in the open. You could tell the people in Dallas were serious about it too. I do remember going downtown not long after I got there, and there were separate drinking fountains and bathrooms.
>
> I would walk into a store in Dallas and see the "whites only" and "colored" drinking fountains, or the separate restrooms. I had never seen this before. Was someone going to be lynched next? In the end, the fact that Dallas was still segregated didn't matter that much. I knew there were certain places I couldn't live, but I made the most of it. I found out I was not welcome in North Dallas, which was where the whites lived and was close to the Cowboys' practice facility. Blacks were welcome in South Dallas. I was worried about making the team and playing football, not being involved in the civil rights movement. When the season was over, I went back to Cleveland.

Pro Football Hall of Fame defensive back Mel Renfro came to the Cowboys from the University of Oregon in 1963. Although segregation was in its dying days in Dallas, its remnants still lingered. Renfro recalled,

> I wasn't in Dallas long before I found out about Jim Crow. I was right on the outskirts of South Oak Cliff, where the blacks lived, and I went into a restaurant. Turns out it was a white restaurant and they said, "We don't serve coloreds here. You have to go next door." There was a black restaurant next door, so I had to eat there. I learned pretty quickly early on in Dallas to not cause any trouble and to go to places where I would be accepted.

The 1960 Dallas Texans had five African Americans on their roster, all of them with ties to Texas and HBCUs in Texas: defensive tackle Walt Napier from Paul Quinn College in Dallas; safety Dave Webster, defensive tackle Rufus Granderson, and running back/defensive back Clem Daniels, all from Prairie View A&M University; and running back Abner Haynes, who in 1956, along with Leon King, became one of the first African Americans to play college football in the South at a four-year school when he suited up at North Texas State College.

Haynes became the star of the early Texans teams and for the AFL as a whole. He had his most productive years in the three years the Texans were in Dallas before their move to Kansas City in 1963.

In forty-two regular-season games with the Texans, Haynes rushed for 2,765 yards, had 1,707 receiving yards, and racked up 5,733 all-purpose yards, the most in the AFL in that three-year span. Haynes won the AFL's inaugural Most Valuable Player Award after the 1960 season.

Haynes's teammates on those early Texans teams attested to his ability on the football field. Cotton Davidson was the quarterback on the 1960 and 1961 Texans, making the Pro Bowl after the 1961 season. Davidson recalled about Haynes,

> Abner was a great ballplayer. He was the most complete player we had. Abner was a great pass receiver, and he was also a very good blocker. You couldn't find a lot of flaws with Abner. I played with the great Lenny Moore when I was with the Colts in 1957, and Abner was just as good as Lenny was.

Fred Arbanas from Michigan State was a rookie with the Texans in 1962. A tight end, Arbanas was a three-time all pro and five-time Pro Bowler with the Texans (and later the Chiefs). He said, "Abner Haynes was fantastic. You gave him a six-inch hole to go through, and he was gone. Abner was the star in the AFL while we were in Dallas, kind of like Jim Brown was in the NFL at the same time. Abner was also a better person than he was a player. He was a real leader, a super guy."

Haynes spoke positively about playing in the AFL and in Dallas, where he moved with his family from nearby Denton as a youth:

> I thought if you came to the AFL, you came to the New America. I had been drafted in the fifth round of the NFL Draft by the Steelers. In 1960, though the NFL had a quota system, the Redskins still didn't have any blacks on their team. We felt welcome in the AFL. That's why I played in the AFL. When Lamar Hunt announced there was going

to be a new league and it would be integrated, I really wanted to go to Dallas. I didn't like the way things were going in the NFL. When Mr. Hunt came out with his decision to form the AFL, I changed my life goals from becoming a minister like my father had to giving professional football a try.

Clem Daniels, who spent his rookie year with the Texans before going to Oakland, said,

> People tend to forget that Houston and Dallas were still segregated when the Oilers, Texans, and Cowboys came into the league in 1960 and the ways of the South persisted. An example was in our first year in Dallas; the Texans would stay at the Ramada Inn out by the airport, Love Field, the night before a game. We had an agreement with the hotel that the whole team would stay together.
>
> Well, one evening, one of our black players, Walt Napier, all 6'4", 275 pounds of him, put on a swimsuit and jumped into the hotel swimming pool. People started calling the front desk saying, "You've got a nigger in the swimming pool and we want to go swimming!" The hotel called a pool service company to come out and drain the pool so the whites could go swimming again. That was just the tip of the iceberg in Dallas. We dealt with it, though. The Hunts were instrumental in dealing with problems. H. L. Hunt was able to open doors. He was able to shelter us from a lot of the problems.

Chris Burford was a rookie receiver with the Texans out of Stanford in 1960. He recalled his early days in Dallas:

> When I got to Dallas, that was an eye-opener too. Things just felt different. Training camp had been in Roswell, New Mexico, so the blacks faced some but not too much discrimination. When they arrived in Dallas, it was like the pressure was on them. It was like, "Go to the back of the bus." Speaking of buses, I saw my first "Colored" and "Whites Only" drinking fountains at the bus station in Dallas. Eventually, though, we helped change things.

Another issue faced by the African American Cowboys was the housing situation in Dallas. The white players mostly lived in North Dallas, close to the team's practice facility. Most of the black players lived at least half an hour away in South Dallas. Cornell Green recalled, "We had to go through town on the Central Expressway to get to practice. If there was a traffic jam or an accident, we'd be late and Coach Landry would fine us."

According to Don Perkins,

> Dallas was very polarized back then. We lived mostly in Oak Cliff in
> South Dallas; the whites lived north close to the practice facility. We
> saw each other at practice, but then we went our separate ways. Coming
> to Dallas wasn't entirely a shock. I'd been called "nigger" before, and I
> had been places where I couldn't use the same bathroom as a white or
> eat in the same restaurant.

Later in his career in Dallas, Mel Renfro decided to take on the issue
of fair housing in the city. The black Cowboys lived in the south part of
Dallas near Bishop College until 1968, when Renfro was denied a townhouse in North Dallas and challenged the status quo.

Although he was born in Houston, Renfro had moved to Oregon
with his family at age two on the recommendation of his older brother's
doctor. In Oregon, Renfro grew up in a mostly integrated society. A North
Dallas builder had agreed to rent the townhouse to him but reneged at the
last minute. "It had happened so often before," Renfro said, "and this time
it was so blatant and it pissed me off so bad that I just said, 'Okay, this is it.
I'm not standing for this anymore.'"

Renfro sued in federal court, citing the Fair Housing Act, and won an
injunction. "I opened a lot of doors for a lot of people," Renfro recalled.
"I frightened those white folks to death, those real estate people, the de-
velopers. I got a lot of positive mail from people of color that said because
of what I had done they could live where they wanted. It made a mark on
that community." After Renfro's lawsuit, the other black Cowboys moved
out of South Dallas and found housing nearer to the team's practice facility
in North Dallas.

Besides facing problems with housing in Dallas, Cornell Green
brought up another area where black players encountered de facto discrimination. Black players were limited in the job market in Dallas, both when
trying to obtain secondary jobs to supplement their income and also in their
endorsement deals. Green said,

> Frank Clarke had a radio show, but that was about it. The black players
> were very limited as far as endorsement deals, off-season jobs, and radio
> shows. I'll give you an example. Local car dealerships used to let the
> white players drive cars—even the benchwarmers. But players such as
> myself, Mel Renfro, or Don Perkins? Forget it.

In spite of the aforementioned problems, there were of course some positives that came out of the NFL and AFL placing franchises in still-segregated Dallas. The Cowboys and Texans were two of the first organizations in the city to begin to create an integrated environment. Several of the Cowboys and Texans from that time period saw themselves as agents for change in Dallas.

"A lot of the things that had existed in Dallas when we got there—the colored water fountains and such—came down. There is no doubt we were a part of that," said Frank Clarke. "It was pretty wild, in the first place, that the NFL decided to bring a franchise into the South when there was still segregation. Some of the black players were fearful at first, but we were able to work our way through it and make some changes in Dallas and within our team. We learned to coexist."

Cornell Green added,

I came from Southern California and then went to college at Utah State. I had mostly white teammates in high school and college. In Dallas, I pretty much had to live on the south side, but other than that, by 1962 I was pretty much able to go where I pleased. There were some things that were different in the South and Dallas. One, I had never seen an all-black college before like Bishop College. I didn't know they existed. The other was, like I said, people having to live in certain sections of the city.

When we came to Dallas, in our own way we were fighting the system. It was being fought at every turn, and we were a part of it. We would go against the grain and challenge the way things were in Dallas because I was a Cowboy and I could get away with it.

There was a friend of mine on the Cowboys, Mike Gaetcher, who was also a rookie in 1962. He was from California, too, and played in college at Oregon, so he had never been exposed to the segregation issue. We went all over Dallas challenging things, going into public places like restaurants together. Nobody ever said anything to us. I guess in our own way, we helped integrate Dallas.

Abner Haynes recalled,

My dad, who was a prominent minister in Denton and in Dallas, knew Lamar Hunt's dad, H. L. Hunt. My family was comfortable with the Hunt family. My family and I talked it over, and we thought my signing in Dallas could help effect change and growth in the city. Kids in Dallas already knew me and who I was. So my playing for the Texans wasn't just to play football. It was to help and try to build the city and community that we lived in. I had done that at North Texas State. My dad had churches in Dallas and Denton. If I could go through North Texas and show the kids I could get an education and that you could go to school with whites and enjoy each other's company, I figured I might be able to do the same thing in Dallas with the Texans. None of this was happening anywhere else in the South. My family had raised me to appreciate everybody and show no hatred toward anybody. It was just an interesting time to live in Dallas in 1960. Times were changing. I felt it was time for me to step up and do something for the community. It made me decide to go to the new league.

Playing football in Dallas in the early 1960s was exciting. We made some progress, race-wise, in this part of the state. It wasn't about me. It was about the community. I felt the Texans helped push integration in Dallas, and I was a vehicle to help get that done.

We learned how to beat the racism. I had teammates, like Jim Tyrer, who would go off if we went to a restaurant and I wasn't served. Fred Arbanas was another one. It eventually got to be that I started being served in Dallas restaurants because of their help.

Chris Burford was a rookie with Haynes in 1960, and the two became fast friends and remain so to this day. Burford described an incident from their early days with the Texans:

I knew Abner better than anyone. Going to Dallas was a big deal for Abner and the other black players. It was a big deal for me too. I'm from California. At Stanford we always played integrated teams. California was open compared to other places. I went to high school in Oakland. We had blacks at our school. We used to always play McClymonds High School all the time, and they were mostly black. I didn't grow up with any attitude toward blacks. I wanted to play with and against the best athletes, regardless of color. We used to go play pickup basketball games all over Oakland; it didn't matter.

When I got to Dallas, I hit it off with Abner. We were a couple of rookies, just twenty-two years old. One day, my wife and I invited Abner and his wife over for dinner. I didn't think it was a big deal. In Dallas, though, it was a big deal. It was kind of unheard of, a white person inviting a black person over to their house as equals.

As it turned out, the dinner meant a great deal to Abner Haynes. "I never told Chris the whole story," Haynes recalled.

I just love him for it. Chris and I used to sit around and talk about things, and the next thing I know, he's inviting me to dinner. No one, especially a white guy, had ever invited me to dinner before. When I got home, I called my parents and talked to them for hours about it. My father was a very prominent pastor in Denton and Dallas and was pretty well known in the white and black community. They had never had dinner with a white person before. In a small way, our dinner brought blacks and whites in Dallas a little closer together.

Fred Arbanas added to the topic of how the Texans helped push toward integration in Dallas. He recounted,

> I was raised in Detroit and had always had black teammates, so I wasn't used to the segregation and discrimination in the South when I went to the pros. I got my first taste at the Senior Bowl in Mobile. My eyes opened to segregation. There were signs all around the stadium saying, "Whites Only" or "Colored," on the bathrooms and water fountains. I remember the segregated seating in the end zone also. My first exhibition game with the Texans was in Atlanta. That was a different experience too. The black players had to stay in a separate hotel.
>
> Then when I showed up in Dallas in 1962, things were changing, but there were still a lot of places blacks couldn't go. Restaurants and bars were pretty much off limits. Me and a few of the other white players started going with Abner and some of the other black players to black bars and clubs to listen to music and have a good time. Eventually we got Abner and some of the others to start going into white places of businesses. It helped that Abner was very popular in Dallas. He was like the unofficial mayor. There was even a song on the radio in Dallas called, "Little Abner Haynes." I felt we had a small hand in bringing people together in Dallas.

After the 1962 season, in which the Texans won the AFL title when they defeated the Houston Oilers, 20–17, in overtime on December 23, the Texans decided that Dallas was not big enough to support both their franchise and the Cowboys. Texans owner Lamar Hunt decided to move the team to Kansas City, where they would become the Chiefs. As the Texans had in Dallas, the Chiefs brought change to Kansas City.

Arbanas described how the integrated Chiefs affected Kansas City:

> Some people don't realize there was an adjustment period when we moved the Texans to Kansas City. Where we trained, in Liberty, Missouri, the black players weren't allowed in bars or restaurants. I remember my roommate, Jim Tyre, went into a place with a couple of black players, and they weren't going to serve them. Well, Jim took care of that problem, and slowly other places started letting the black players in.

Fred Arbanas, Dallas Texans. *Michigan State University Athletics*

In Kansas City things started getting better, with the Civil Rights Act of 1964 being passed. That, and with our black players going out into the community and meeting people, the whites came around. I felt our team opened up integration in Kansas City.

Even as late as 1963, some establishments in Kansas City still practiced de facto discrimination. "It turns out after we moved to Kansas City, we changed some things racially there also," Chris Burford said.

We went up to Kansas City with Lamar Hunt. There were five of us players that went. Abner and Curtis McClinton were the two black players. We all attended a luncheon with some VIPs from Kansas City.

When we arrived, we went up to the bar to get a beer. Well, the bartender refused to serve Abner and Curtis. The mayor of Kansas City happened to be there, so we complained to him. We more or less informed him we wouldn't be coming to Kansas City if we had to put up with this kind of stuff. So right then and there, the mayor integrated that restaurant. It changed things in Kansas City after that, because we started going to other bars and restaurants in town and integrated them too.

Although African American NFL and AFL players, both those from visiting teams and those who lived in Dallas, faced the pressing issues of segregation and de facto racism throughout the city, in the end the Cowboys and Texans helped bring some positive changes to the city in the early to mid-1960s. Meanwhile, 250 miles down the road in Houston, black players faced some of the same issues, plus some new challenges, as the Houston Oilers franchise staked its claim in East Texas.

6

AT HOME IN EAST TEXAS

The Oilers Take the Field in Houston

Houston after World War II was a typical southern city in every part of life as far as black and white social interaction was concerned. There just was not a lot of contact between the races. There were white neighborhoods and there were black neighborhoods. Except for maids or those who worked for a white family in some other capacity, African Americans really had no contact with the white world.

As the 1960s approached, Houston remained a segregated city, but times were changing. On March 4,1960, about a month after North Carolina A&T students had tried to integrate lunch counters in Greensboro, Texas Southern University students staged the first civil rights sit-in west of the Mississippi River when they walked from the TSU campus to several area drug stores in an attempt to integrate Houston lunch counters. They were led by student activist Eldrewry Stearns, head of an on-campus organization called the Progressive Youth Association (PYA), and Quentin Mease, director of Houston's African American YMCA.

After being unsuccessful in their first attempts at desegregation, in the summer of 1960 the TSU students attempted to integrate the downtown Houston lunch counter at Woolworth's. Through their efforts, along with the actions of many others, on August 25, 1960, seventy downtown lunch counters, department stores, drugstores, and supermarkets desegregated.

Thus, Houston was in a time of great transition when the AFL decided to place a franchise there for the 1960 season. Of the three Texas franchises that began play in 1960, the Houston Oilers were the most successful. The Oilers won the first two AFL championships in 1960 and 1961 and lost the 1962 Championship Game to the Texans in double overtime. The 1960 Oilers posted a 10–4 record and defeated the Los Angeles Chargers, 24–16, in the inaugural title game.

The First HOUSTON OILER Football Team and Coaching Staff
AFL Champions—1960

First Row: (L to R)   Jim Norton, Bobby Gordon, Tony Banfield, Billy Cannon, Dennit Morris, Charles Tolar, Julian Spence, Gary Greaves, George Shirkey and
Allen Hurst, Assistant Trainer

Second Row: (L to R) John Carson, Ken Hall, Bob Talamini, Charles Kendall, Bob White, Hugh Pitts, Al Witcher, Jacky Lee, Dave Smith, Bill Groman, and
Don Floyd

Third Row: (L to R)   Coach Fred Wallner, Charles Milstead, George Belotti, Mark Johnston, Hogan Wharton, Charles Hennigan, Doug Cline, George Blanda,
Rich Michael, Phil Perlo, Trainer Bobby Brown and Coach Walt Schlinkman

Fourth Row: (L to R) Head Coach Lou Rymkus, John White, Dalva Allen, Al Jamison, John Simerson, Jerry Helluin, Mike Dukes, Dan Lanphear,
Coach Mac Speedie, Coach Wally Lemm and George Greene, Equipment Manager

1960 Houston Oilers. *Robert Jacobus*

The 1961 Oilers started out the season 1–3–1 before catching fire and winning their last nine contests. The Oilers offense, led by quarterback George Blanda, set a professional record for points in a season, with 513, and Blanda set a record for touchdown passes thrown in a season, with 36. The Oilers defeated the Chargers again, this time 10–3, for their second straight title.

Their success on the field, however, appeared to have no correlation with the number of African American players on the team's roster. In their championship seasons, the Oilers carried the fewest African American players of any of the AFL franchises. In 1960, the black players on the team were defensive back Julian Spence, from now–defunct Samuel Huston College in Austin, and tight end John White, who had played his college ball at Texas Southern University in Houston. In 1961, defensive tackle Bob Kelly from New Mexico State also joined Spence and White on the Oilers, giving the team a total of three African American players.

By 1962, Spence and White were gone from the Oilers and Kelley was the only African American player on the roster. He appeared in only three games. In comparison, by 1962 every other AFL team had anywhere from six to ten African American players on their roster.

It remains unknown whether this was a deliberate move by the Oilers. Houston was the largest segregated city in the South and the southernmost city with a pro football franchise. Having a limited number of African American players on the roster thus may have been no coincidence, with the owners trying to appease their white fanbase. However, the jury is still out, as the Oilers may have been going after the best player regardless of color. One just can't argue with their early success in spite of having few black players.

Unfortunately, John White died in 1988, Julian Spence in 1990, and Bob Kelly in 2014, so they were unable to convey their thoughts about living and playing in Houston while the city was still segregated. However, some of their former teammates and friends gave some insight on the lives of these pioneer players in their early years.

White came to Texas Southern in 1956 from Tampa, Florida, and signed a free agent contract with the Oilers for their inaugural 1960 season. Although he came from a segregated society in Florida, this did not seem to make his transition to life in Houston any easier. While he was a member of the Oilers, White's wife went into labor in a Houston hospital. White was asked to leave the waiting room because blacks were not allowed in it.

After White's career with the Oilers ended in 1962, White stayed in Houston and in the early 1970s helped cofound the Professionals United Leadership League (PULL), a program for troubled young men. His notable cofounders included former Chargers All-Pro turned professional wrestler Ernie Ladd and prominent local black doctor John B. Coleman, who has a library in Houston named after him. In 1973, even future president George W. Bush worked for the organization.

Robert Brown, who played football at Texas Southern University with John White in the late 1950s, recalled,

> Both Julian and John loved sports. I knew both of them. I actually went to TSU with Julian's wife, who was a year ahead of me. John was a senior on the TSU football team when I was a freshman. I knew John pretty well. He ended up having a house just a mile and a half from me in the Third Ward. At first, when John was with the Oilers he actually stayed at Jones Hall, which was the athletic dorm at TSU. Eventually he married a TSU cheerleader and they moved into the Third Ward, only about a half mile from Jeppesen Stadium, where the Oilers played.
>
> John used to come by our TSU football practices when he was with the Oilers. He would help coach us. He liked to give back to his school.

Sometimes he would work out with the team too. John was a tight end, and I remember one day in practice he caught a pass and I tackled him low around the legs. He got up and said, 'You're hurting my money,' which meant that as a pass catcher, he needed good legs to be able to run and didn't want to get injured. John never really talked much about his playing with the Oilers and what he faced segregation-wise. It's just the way things were back then. We really didn't sit around talking about things like that.

Robert "Boo Lee" Williams knew John White as a youngster growing up in the Third Ward, which is where Texas Southern University is located and was just across Scott Street from Jeppesen Stadium. Williams was a 1967 graduate of Yates High School, which was a block from Jeppesen Stadium and the University of Houston. Williams was in the last graduating class of Yates before the desegregation of Houston high schools in the 1967–1968 school year.

Williams remembered White from when he played at TSU:

I knew all about John White when he played for Coach Durley at TSU. He was a heckuva pass catcher and player in the SWAC. Unfortunately, when he went to the Oilers, I don't think they used him enough. George Blanda hardly ever threw to him. I knew him a little bit. I was only ten or eleven years old when he played for TSU, but he was always nice to us kids. All of us Third Ward kids were thrilled to see him play for the Oilers.

Charlie Hennigan came to the Oilers in 1960, as an unheralded wide receiver from Northwest State College in Louisiana. Hennigan became a five-time Pro Bowler and three-time first team All-Pro with the Oilers. He reminisced about his early black teammates:

Julian and John were my teammates. I didn't have a problem with either of them. It was not a big deal. To be honest, before I joined the Oilers, I hadn't been around blacks very much, being from Louisiana and all. They were good guys, as was Bob Kelly when he joined the team. I like to win, and we had a saying back then, "If you can play, you can stay." If those guys could help us win games, they were okay in my book.

I do remember one exhibition game in New Orleans where Julian and John had to drive in from a black motel to the game, since they couldn't stay with us. Eventually, though, that came to an end and the black players could stay with the whites. When you think about it, we did represent a transition group on the way to integration, and that was something to be proud of. We helped bring change.

Bill Groman, the other half of the Oilers' all-star receiving tandem and one of Julian Spence's closest friends on the Oilers, also spoke about his African American teammates:

> I hung out with Julian Spence much more than with John White. John was a nice guy, kind of quiet. My wife and his wife eventually taught school together. Julian and I would hang out on the road sometimes. He loved jazz, and he knew all of the clubs to go to when we went to New York. Everyone called him "Spender."
>
> I'm from Ohio, so I grew up in integration. My best friend when I was fourteen was black. There may have been some players from the South on our roster who didn't like John and Julian being on the team. It helped, though, that we had a good mix of guys that came from northern colleges, and they were pretty smart and accepting of Julian and John. Al Jamison was from the Ivy League and Mark Johnston was from Northwestern.
>
> When we were playing for the Oilers in the early 1960s, most of us lived in apartments. I never saw anything directed at Julian and John. Then again, I never saw much of them after practice. I guess they went to some segregated apartments somewhere. I know they weren't able to go to a lot of restaurants in Houston because they would get kicked out of them. We never sat down and talked about race, though. Even though we knew the issue was there, it was never brought up. Looking back, we probably should have.

Offensive left guard Bob Talamini was another All-Pro who came to the Oilers in 1960 out of the University of Kentucky. After eight years with the Oilers, Talamini ended his pro career as a member of the Super Bowl III champion New York Jets.

"John and Julian were great players and good guys," said Talamini.

> I played at Kentucky, where obviously we didn't have any black players. Playing with and against blacks was a new experience for me. John and Julian were both very likeable. They were kind of quiet, though—not real aggressive. Lou Rymkus, our coach the first year, seemed to like them a lot. Julian was just a little bitty guy. He was the first Oiler on that 1960 championship team to pass away.

Offensive left tackle Al Jamison from Colgate lined up next to Talamini and was another Oiler All-Pro. He recalled,

I knew both Julian and John very well. John White was basically an offensive tackle playing tight end. He was a good player. Very dependable. Julian was very pleasant, very likeable. He was also very small—one of the smallest players in the league. Julian was also dependable. He didn't do anything outstandingly well, but he did it well enough to help us win. I never got a smack of any kind of integration problems on the Oilers.

Although the city of Houston started the desegregation process in 1960, racist attitudes persisted throughout the 1960s and beyond. On October 9, 1960, the inaugural season Oilers played against the New York Titans at Jeppesen Stadium on the campus of the University of Houston. The Titans' black offensive lineman, Howard Glenn, age twenty-four, suffered a broken neck during the first half of the game. Legendary *Houston Post* sportswriter Mickey Herskowitz recalled the incident:

> The press box learned Glenn died from the injuries and announced the news to the sportswriters covering the game. In the early days of the American Football League, the writers always chose a player of the game. I heard one of my colleagues remark, "I can't cast my vote until I find out who killed that nigger!" It was taken as a joke but reflected the attitude toward black athletes that persisted during this time period.

It was under the shadow of attitudes like this that African American players from the different AFL franchises traveled to both Houston to play the Oilers and Dallas to play the Texans. Several of those players reminisced about their time in Houston.

Some African American players, such as Pro Bowl running back Larry Garron of the Boston Patriots, were able to draw support from their families and essentially avoid the conflicts and hardships endured by some of their teammates and other African American players. Garron went to Dallas and then Houston two weeks later in the 1961 season. He said of his experience, "I really don't remember Dallas or Houston that much and how we were treated. I had family in both cities, so I just stayed with them instead of going to a black motel or staying with a black family. My dad was in Dallas, and I had a cousin in Houston. I don't recall any problems at the games either."

In 1960, Abner Haynes of the Dallas Texans made a trip to Houston to play football, just like he had the previous season. In 1959, Haynes had been a member of the North Texas State Eagles when they came to Houston to play the Cougars on October 24. The Eagles improved their record to 6–0 with a hard-fought 7–6 win. Haynes spoke about his 1959 North Texas experience, followed by his 1960 trip to Houston with the Texans on October 16, a 20–10 Oilers victory.

What upset Haynes about his 1959 visit was that he was not able to stay with his teammates in Houston:

> Although I had been born in Denton, I had visited Houston a lot growing up. My dad had a friend there, Bishop Galloway. I had sung in the choir at his church there. My family liked to sing. In fact, my first cousin is Sly from Sly and the Family Stone. I felt comfortable there in Houston.
>
> However, before we went to go play the Cougars my senior year, I was surprised when the college president and Coach Mitchell came to visit me a few days before the game and they told me I couldn't stay with the team in Houston. I was shocked. President Matthews told me, "Abner, we've been looking all week for a place where the team can stay together, but we can't find one." I was shocked. Once again, I felt comfortable in Houston; it was almost like home. It was like they turned their back on me. I have to admit, it hurt a lot.
>
> My white teammates tripped out when they found out I couldn't stay with them. They came to my rescue. Then when the students at North Texas found out the situation, a bunch of them rode down on the train together with us to Houston, to make sure we were all right.

Haynes then spoke about 1960:

> There wasn't anything out of the ordinary when we went to Houston. Just like in college, we didn't get to stay with our white teammates. They stayed at the University of Houston, which was where the stadium we played at was, while we stayed at Texas Southern University. Texas Southern is almost right across the street from where we played, so we never really ventured out into the city of Houston for anything. So, in a way, by staying at Texas Southern and playing our game right there, we weren't exposed to any real discrimination while we there—besides being apart from our teammates.

Clem Daniels, who was Haynes's roommate, also spoke about his Houston experience:

> With the Texans, my first year, we had to stay at Texas Southern University, while the whites stayed at the University of Houston. I had been to TSU before because we used to play them when I was with Prairie View. I really didn't complain about us staying apart because I was not

established as a pro yet. If I spoke out, I could get in trouble. Later, though, once I became an All-Pro, then I started speaking out against what I thought was wrong.

In 1961, I didn't go to Houston with the Raiders for the season opener because I had just signed my contract with them. I believe they did stay apart, just like the Texans did in 1960.

Now, by 1962, we were able to stay as a team at the Shamrock Hilton Hotel. I think part of that had to do with Barron Hilton, the owner of the San Diego Chargers, owning the hotel.

Another reason for the desegregation of Houston hotels had to do with Major League Baseball making its debut in Houston for the 1962 season. In April 1962, the Houston Colt .45s, the precursor to the Astros, began their inaugural baseball season in the National League. As it turned out, a controversy could have potentially erupted if Houston's hotels were not integrated.

Quentin Mease, a black activist in Houston, reasoned at the time, "National League stars like Willie Mays and Hank Aaron would soon be coming to Houston on road trips, and they would not tolerate staying in a segregated hotel."

Houston leaders realized this, and on April 1, 1962—ten days before the Houston Colt .45s played their first home game—the Rice Hotel in downtown Houston, the Shamrock Hilton Hotel (where National League teams were booked to stay), and several other hostelries accepted their first black guests. That's why, when Daniels came to town with the Raiders in 1962, he was able to stay with his white teammates.

Gene Mingo and Lionel Taylor of the Denver Broncos shared their 1960 Houston experiences. They came to Houston twice that year: once during the preseason on August 20 when they lost to the Oilers, 42–3, and then during the regular season on November 20 when they dropped a 20–10 decision to the Oilers.

Mingo recalled,

When we went to Houston in 1960, the black players stayed at Texas Southern University, and the whites stayed at the University of Houston. Both were really close to Jeppesen Stadium, where the Oilers played. We went down to Houston and practiced there most of the week. We practiced at a park close to UH and TSU—I think it was MacGregor Park. They had a rec building there.

Man, it was hot in Houston when we went there in August. I remember after practice we would go get a towel from the trainer and take a shower. After we dried off and took the wet towel back to the trainer, we were already drenched with sweat, and we needed another towel for that. We also went to an off-campus barbeque place somewhere by TSU; it was good.

It rained when we played the Oilers in August. The rain was blowing sideways and coming down hard. It was difficult for me to try field goals and extra points. A lot of people don't know it, but I'm the first black field goal kicker in pro football history. I also had the first punt return for a touchdown in AFL history—76 yards against Patriots. I'm also the only person in pro football history to score in six different ways. I also led the league in scoring in 1960.

One thing that sticks out about going to Houston was that there was segregated seating at Jeppesen Stadium. The blacks were in the end zone. I also remember before we went there, the team advised us how to act and where we could and couldn't go around Houston. We were lucky we had a couple of black guys on our team who had been to the South, so they could advise us as to what we could and couldn't do. Chuck Gavin was from Mississippi and played his college ball at Tennessee State, and Lionel Taylor had played with the Bears in 1959 and came to Houston to play a preseason game.

Taylor recalled his trip to Houston in 1959 with the Bears, as well as in 1960 with the Broncos:

We stayed at TSU that first year. I really don't remember too much. We really didn't experience Houston much, since we stayed right across the street from the stadium. I had been with the Bears the year before and we played in Houston in an exhibition game, so I knew what to look out for. We stayed at TSU then too. The black veterans on the Bears like J. C. Caroline and Willie Galimore took good care of me. They watched out for me. Unlike with the Broncos in 1960, we went out in the evening. One good thing about staying apart from our white teammates was that we really didn't have a bed check or curfew. Nobody from the team wanted to come over to the black part of town. In Houston we decided to go see Ruth Brown perform at some club. Needless to say, we didn't get in until very late.

Blanche Martin, a visiting player with the Los Angeles Chargers, vividly recalled his encounter with a Houston cab driver on New Year's Day in 1961, just hours after the Chargers had lost to the Oilers, 24–16, in the AFL Championship Game:

I needed to get back to Michigan State after the game because I was trying to get enrolled in graduate school to get my master's. I had sustained
a knee injury and knew I wasn't going to make it in pro football. I had
about two hours to spare, so I figured I had plenty of time. Well, I was
trying to hail a cab and they all kept passing me by. Finally, a white cab
driver pulled over and asked me, "Boy, what's your problem?" I explained how I had to catch a flight so I could go to graduate school. He
came back with, "You don't understand, do you?" "Understand what?"
I asked him. He said, "We don't tote no coloreds!"

Well, I had twenty dollars, which was a nice amount of money
back then. I told the driver I would give it to him if he took me to
the airport. He thought about it for a minute and said, "Get in and get
down!" I guess earning some extra money trumped the segregation laws
in Houston. He ended up getting a twenty-dollar tip on a sixteen-dollar
fare! Long story short, I made my flight, I went to graduate school, and I
became a dentist in East Lansing for more than forty years. I also promised myself I would never go to the segregated South again.

Despite these various stories of racism and inequality, longtime Oilers affiliate Boo Lee Williams maintains a positive perspective about what
it was like for African American players in Houston. When Williams was
twelve, he was hired by the Oilers training staff to assist the opposing team
when they came to town. Williams got to spend game day on the sidelines
with some of the biggest stars in the AFL.

He recalled,

I worked for the Oilers' trainer, Bobby Brown, for their first three
seasons. Whenever the Oilers would have a home game, I would go to
Jeppesen Stadium on Saturday morning and help wash all of the practice
gear that the opposing team had used that week. Then, before I went
home on Saturday night, I would help lay out the jerseys and equipment
for the opposing team, so they would be ready when they arrived at the
stadium on Sunday morning.

Once the game started, I would assist the other teams' trainer. I
would get water, towels—whatever they needed. It was pretty cool. I
got to see star black players like Ernie Ladd and Paul Lowe of the Chargers, Abner Haynes of the Texans, and Cookie Gilchrist of the Bills.

One thing I noticed when I worked the sidelines at the Oilers games
was that I never heard the white fans give the black players a hard time.
Believe me, I would have been the one to hear it. To me, Houston and
Dallas weren't as Deep South as New Orleans or Atlanta. One other
thing I noticed was that on all of the opposing teams, the white and
black players would sit on the bench together. When the fans saw this,

Blanche Martin, Los Angeles Chargers. *Michigan State University Athletics*

it helped diffuse things racially. I think part of the reason the players were so unified goes back to the fact that they all had to stick together. Most of the early AFL players, both white and black, had not been wanted by the NFL teams. The early AFL guys sort of formed a bond with each other.

Yet, while the benches were integrated along the sidelines of the Oilers' Jeppesen Stadium, the stands and fan seating still remained segregated. This was a Houston-centric issue; by the early sixties, all other cities with professional sports franchises had integrated their stands. It seems that the Oilers were the last major-league sports franchise to practice segregated seating—a practice that lasted through the 1963 season. In spite of pressure from the local black media and the NAACP (among other organizations), Oilers owner Bud Adams insisted he had no control over the seating arrangements. Jeppesen Stadium at that time belonged to the Houston Independent School District, and school district policy called for segregated seating at sporting and other events.

Modern testimonials regarding segregation in the stadium are often skewed along racial lines, with white players generally downplaying or remaining unaware of the issue. White player Bob Talamini said, "I didn't realize that seating was segregated at Jeppesen Stadium. I guess since it didn't really pertain to me, I didn't even think about it. That's a shame because when I think about it, that had to be something the black players knew about and it probably upset them."

Another white player, Bill Groman, noted, "I guess I was kind of aware there was segregated seating at Jeppesen Stadium. I remember blacks sitting in the end zone. Back then, I really thought it was more of a money thing—you know, end zone seats being cheaper and all. It really didn't sink in back then as to why they were really sitting there."

Despite the incognizance of many white players and spectators, the black community in Houston was well aware of the issue. Boo Lee Williams gave his take on segregated seating at Jeppesen Stadium:

> The blacks couldn't sit with the whites. They had to sit in the end zones. I had friends growing up who would occasionally go to Oiler games and would sit in the segregated section. I never sat in the end zone where it was segregated, because I was on the sidelines working.
>
> Growing up, we really didn't think about it very much. That's the way it was back then, and segregation had been our way of life from the time we were born. There were never very many black fans at Oiler games, though. Some of that may have had to do with newspaper

columnist Lloyd Wells telling blacks not to go to the games. He had done the same back in the fifties with segregated seating at Houston Buff baseball games.

As noted by Williams, the black media in Houston admonished Adams and the Oilers over their seating policy. There were two African American newspapers in Houston during this time period: the *Houston Informer* and the *Houston Forward Times*. The *Informer* featured sportswriter and columnist Lloyd C. A. Wells, who was also a mentor to young African American males in Houston during this time period and eventually went on to become a full-time scout for the Kansas City Chiefs in the 1960s and 1970s. Wells supplied the Chiefs with numerous African American players on their Super Bowl IV winning squad, including Otis Taylor, Jim Kearney, and others. He later became part of Muhammad Ali's entourage in the late 1970s.

A couple of months before the Oilers' home opener in 1960, Wells began his onslaught on Jeppesen Stadium segregation. In his weekly *Informer* column on July 9, 1960, he wrote,

Lloyd Wells with Hank Stram, circa 1966. *Melody Wells Ratliff*

If there is any doubt in your mind about the seating policy the Houston Oilers have set up for the Negro citizens here, let it be quelled with this current information I received from their ticket office. As for the air-conditioned loges, mid-stadium box seats, observation deck seats, lower level box seats, blue ribbon reserved section and reserved grandstand seats, Negroes won't be permitted to go near any such seats . . . under no conditions. As the ticket office will tell you, the only sets available for Negroes, will be the east side "End Zone Area."

If you are the kind of person who will take whatever is shoved off on you, it will cost $4.00 to sit in the Jim Crow section where you will need tele-photo and wide-angle eyes to see the action. I'm just wondering if the Dallas Texans are going to have their seats in the Cotton Bowl on a segregated basis. As such, we made a quick call to Dallas and Publicity Director Bob Halford of the Texans informed us that Negroes can sit anywhere they want to in the Cotton Bowl. He said the seating would be on an integrated basis.

In the August 20 edition of the *Informer*, Wells voiced his displeasure at some black fans in Houston who were going to go to Oilers games and accepting the segregated seating arrangement. He exclaimed, "It's no use urging Negroes not to attend the Oilers from the attitudes of several I've talked to, they will be out there like the white man wants them . . . hat-in-hand, down in the end zone cooped up like chickens."

Wells went on to say,

I have expressed my attitude toward the Oilers and their segregation policies, all I say now is those who don't believe in the Sit-In movements of Negro college students throughout the USA and the Alabama Bus Strikes and all the other protest movements made by Negroes throughout the USA in the past few years, then I'm quite sure you will feel no qualms about going out there and sitting in "your place."

The *Informer*, on August 27, contained this snippet from Wells's column:

Now that the Houston Oilers have a clue with what they can do with their segregated ball club, I'm sure lots of white people in Houston who were of the school of thought that Negroes would accept continued rank treatment from teams like the Buffs and Oilers, have more respect for us as a race. I'm hoping that at the next Oilers home game, instead of 50 Negroes, there won't be one dark face in the stands. I hardly think anyone can say that they don't know what is going on because of the full coverage we have given this.

I doubt it, but I think the Oilers should make some kind of statement, or change of policy to the Negro fans in Houston. Let's see if they are big enough.

Sports columnist Bud Johnson, while not quite as zealous as Wells, gave his opinion on the Oilers and segregated seating in the August 27 edition of the *Forward Times*:

> It is apparent that the Houston Oilers front office does not consider the Negro fan essential to the success of its team . . . although I had given K. S. "Bud" Adams and his cohorts credit for having more sense than they have displayed. I guess they are not as broadminded as I supposed.
>
> There is only one position for us to take from this point and that is to turn thumbs down on them. Since it is really known what direction the Oilers will go, we can do whatever is necessary to combat the segregation policy.
>
> If I were just an ordinary fan it would be a welcome relief to me to sit at home and watch the top NFL football teams in action instead of braving cold, rain, segregation and inflated prices to see a bunch of Class D college boys try and act like professional football players.

A week before the first-ever regular-season Oilers game, the team traveled to Dallas to take on the Texans in their last preseason game. The Texans, led by Abner Haynes, beat the Oilers, 24–3, in front of fifty-one thousand fans at the Cotton Bowl. Lloyd Wells noted in his September 10 column in the *Informer*,

> It was noteworthy to see that of the 51,000 Dallas Texans grid fans in the Cotton Bowl, at least 6,000 were Negroes and they were sitting all over the stands as they choose. Or, in other words, there was no segregation and/or block seating. Maybe that is the reason we aren't saying there were more Negroes present at the contest.
>
> They always did say Dallas was bigger in every respect except size over Houston . . . seeing their seating and the large crowd they had at the Cotton Bowl Friday night makes it evident why. If Houston is going to try and go "Big League" . . . then they should go all the way.
>
> I couldn't think of anything better I'd like to do, then go out to Jeppesen Stadium next Sunday and see the Oilers play the Los Angeles Chargers, but not so bad that I'll go under the present setup. If I did, and you do . . . it will be like giving all those kids who went to jail all over the South last year fighting for their rights in public places, a swift kick in the pants.

In the September 24 edition of the *Informer*, Wells wrote,

> It is clear now, that the vast majority of Houston Negroes aren't going to take the type of treatment Houston's Oilers are laying down. Everyone in Houston, who has any kind of knowledge about local football games, will point out to you that the approximately 50 Negroes on hand at last Sunday's games, hardly represent the Negro football fans in this city. If the Oilers would just be fair, instead of having headlines about a meager 20,000 at a stadium that seats 35,000 . . . in perfect weather . . . Negroes would fill those seats and make them the success they need to be, to end up in the black at the end of the season.

Wells continued to admonish the Oilers via several articles in October 1960, rallying against "Uncle Tom" fans and calling out team owner Bud Adams. His campaign continued well into 1961. On June 10, 1961, Wells even used his platform with the *Informer* to initiate the first organized boycott of an athletic event by African Americans in the United States, a track event at Jeppesen Stadium called the Meet of Champions. A large contingent of black fans (about eight thousand) was expected at the meet, especially since the neighboring Texas Southern University track team had entered several world-class athletes. Wells called on the NAACP, the Congress of Racial Equality (CORE), and the powerful student-led PYA from Texas Southern University to assist with the boycott. In the end, the protesters were even joined by black track stars Ralph Boston and Ralph Thomas, initially slated to compete on the field. When all was said and done, only three black fans attended the meet.

With the apparent success of the Meet of Champions boycott behind him, Wells focused on the upcoming Oilers home opener against the Oakland Raiders on September 9. He tried to get the African American players on the Raiders to boycott the game.

In the end, much to the chagrin of Wells and others, the Raiders' black players did play in the game. Wells wrote in an article for the *Pittsburgh Courier* on September 16, 1961, "In appearing before a crowd that numbered only 25 Negroes in a city of 250,000 Negroes, these athletes gave every one of them a slap in the face by competing before a segregated crowd."

Although Wells never asked the three black Oilers to boycott the 1961 opener against the Raiders, Julian Spence, John White, and Bob Kelly were asked by the NAACP to boycott the game. Like the Raiders players, they also decided to play.

Bob Kelly recalled, "That was the worst situation for me. I was one of only three blacks on the Oilers. There wasn't much we could've done to make a difference. We had to get on with our lives." Spence, White, and Kelly also probably came to the realization that if they boycotted the game, they stood a good chance of being released by the Oilers.

A couple of the 1961 Raiders recalled the team's trip to Houston. Quarterback Tom Flores said, "I do remember the NAACP trying to get our black players to not play in Houston in 1961. The boycott never came off, though, so it wasn't a big thing. What I remember the most about that game was that it was really hot in Houston and we got killed, 55–0."

Clem Daniels recalled,

> I remember the NAACP trying to get the black Raiders to boycott the Oilers game because of segregated seating. However, I didn't make that game to Houston. I had just come to Oakland from Dallas, and I hadn't even signed my contract with the Raiders yet, and I wasn't even activated, for that matter. I really couldn't tell you one way or the other if I would have boycotted the game if I had gone to Houston. Like I mentioned earlier, I was just trying to make the team, so I probably wouldn't have risked it. It was a couple of years later when I became an All-Pro that I started speaking up.

The next organized potential boycott of the Oilers' segregation policy at Jeppesen Stadium occurred on December 3, when the San Diego Chargers, with a large contingent of African American players (including AFL legends Paul Lowe and Ernie Ladd), came to Houston sporting a perfect 11–0 record.

Wells wrote in the November 25 edition of the *Informer*,

> Every Negro in the American Football League that has played here against the Houston Oilers is an insult to the actions of the hundreds of Negro youth who have made great personal sacrifices for the principles of human rights and gave up their chances at completing their education . . . and in some cases the right to attend school and served jail time in fighting for those principles that benefit all Negroes.
>
> Abner Haynes, as the biggest star the AFL, could have gained the admiration of the nation by refusing to play here, but just like a coward he went out and looked worse than he ever has in his entire football career.
>
> I still say this injustice toward Negroes is going to cost the Oilers in the long run. We'll see . . . watch for our stand relative to the San Diego Chargers coming here and playing.

With the help of the NAACP and the PYA, Wells had asked the nine black Chargers to boycott the game. Lowe informed Wells by phone the Wednesday before the game that after a nine-hour meeting, the Chargers had decided to play the game, but they wrote a letter to AFL headquarters stating they would protest playing in Houston in the future if the segregated seating policy didn't change. Lowe also expressed that the nine black players could be fined or suspended by the league if they refused to play.

Wells responded, "The players are only thinking of their personal loss or gain. We pointed out to them if that the hundreds of freedom riders and sit-in strikers would have had their feeling, Negroes would still be far behind in the many things these fearless kids made possible by making personal sacrifices."

Years later, San Diego's Ernie Ladd commented on Wells and his comments about the nine black Chargers crossing the picket line: "Lloyd Wells . . . was calling us every name in the book because we went ahead and played with our brothers and sisters sitting in the end zone. That was an embarrassing moment for me. But Lloyd Wells was right."

Possibly distracted by all of the publicity, the Chargers stumbled to their first loss of the season to the Oilers, 33–13.

Clem Daniels told one more story about segregated seating at Jeppesen Stadium. Daniels played his college football at Prairie View A&M University for the legendary Billy Nicks. Nicks is a legend among football coaches, both black and white, for winning five black college national championships while at Prairie View. Daniels, who played on Nicks's 1958 championship team, spoke about when he was with the Oakland Raiders and they came to Houston to play the Oilers in 1964:

> When I was playing with the Raiders in the early 1960s, we would come to Houston to play, and no one from Prairie View would come to the game because there was still segregated seating at Jeppesen Stadium. . . . Coach Nicks, who actually lived in Houston, would drive the fifty or so miles up to Prairie View every day. He would either come see me at the hotel the day before the game or we would go out to his house on Rosedale Street in the Third Ward. Coach Nicks told me he supported me but he refused to come watch me play as long as Jeppesen Stadium was still segregated.
>
> I think it was 1964 when segregated seating ended at Jeppesen and Coach Nicks came to the game. Now, our coach Al Davis knew all about Coach Nicks and was a big supporter of his. After the game, Coach Nicks came into the locker room, and Al Davis went berserk

because he got to meet Coach Nicks. He asked Coach Nicks, "How come you haven't been to one of our games here before?"

Coach Nicks replied, "Well, circumstances prevented it." On the plane ride back to Oakland later that night, Al Davis had me summoned up to the front of the plane to talk with him. He asked, "What did Coach Nicks mean by what he said?" I explained to Davis that Coach Nicks refused to go to the games as long as the seating was segregated. Coach Davis's reply was, "Well, those sons of bitches!"

With the city of Houston finally becoming desegregated in the early 1960s and Jeppesen Stadium doing away with segregated seating by 1964, the stage was set for Houston to step up in early 1965 when controversy rocked the AFL All-Star Game in New Orleans. Just a couple of years before the incident in New Orleans, Houston had been the nation's largest segregated city, and now it would step to the forefront of the civil rights movement.

7

THE GOOD, THE BAD, AND THE UGLY

Team Management and the Fight for Equality

By the late 1940s and stretching into the 1950s and 1960s, African American football players gained increasingly more rights when they traveled down South. The journey toward equality was a slow and steady process, with brave players protesting and standing up for their rights, along with the rights of black fans in the stands and the black community in general. Fortunately, these players were not alone in this struggle. Some of the earliest forms of protest against de jure and de facto racism on and off the playing fields of the Jim Crow South were surprisingly led by team coaches, owners, and general managers, who stood up and spoke for the rights of their African American players at a time when it could prove dangerous or even deadly for these players to speak out on their own. Eventually, as the civil rights movement heated up, black players were able to stage their own demonstrations against conditions in the South without as much fear of retaliation. But particularly in the decades of the forties and fifties, many team higher-ups and managers played significant roles as allies in the struggle for racial equality.

One need only think of the previously noted actions of team officials from the 1949 New York Yanks, who went lengths to arrange alternate transportation for African American players Sherman Howard and Buddy Young to Washington, DC, from New York so they could avoid segregated conditions. The list goes on, with a multitude of team owners stepping in to face the challenges posed by segregation.

However, great change is often met with equal resistance. And while it is true that many team managers assisted African American players in their fight for equal rights, not all team owners, management, or coaches supported the players. Some still held on to the Jim Crow way of doing things.

As detailed by African American player Bobby Watkins, Chicago Bears owner and head coach George Halas was notoriously indifferent to his black players when they traveled to the South for exhibition games. Halas brushed off Watkins with the excuse, "That's just the way it is down here, Bobby."

Lenny Moore also recounted how team owners didn't care about the plight of black players in the South:

> As far as going into the South to play a preseason game or putting franchises in the South, the owners and the NFL didn't care about us. That's where the money was. They didn't care that it was racist down there. It was all about the money. In spite of it all, we, the black players, hung in there. In the end, if you want to win, you're not going to bypass talent. Case closed. The truth was back then, and even today, the success of any ball club depends on the brother.

Here, Moore emphasizes the unparalleled contribution of African American athletes to professional football, who have forged a tradition of excellence and innovation in the sport, beginning in the integrated NFL after World War II and continuing to the present day.

Despite this fact, discriminatory white owners, such as the Washington Redskins' George Preston Marshall in the forties through the sixties, still questioned the merit and value of African American players. Eventually, his racist attitude led to the downfall of the Redskins franchise after the NFL integrated in 1946. When the NFL was strictly composed of white players, the Redskins were one of the NFL's top teams, compiling an 82–43–6 record from 1934–1945; they went to the NFL Championship Game six times, winning titles in 1937 and 1942. Yet, from 1946 (when the NFL was integrated) until 1961, their record was a dismal 69–116–8, with a 1–12–1 record in 1961.

In the 1961 NFL draft, a record thirty-eight African American players were selected. Of course, in line with their prejudiced track record, the Redskins did not select a single black player. The team had the number two pick in the entire draft and chose to select quarterback Norm Snead out of Wake Forest, who became a journeyman quarterback. The Redskins could have chosen Hall of Fame African American defensive backs Herb Adderley or Jimmy Johnson, but passed on both of them.

That same year, a total of eighty African American players dotted the rosters of NFL teams—the most ever up to that time. None wore the Redskins' uniform. Instead of finding the best player available after the NFL integrated, Marshall was adamant about keeping the Redskins lily-white, in part to appease his fans in the notoriously prejudiced South. When the Redskins moved to Washington in 1937, they became the southernmost NFL team, a distinction they held until the Dallas Texans joined the NFL in 1952 for their one fateful season. After the Texans left for Baltimore in 1953, the NFL did not place another franchise in the South until the Cowboys arrived in Dallas in 1960. By 1956, Redskins exhibition and regular-season games were broadcast to sixty radio and twenty-nine television stations throughout the South.

Marshall had made his stance on segregation well known throughout the years. Ric Roberts, reporter for the *Pittsburgh Courier*, quoted him in 1941: "Negroes will never play in our league again, because the white players would not stand for it."

Marshall was also quoted by Roberts in 1950 as saying, "I have nothing against Negroes. I am very friendly with Buddy Young and Marion Motley, but I want an all-white football team. I believe in states' rights, both in government and in football."

Marshall also publicly claimed on many occasions that the Redskins would remain all-white, because the Redskins were the "Team of the South." Marshall did not want to offend his southern fans by having black players on his roster.

A couple of African American players from the early 1960s who were associated with the Redskins—Lonnie Sanders and Billy Joe—discussed Marshall's marketing of the Redskins as the "Team of the South."

In 1963, Sanders, a defensive back out of Michigan State, became the second African American ever drafted by the Redskins to actually suit up for the team. He said,

> George Preston Marshall was a great marketing guy. He wanted the Redskins to be the South's team. You have to remember, there was no Miami, Atlanta, New Orleans franchises yet. The fight song, "Hail to the Redskins," used to say, "Fight for Old Dixie" in the lyrics instead of "Fight for old DC." Marshall used to bring busloads of fans up to Redskins games from the South, so they had fans in the southern states all up and down the East Coast. So really, one could see why he didn't want black players on his team, or, for that matter, why I don't think he cared about what we had to put up with when we played in the South.

Joe, a running back from Villanova, was also selected by the Redskins in 1963, but he didn't sign with them. He instead opted to play for the AFL Denver Broncos, where he garnered Rookie of the Year honors. He explained,

I didn't want to sign with the Redskins out of college. They were a racist organization back then, even though they had signed Bobby Mitchell the year before. I ended up with Denver. The AFL was signing a lot of black players. The Redskins tried to offer me more money, but I didn't want to go there. They were considered the South's team. From what I understand, one of the reasons they didn't sign black players was because their games would be televised in the South and George Preston Marshall thought having blacks on the roster would offend southern viewers.

The numbers back up both Sanders's and Joe's testimonies about the culture of the "Team of the South." In 1950, the NFL became a twelve-team league with the addition of the Browns, 49ers, and Colts from the AAFC. From that point until 1965, when segregation was finally dying away in the South because of protests and legislation like the Civil Rights Act of 1964 and the Voting Rights Act of 1965, the Redskins played thirty-nine of their eighty-six preseason games in southern cities—more than 45 percent of their total games. The next closest team during this time period was the Chicago Bears, with twenty-six southern preseason games. On the other end of the spectrum were the 49ers, who were on the West Coast and more than two thousand miles from the South, and the Browns, who declined to play in the South because of Paul Brown's policy not to have his team stay in separate facilities; each team played only one time in the South from 1950 to 1965.

In 1961, Marshall's hand was finally forced, and he integrated the Redskins in a scene reminiscent of when the Los Angeles Coliseum Commission agreed to integrate the Coliseum in 1946. The Redskins were slated to begin playing at the new Federal Field (later renamed RFK Stadium) that was to be christened in 1961 in DC. Stewart L. Udall, secretary of the interior under President John F. Kennedy, warned Marshall that the new stadium was not built to perpetuate racism and that the Redskins must hire black players. Udall said the Redskins could use the stadium only if they complied with federal law, which prohibited discriminatory practices in the hiring of employees. Udall said the Redskins could play there in 1961 only if they promised to sign black players.

In addition, the NFL forced Marshall's hand when the league signed a huge television contract with the networks in 1961. Congress had ruled that professional sports leagues could negotiate their own contracts with the networks, so the NFL signed a two-year, $9.3 million deal with CBS. Although paltry by today's television deals, this agreement brought the NFL into the big time. To help complete the deal with CBS, NFL owners urged Commissioner Pete Rozelle to meet with Marshall to get him to desegregate. Rozelle did so in August, and although Marshall exclaimed, "I didn't know the government had a right to tell a showman how to cast the play," he nonetheless finally relented. With the threat of not being able to use the new Federal Field hanging over his head, in addition to potentially putting the NFL's new television contract in jeopardy, Marshall finally integrated his team.

Since the Redskins had the worst record in the NFL in 1961, they had the first choice in the 1962 draft. Marshall made good on his promise to integrate by drafting running back Ernie Davis from Syracuse, who had won the Heisman Trophy for the Orangemen in 1961. However, the Redskins subsequently dealt Davis to the Cleveland Browns for Hall of Fame halfback/receiver Bobby Mitchell. In 1962, Mitchell, fullback Ron Hatcher, and guard John Nisby became the first African American players for the Redskins.

The addition of Mitchell paid immediate dividends, as he was moved to receiver and enjoyed an All-Pro season when he caught 72 passes for 1,371 yards and 11 touchdowns. More importantly, the Redskins improved their record to 5–7–2.

George Preston Marshall was matched by several other coaches in the NFL who were thought to be racist. One example was the Minnesota Vikings' first head coach, Norm Van Brocklin. Van Brocklin enjoyed a Hall of Fame career as a quarterback with the Los Angeles Rams and Philadelphia Eagles. After leading the Eagles to the 1960 NFL championship, Van Brocklin retired and, in 1961, became the coach for the expansion Minnesota Vikings. Several African American players brought up Van Brocklin's name without hesitation when speaking about racism and discrimination in the NFL.

Offensive tackle Proverb Jacobs, who, in 1959, was trying to stick with the Eagles for a second season after being their second-round pick in the 1958 draft out of the University of California, said about Van Brocklin,

> I had trouble dealing with the blatant racism that was going on. There was this great punter and kickoff guy trying out for the team from Southern University, an all-black college in Louisiana. His name was Dick Williams. He was six feet, four inches tall and could catch the football—he was an end. I think he was from Port Arthur, Texas. He would kick booming punts 60 yards or more in the air; likewise with field goals. He was good.
>
> I watched Van Brocklin destroy him. He would call a pass pattern where Williams was the secondary receiver and then he would drill to

him just as he was making his break and before he could react. The ball would pop off his fingers. Van Brocklin would then say, "Oops, bad hands." After a while, Dick's confidence was completely broken. I would make comments about this in the huddle, and Van Brocklin didn't like it very much. He was trying to protect Bobby Walston, who was the placekicker and kickoff man on the team, and himself, who was the punter. Dick Williams lost all confidence in himself and was later cut from the team [as was Jacobs, right before the Eagles opened their 1959 season].

Bobby Reed was a halfback out of the University of the Pacific who played for the Vikings and Van Brocklin in 1962 and 1963. Reed said,

The Vikings had a prejudiced coach. Norm Van Brocklin was very prejudiced. The civil rights movement never made it to the Vikings. Coaches ran the NFL back in those days. If they didn't like you, they could blackball you. We had a bunch of brand-new guys because it was an expansion franchise. We really didn't have any black veterans on the team to help with any problems that might arise race-wise. After a while I got tired of Van Brocklin. He was a cocky little prick. All of his assistant coaches were from the South, so the black players had to put up with their bullshit too. I ended up going to Canada to play. They were more open racially, and they paid better.

Reed's roommate in camp in 1963 was tackle George Balthazar from Tennessee State. Balthazar was giving the NFL one more shot in 1963, after being cut by the Steelers in 1961 and the Colts in 1962. Balthazar did not hold back in his feelings about Van Brocklin:

Norm Van Brocklin was the most prejudiced SOB I've ever met. I was in camp with the Vikings in 1963. In team meetings, he would freely use the word "nigger." It was not directed at his own players, but he would use it describing black players on opposing teams while we were watching game films. For example, we might be watching film on the Chicago Bears, and one of their black defensive backs was J. C. Caroline. He was one of the best in the league. Van Brocklin would say something like, "You can fake that nigger and he doesn't know which way to go."

I may also be the only black man cut in NFL history because I wasn't dark enough. I'm a Creole, and I'm a very light-skinned black. There have been times I've passed for white. I could go just about anywhere and not have any problems. Walt Yowarsky, our offensive line coach, came to me with tears in his eyes after I'd been cut in training camp

and said to me, "You're the first person I know who was released because you weren't black enough." I said, "What do you mean?" Coach
Yowarsky said, "Van Brocklin wanted his players blacker for his quota
system. He wanted no doubt who was and wasn't black on his team."
I had started a preseason game against the Giants on August 25th. I
was cut on the 27th. I had been having a good camp—I was starting.
It makes you wonder about what Coach Yowarsky said. Maybe there
was some truth to it.

All things in balance—where there is darkness, there is light, and when
there is bad, there is good. Despite the detrimental tyranny of higher-ups in
pro football like Marshall and Van Brocklin, between the 1940s and 1960s
there arose an increasing number of owners, coaches, and people in management who assisted and protected African American players when they
went to live or play football in the South.

Team owners were some of the first to stand up for the rights of their
African American players when they ventured to the South to play preseason games. One of the first recorded incidents involved the New York

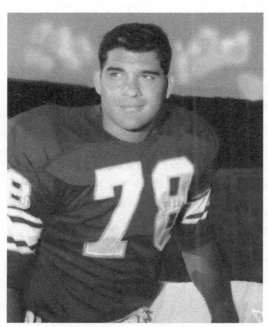

George Balthazar, Minnesota Vikings, 1963. *George
Balthazar*

Yanks owners and management coming to the aid of Sherman Howard and George Taliaferro when they traveled to Baltimore by train in 1949. At first, coaches were generally reluctant to join in, because if a coach tried to help or defend one of his black players, he too could lose his job and face being blackballed from the league. In the early years of integration after World War II, the only exception to this was Paul Brown of the Cleveland Browns. Brown was able to have a say about how his black players were treated without fear of reprisal because he was part team owner—he had cofounded the Browns and owned 5 percent of the team.

One of the earliest owners who stood up for his African American players when they traveled to the South was Tony Morabito of the San Francisco 49ers. At age thirty-six, Morabito became the founding owner of the 49ers when they began to play in the AAFC in 1946. The 49ers then joined the NFL when the AAFC folded after the 1949 season.

As previously mentioned, the 49ers played only one exhibition game in the South after World War II, a 1953 contest against the Eagles in San Antonio.

Charlie Powell, along with running back Joe Perry, was one of the two African American members of the 49ers at that time, playing defensive end for them from 1952 to 1957. The older brother of Art Powell, Charlie Powell also tried his hand at professional baseball, in addition to trying professional boxing in the late 1950s—even boxing against Cassius Clay (who would later be known as Muhammad Ali).

Powell mentioned the supportive role played by Morabito when they traveled to the Alamo city:

> I'll never forget one time when we were going to play an exhibition game in San Antonio in 1953, and the promotor called up team owner Tony Morabito and said, "It sure is going to be a nice exhibition game, but leave those two colored boys there. Don't bring them down here." Morabito told us the whole story in a team meeting. He told the guy he could take the game and do what he wanted with it—that the 49ers weren't coming. All the guys clapped, and it was good because it kept the team together.

Powell added,

> It was the same way when we got to the city and they told us that me and Joe Perry couldn't stay at the hotel with the white players. Morabito said something along the lines of, "You mean you're going to rent rooms to all these players and not these two? Well, I'll tell you what.

You just lost your money for everybody." And he threatened to find a resort hotel or a country club or some kind of place and rent the damn thing to keep the team together. The hotel relented, and we got to stay together with the white players. It was nice.

Another owner who facilitated the equal treatment of black players was Baltimore Colts owner Carroll Rosenbloom. George Taliaferro spoke about an encounter he had with Rosenbloom and white teammate Gino Marchetti after the Dallas Texans moved to Baltimore for the 1953 season:

> There was one other incident after we left Dallas and went to Baltimore that stands out. It also showed me that Gino Marchetti was a godsend as a human being. We were going to Baltimore for the first time to play the Redskins in an exhibition game. We left our training camp in Hershey, Pennsylvania, and got on buses to take us to Baltimore to play the game. Besides Buddy Young, we had some other black players on the team—Mel Embree, a wide receiver from California, and Charles Robinson and George Rooks, two guys who had played at Morgan State in Baltimore.
>
> When we got to the Lord Baltimore Hotel, our road secretary, Sam Banks, told Mel and I we weren't staying there; we were going to a black hotel. Buddy Young had already bought a home in the Baltimore area, and Robinson and Rooks stayed with family there since they were from the area. I told the Colts, "The hell with you; I'm not playing if I can't stay with the team!" The team said, "Your contract says you have to play, we can force you to." I said, "Like hell you can!" I ended up staying at Charlie Robinson's home.
>
> On game day, I showed up at the stadium and I stayed in my street clothes. They weren't going to force me to play. When I was sitting there, Gino Marchetti was the only teammate who showed concern. He sat down next to me for a minute and said, "I wish I could do something to help." The other guys on the team didn't want to get caught up in the middle of all of this. They didn't go out of their way to help me. They knew what was going on. A lot of those guys on the team grew up in the South with segregation, and they knew how myself and the rest of the black players were treated. They weren't going to jeopardize their careers for us. Gino didn't give a shit, though. He stood by us.
>
> What happened in the end was that our new owner, Carroll Rosenbloom, came into the locker room and saw me sitting by myself. He sat down next to me and said, "I know how you feel; I'm Jewish." I told him, "You have no idea what it's like for me. At least being a Jew, you have the money to own a team. I can't." With that, Mr. Rosenbloom pulled three $100 bills out of his pocket and gave them to me to get me

to play. I ended up playing and scored three touchdowns. That $300 made a big difference to me, as did Rosenbloom showing that he cared.

Lenny Moore also spoke about Rosenbloom and how he came to the aid of his black players when they traveled to Miami in 1960, to play the Steelers in a preseason game. Moore spoke about a mix-up in hotel reservations and the resulting aftermath:

> In Miami we somehow got booked together as a team at the previously all-white McAllister Hotel in downtown Miami. By mistake, we ended up being the team that broke the color line in Miami. Although we were allowed to stay there, we had to stay in our rooms and couldn't use any of the hotel facilities. We couldn't even take a cab over to the black part of town so we could have a little fun.
>
> We ended up having a meeting with Carroll Rosenbloom, the owner, and Weeb Ewbank, our coach, about our situation. I remember Rosenbloom sympathizing with us because he said he had faced discrimination as a Jew. Carroll eventually got some cabs to come take us to the black part of town. Even though Carroll helped us, we were always subjected to these types of situations down South. The white players on the Colts didn't have to put up with the stuff we black Colts had to endure.

Art Rooney of the Pittsburgh Steelers was another owner who sympathized with his African American players, taking a stand as an ally in the fight for equality. Lowell Perry, a receiver out of Michigan, and his wife, Maxine, spoke highly of Rooney and his supportive efforts. Perry was an eighth-round pick of the Steelers in 1953. He didn't get to play for the Steelers until 1956, because he served three years in the Air Force ROTC. In his sixth NFL game he fractured his hip and pelvis squared up against the New York Giants, ending his playing career.

Maxine Perry said about her husband's injury,

> It was frightening and heartbreaking. Thank God for Art Rooney. He visited Lowell daily and assured him he would always have a job in the Steelers organization. Mrs. Rooney would visit also. She baked pies and cakes. It was unbelievable. Art Rooney will be with me forever. I can't even think about him without getting emotional.

Rooney, true to his word, gave Perry a job. In 1957, after it was determined that his injury would prevent him from playing football, Perry became the first black assistant coach in modern NFL history. He coached receivers.

Before granting Perry his assistant coach position, Rooney consistently stood up for the rights of black players. Maxine Perry recalled an incident when the Steelers were Jacksonville bound for an exhibition game against the Bears in 1957. Jacksonville planned to host a parade for the players on the Steelers and the Bears. But as it turned out, the parade was reserved for white players only. The black players had to stand on the curb and watch.

Maxine Perry said,

> The white players didn't know what was happening. They wanted my husband to join the parade, but the black players weren't allowed. They also had to stay at a different hotel. When Mr. Rooney found out about it, he was livid. He flew down the next day and told the team they would never be victims of discrimination again.

The very next year, the Steelers had a scrimmage scheduled in Atlanta. When Rooney found out the black players would be staying separate from their white teammates, he canceled the game.

Rooney would go on to uplift African American players in other ways. In the mid-1960s Steelers defensive back Brady Keys was turned down ten times by bankers for a business loan to start his restaurant because they didn't want to loan money to a black man. Rooney loaned Keys the money, and he went on to start All Pro Fried Chicken in San Diego in 1967. Keys said, "Art Rooney was sent from God." Rooney would never accept repayment of the loan from Keys. In 1970, Keys became the first African American to be awarded a Kentucky Fried Chicken franchise in the United States. He eventually headed the Keys Group, and his corporation owned numerous KFC and Burger King restaurants throughout the country. Keys went on to become one of the wealthiest and most influential black men in the United States.

By the early 1960s, NFL teams started fighting back against segregated seating in southern stadiums. In November 1961, the Philadelphia Eagles canceled an exhibition game with the Redskins over that very issue. The Eagles were scheduled to play the Redskins at Forman Field in Norfolk, Virginia, on September 1, 1962. Eagles general manager Vince McNally said he didn't want any of the Eagles players "to be embarrassed by incidents which could occur." McNally returned the contract for the game to Redskins owner George Preston Marshall.

After the Eagles canceled the game in Norfolk, they also adopted a team policy to play no more preseason games in the South if the venue was to have segregated seating. The Baltimore Colts soon followed suit. Marshall, in turn, got the Chicago Bears, who had not yet adopted an anti-segregated-seating policy, to fill the Eagles' spot in Norfolk.

As far as head coaches are concerned, Paul Brown stands out as a pioneer in the early days of integration. Brown spoke about his ground-breaking and at times controversially progressive policies and actions:

> One of the reasons I was so successful in dealing with our players was that I had complete authority. . . . Everything pertaining to football was under my control.
>
> I never considered football players black or white, nor did I keep or cut a player just because of his skin color. In our first meeting before training camp every year, I told the players that they made our teams only if they were good enough. I didn't care about a man's color or his ancestry. I just wanted to win football games with the best people possible.
>
> We became the first pro football team of the modern era ever to sign black players, and I think the delicate way in which we helped Marion Motley and Bill Willis helped them escape the tremendous pressure they faced. Some people in the league resented this action . . . and I felt it was best answered by the players themselves when they played against these teams.

Brown made a special rule for his team. Whenever a rookie from the South first reported to the Browns, he first had to look up African American players Marion Motley and Bill Willis, introduce himself, and shake hands. It broke the ice and proved effective.

Several of Brown's African American players reminisced about their interactions with him. "Because of Paul Brown, every place we went we stayed together," said Jamie Caleb, a halfback from Grambling State University who played for Brown in 1960.

Pro Football Hall of Famer Bobby Mitchell played halfback for Brown from 1958 to 1961. He added, "Paul Brown always made sure we stayed together. We were the only team that did that in the early days."

Sherman Howard, who suited up for Brown in 1952 and 1953, said,

> When I was with the Browns, we went to Houston for an exhibition game, I think it was in 1953. They wouldn't let the blacks stay at the Shamrock Hotel—myself, Marion Motley, Bill Willis, and Horace Gillom. Since we couldn't stay together, that meant we couldn't eat

together, and Paul Brown didn't like that. He said, "We won't do this again," and we didn't.

Paul Brown liked to control the environment around him, and when the team couldn't stay or eat together, that just wouldn't work for him. Coach Brown was somewhat advanced as far as signing and playing African Americans, and having the whole team stay and eat together. In my opinion, though, it was more of a case of his controlling the environment and finding the best player possible—he didn't necessarily implement his policies out of a compassion for blacks.

Guard Harold Bradley Jr., from the University of Iowa, played for Brown from 1954 to 1956. Bradley and his father, Harold Bradley Sr. (who played for the Chicago Cardinals in 1928), were the first African American father-and-son duo to play in the NFL. After his 1958 season with the Eagles, Bradley abruptly retired from the NFL and moved to Italy, where he became an actor, painter, singer, and artist. He continues to reside there today.

"Paul Brown was acknowledged as one of the most liberal-minded coaches by the media," Bradley said:

He was cited as having an "open door" policy to black players. This went back to his days as a high school coach at Massillon, Ohio, and then at Ohio State. There were stories circulating around the sports world in the late 1940s, early 1950s that communicated Paul Brown's "open door" commitment to integration and how that contributed to his winning ways.

Mr. Brown was proud of that contribution, although as far as I know, he was shy to carry on in public about it. He seems to have been identified as a fair and open-minded football coach who quietly helped integrate pro football after World War II. Playing for Paul Brown and the Browns proved to me that integration is great stuff. It proved that people can work together. With the Browns, there were no racial problems while I was there. The white guys respected me, and I respected them.

John Wooten, who played guard for Paul Brown from 1959 to 1962, said,

Paul Brown would not accept segregating his team. We never played exhibition games in the South because of that. He used to always say, "I don't have any white Browns and I don't have any black Browns—I just have Cleveland Browns." When Paul Brown came to the NFL from the AAFC, there were very few blacks in the NFL. The AAFC was more liberal toward blacks, like the AFL a few years later. George Halas and George Preston Marshall basically ran the NFL back then. When Paul came in, he basically told them, "You're not going to tell me who's on my team."

When the AFL came into existence in 1960, there were several owners and coaches who came to the aid of their black players. From its humble beginnings, the AFL developed a reputation as being more open-minded than the NFL when it came to signing, treating, and coaching African American players. One of the more progressive AFL coaches was Hank Stram of the Dallas Texans/Kansas City Chiefs.

Abner Haynes said about Stram, "Hank didn't give a damn. He didn't care about the color of your skin. Hank was always a straight shooter."

In addition to Stram, Haynes also spoke highly of Texans owner and AFL founder Lamar Hunt:

> Lamar Hunt was a great person to work for. He would guide you and help you. He was like an older brother, a friend. He loved Dallas. He was concerned about the community. This new team was a way to show the Dallas community how we could work together. I loved Lamar and Hank Stram. A lot of white coaches would belittle black players at practice and during games. Hank never did that. He and Lamar brought brotherhood to the organization. They both came from good families. If there was a problem on the Texans, we came together. I continue to use those lessons they taught me today.

The statistics bear out what Haynes said about the Texans/Chiefs being more progressive than other teams. They always had a larger percentage of black players on their roster, even in the more racially diverse and progressive AFL. In the mid-1960s Stram also hired the first full-time African American scout in pro football history—journalist and activist Lloyd Wells. Wells helped bring eight African American defensive starters to the Chiefs' Super Bowl IV championship team, including Hall of Famers Buck Buchanan and Willie Lanier. On the offensive side of the ball, Wells got All-Pros like receiver Otis Taylor to sign with the Chiefs.

Sid Gillman of the San Diego Chargers was another AFL head coach who ran his team seemingly unfazed by skin color. Ernie Wright, an African American Pro Bowl offensive tackle, played for Gillman for eight seasons. He said of Gillman's color-blind attitude,

The Chargers never had any racial conflicts within the team itself. . . . I don't believe that Sid Gillman has ever had a prejudiced bone in his body.

When I started in 1960, we all knew that the NFL had a quota for blacks. There was always an even number of them, so when you were on the road, you'd always have two blacks together. There were no blacks that were on the bench. Everybody that was black on the team was playing. They weren't developmental players, they weren't reserves, they weren't backups. If you were black, you were playing. From the day you started, you could room with anybody you wanted to. Sid's only prejudice was against people who wouldn't play and wouldn't work at the game. He loved to be around talented people. He loved to be around people who wanted to win.

Al Davis was another integration pioneer in the AFL. Davis was first head coach of the Oakland Raiders and eventually became the owner of the franchise. Davis refused to accept segregated hotel accommodations for his players. He was also a pioneer for black players in other ways. In 1968 Davis was the first to draft an African American quarterback in the first round of the AFL/NFL draft when he selected Eldridge Dickey out of Tennessee State University. In the early to mid-1960s Davis made a habit of scouting and drafting black players from HBCUs before it became popular, like Art Shell out of Maryland State in 1968. Davis made further history in 1989 when, as owner of the Raiders, he made Shell the first African American head coach in NFL history. That was after hiring the first Hispanic head coach in NFL history in 1979—two-time Super Bowl champion coach Tom Flores. He also hired the first female chief executive in league history when Amy Trask became chief executive officer of the Raiders in 1997.

Clem Daniels said of Al Davis,

Al knew what struggles black players were going through in the early 1960s with the civil rights movement. He always stood by us. I don't know of many owners or coaches who were doing that back then. He took up for us when we protested in Mobile, Alabama, in 1963; he just as easily could have cut us and blackballed us from pro football.

However, the one coach in pro football who consistently stood up for the rights of his black players, without fear of reprisal, especially when his team traveled down South, was Green Bay Packers head coach and general manager Vince Lombardi. Lombardi had a long record of promoting and insisting on equality for Packers players, regardless of skin color. He would not tolerate discrimination against his players.

Lombardi, who set the standard for NFL coaches, was the Packers' head coach and general manager from 1959 to 1967. In that nine-year period, the Packers had an 89–29–4 regular-season record. Lombardi had a 9–1 record in playoff games, winning five NFL championships in a seven-year period (1961, 1962, 1965–1967). The Packers also won the first two Super Bowls after the 1966 and 1967 seasons. The trophy that goes to the Super Bowl champion today is named in Vince Lombardi's honor.

Lombardi's views toward discrimination appeared to partially come from personal experience. Being Italian and growing up in Brooklyn, he knew what it was like to endure racial slurs. In addition, Lombardi felt that discrimination against Italians had prevented him from getting some coaching jobs throughout the years.

In addition, after he became head coach of the Packers, in September 1960 Lombardi was refused service at a restaurant in Winston-Salem, North Carolina, when the Packers were playing the Redskins in an exhibition game. Because his skin was deeply tanned from the summer sun, restaurant staff thought he was black. It gave him some insight into what it was like for African Americans in the South.

Lombardi was said to have treated his players the same, regardless of race. Dave Robinson was a rookie with the Green Bay Packers in 1963. A linebacker out of Penn State, Robinson was one of the anchors of Lombardi's defenses, earning three straight titles from 1965 to 1967. Robinson was elected to the Pro Football Hall of Fame in 2013. Robinson said of Lombardi, "It never entered my mind the reason I was getting chewed out for something was because I was black. Everybody was treated equally."

At his first team meeting as the new head coach of the Packers in 1959, Lombardi said, "If I ever hear 'nigger' or 'dago' or 'kike' or anything like that around here, regardless of who you are, you're through with me. You can't play for me if you have any kind of prejudice."

By his second season in Green Bay, after he had established himself, Lombardi also let local restaurants and bars in Green Bay know that if his black players weren't going to be served at those establishments, then they would be off-limits to the white players as well.

Packers guard Jerry Kramer, who, in 2018, was finally elected to the Pro Football Hall of Fame, said of Lombardi,

> I think part of Vince's open-mindedness toward black players went back to his being denied service at a restaurant in the South because they thought he was black. He also broke down barriers in Green Bay. There was a bar and restaurant there that banned the African Americans

Dave Robinson, Green Bay Packers. *Robert Jacobus*

on the team. It was a very popular place in Green Bay. Well, Vince had a meeting the next day and informed everyone on the team the place was off-limits.

Dave Robinson added,

Supposedly there were seven or eight restaurants in Green Bay that didn't want to serve the black players when Coach Lombardi arrived. Vince handled the problem in about forty-five minutes. He called all of those restaurant owners together one day, and in the meeting he told them, "It's your business, you can serve who you want. As of right now, however, no black Packers will come into your restaurants, nor will any white Packers. They are off-limits to them." Now, Green Bay only had sixty thousand people back then. These owners needed the Packers in their restaurants to help bring people in.

Packers Pro Football Hall of Fame defensive end Willie Davis said,

Coach Lombardi's policy toward racism can be summed up in two words: zero tolerance. I can tell you truthfully that more than a few players were shown out of Green Bay because they weren't buying into Coach Lombardi's policy. I would say nobody had more impact in creating diversity in the NFL than Coach Lombardi. It was partly because he took a new approach—almost playing ignorant to any kind of racial tension in the league. Right from the start, he treated us as equals. We were just players competing for a spot on the team. He chose not to see color in an era where most coaches chose to look the other way in terms of blacks. It was if he felt the best way to fix the problem of segregation and racism in the league was to actually pretend it didn't exist—at least to us.

Center Bill Curry came to the Packers in 1965, as a rookie from Georgia Tech. After his ten-year NFL stint concluded, Curry became a coach, and his stops included Georgia Tech, Alabama, and Kentucky. He said about Lombardi's stance toward discrimination,

There were teams in the NFL when I came into the league in 1965 that had quotas for how many blacks they would have on their roster. With the Packers, it was different. On our forty-man roster we had ten African American players. Lombardi didn't care about the color of your skin. He would have had forty blacks on the Packers if that gave him the best chance to win. He cared if you could play football and whether you were a good person. He had a gift for getting all of those different personalities and backgrounds to work together. Vince didn't tolerate racism. With the Packers, if you said one racist thing, you were cut from the team immediately. He had been discriminated against because his last name ended in a vowel.

Lombardi even dealt with the interracial marriage issue in a different manner than previous owners and coaches had. In the 1950s, both Henry Ford and Milt Campbell had been cut them from their respective teams for marrying white women. In the mid-1960s, Packers defensive tackle Lionel Aldridge questioned if he might meet the same fate.

Aldridge's wife at the time, Vicky, described the events as follows:

> Lionel went in to meet with Coach Lombardi because he had heard
> the first interracial couple that had gotten married in pro football had
> been blackballed from the NFL. It was rumored to be Cookie Gilchrist,
> and he ended up going to the AFL. Lionel wanted to find out from
> Lombardi what would happen if we got married. According to Lionel,
> Lombardi said, "You know what, I don't care who you marry as long as
> you keep the Green Bay Packers team clean, your nose clean, and play
> good football. Don't worry about it—the same thing won't happen to
> you that happened to Cookie Gilchrist."

Thinking they were beyond Lombardi's sphere of influence, the
higher-ups in the NFL even tried to stop the marriage. Commissioner Pete
Rozelle came to Green Bay personally to apply pressure to Lombardi on
the issue. Lombardi told Rozelle, "Absolutely not—this is *my* team. My
team is who my team is, and no one can tell me what I can and cannot do."

Vicky Aldridge added, "Coach Lombardi was totally a racial pioneer.
He stuck his neck out for us, and for his beliefs."

Traveling through the Jim Crow South in 1960, Lombardi saw
firsthand the discrimination his African American players faced, having to
stay in separate hotels and not being able to eat together with the rest of
the team. The Packers opened the preseason in New Orleans against the
Steelers on August 13. When the team bus pulled up to the white hotel in
downtown New Orleans, the white Packers got off the bus and went into
the hotel. Waiting to get situated with his alternative housing arrangement,
Packers African American safety Willie Wood broke a de facto segregation
rule: He entered the hotel lobby when he should have waited outside—in
the August Louisiana heat, no less. After being escorted out of the hotel by
a black porter, Wood then attempted to hail a cab and head to the black
hotel on the other side of town. Unfortunately, he mistakenly got into a
whites-only cab and had to be directed to a black cab.

When Lombardi saw what happened to Wood and his teammates Emlen Tunnell, Willie Davis, and Paul Winslow in New Orleans, he decided
that his team would never stay apart again.

Staying true to his word, in 1961 and 1962 the Packers played preseason games against the Redskins in Columbus, Georgia. Rather than have
his team face being apart, Lombardi had the Packers team stay together at
Fort Benning, a local army base.

Jerry Kramer recalled staying at Fort Benning:

I remember in 1961, in Georgia, we couldn't stay in the same hotel together. We ended up staying in the army barracks at Fort Benning. It was not comfortable. We were big football guys, and we had to sleep on cots. But we did stay together as a team. I also remember in Georgia that the black players had to stay apart from the rest of the players in the back of the restaurant we went to. We all sat in the back, and Coach Lombardi informed us if we went up to the front of the restaurant to order something like a burger, it would be a $500 fine. Vince made it clear that there was to be no discrimination.

Linebacker Nelson Toburen came to the Packers in 1961 out of Wichita State University. He also went to Georgia in 1961 and 1962. He said, "I remember going to Fort Benning in 1962, my rookie year. It was September and the barracks were not air-conditioned. It was miserable. But Coach Lombardi was adamant that we stay together as a team."

On a side note, while he was in Fort Benning, Toburen made an interesting observation about his black teammates. He noted,

There was one other item I noticed when we went down South to play. I could see the attitude of our black players change when we went south of the Mason–Dixon Line. I think they felt they had to act a certain way or risk retaliation. They seemed to become a bit more fearful. I think it was more so that the black players who had been raised in the South acted this way, as opposed to the black players who grew up in the North and West, where they hadn't faced the Jim Crow stuff growing up. I can't say I blamed them.

The Packers were once again slated to play the Washington Redskins in Columbus in the 1963 preseason. However, a little more than a month before the game was to be played, it was moved to Cedar Rapids, Iowa. The venue for the game was Kingston Stadium, a fifteen-thousand-seat facility.

The real reason the game was moved to Iowa is unclear. There were two versions. The first was that the game was moved for financial concerns and poor ticket sales.

On July 20, a few days before the game was moved, United Press International ran a story saying, "The Green Bay Packers and Washington Redskins are seeking a new location for their Sept. 7 game after cancelling the scheduled appearance at Columbus, Ga., due to poor advance sales. Public response to date indicated a grave financial risk to the sponsoring Boys Club."

An Associated Press wire story on July 21 said,

> It was announced at Columbus, Ga., that the community's Boys Clubs
> had withdrawn sponsorship of the Sept. 7 Packer exhibition with the
> Washington Redskins, leaving the teams to look for another site.
>
> The cancellation of the Columbus exhibition, last in a series of three,
> was announced by William Martin, who had served as the sponsor's
> chairman. He said public response indicated a grave financial risk for
> the Boys Club.
>
> He said the Packers and the Redskins had agreed to cancel the game.
>
> The first game, in 1961, drew only 13,000, as the Packers won,
> 31–24, and only 16,000 turned out last year when Green Bay took a
> 20–14 victory.
>
> According to Martin, "We just did not have any indications that the
> game would be as much of a success as it was the previous year, and we
> decided not to risk the loss of $16,000 which had been cleared on the
> two previous games."

The other reason given was because of segregated seating at the stadium in Columbus, coupled with the fact Lombardi did not want his players to stay at the army barracks at Fort Benning again.

On August 1, 1963, an Associated Press wire story said, "The game
was originally scheduled for Columbus, Ga., but was moved because the
two teams were dissatisfied with segregated seating."

On the same day, the *Green Bay Press Gazette* ran a story that said,

> The Packer–Redskin non-leaguer at Columbus, Georgia, cancelled
> because both clubs were dissatisfied with segregated seating, will
> be held in Cedar Rapids, Ia., the same night, September 7th. . . .
> The Packers and Redskins, both with Negro players, stayed at Ft. Ben-
> ning, just outside Columbus, rather than live apart from their Negro
> players. There was some fear of demonstrations, due to separate seating,
> if the game had been played in Columbus.

The Westside Civic Club of Cedar Rapids sponsored the game for
charity. There had been games held at Kingston Stadium the previous
three years, and although those three games cleared a profit, the exhibitions ended after 1962. There were no plans to continue holding preseason
games in Cedar Rapids. However, when the Redskins/Packers game was
looking for a place to move, the Westside Civic Club stepped up and put
on the game. It was announced on July 31 that the game would be held in
Cedar Rapids on September 7.

Dave Robinson recalled his version of the series of events:

> When the Packers played the Redskins in Winston-Salem a year or two
> before the Cedar Rapids game, Vince and his wife Marie went into a
> restaurant, and they were refused service because the maître d' thought
> that Vince was black, due to his dark skin and the tan he had acquired
> being out in the sun during training camp. Vince called George Pres-
> ton Marshall and told him about the incident, and Marshall supposedly
> laughed at Lombardi. Lombardi got back at Marshall with the Cedar
> Rapids arrangement. The Packers were world champions and very
> popular at this time. They sold out stadiums, and the teams would split
> the revenues. Lombardi stuck it to the bigoted Marshall by scheduling
> the game in the fifteen-thousand-seat stadium in Cedar Rapids. The
> Redskins had a large press contingency following them around because
> Frank Budd, the "World's Fastest Human," was trying out for the team.
> There were about a hundred press requests for that little stadium, and
> the press box could only hold about twenty. The place was terrible,
> with cramped locker rooms, and both teams lost money.
>
> Apparently, the Redskins and Packers alternated years in where they
> played the game. Following the Cedar Rapids game, Lombardi went to
> Marshall and informed him that they would play in Cedar Rapids every
> year the Packers hosted the game. Marshall supposedly asked Lombardi
> to cancel the series after the Cedar Rapids game.

Tight end Marv Fleming, the Packers' eleventh-round draft choice
out of the University of Utah in 1963, was one of three African American
rookies to make the team—the others being Lionel Aldridge and Dave
Robinson. Fleming recalled the game in Cedar Rapids:

> The Cedar Rapids game was my rookie year. I didn't go to Fort Ben-
> ning the previous couple of years, but I do know that in prior years
> playing the Redskins in Georgia, there were some problems and the
> team stayed at the army base so they could stay together. Coach Lom-
> bardi frowned upon the team not being able to stay together. I grew up
> in LA and went to college in Utah, so being separate from my white
> teammates would have been foreign to me if we had played down
> South. In fact, when we played in Cedar Rapids, there were about
> three buses full of my supporters from Utah who came to cheer me on.
>
> The real reason I remember Cedar Rapids is because it was where I
> made the team. You have to remember that was my prime concern—
> not the fact that we moved the game. It was the last exhibition game
> before the regular season the next week. I got lucky because our regular
> tight end, Ron Kramer, got sick and I took his place and had a great

game. After the game, Willie Wood came up to me and said, "Welcome to the Green Bay Packers." I asked, "What do you mean?" He said, "Look at how well you played compared to your competition." I did actually play much better than my competition for the spot behind Kramer, Jan Barrett.

Jerry Kramer added,

The game in Cedar Rapids was nothing special. There wasn't much of a crowd. We had played in a place like that before, against the Giants in 1959, in Bangor, Maine. I guess I didn't realize we played the game there because of the conditions for the black players in Georgia. What Coach Lombardi did by moving the game was completely in his character, though.

After Cedar Rapids in 1963, the Packers encountered an unexpected bout with discrimination when they returned to New Orleans in 1964, to play in a preseason game against the St. Louis Cardinals.

Dave Robinson spoke about going to New Orleans in 1964, and also recalled an earlier experience down South when he was in college at Penn State:

I wasn't new to integrating the South. At Penn State I integrated the Gator Bowl in Jacksonville at the end of the 1961 season. I found something interesting. We were down in Jacksonville for ten days, and the only time I felt comfortable was those three hours I was on the football field. Jacksonville was segregated, obviously. We stayed in San Augustine, Florida, at a place called the Ponce De Leon Hotel. I had a room to myself.

There was an article in the paper about me integrating the Gator Bowl. I didn't know it at the time. I remember when they wanted me to go to the press room at the hotel but I wasn't allowed to be in the lobby. I had to take a freight elevator and go in the back way so I wouldn't be seen.

We also got to meet the Gator Bowl queen. She was giving the players on both teams a kiss on the cheek as we were in line being introduced to her. She kissed the guy before me and after me, but not me. It's been like this my whole life.

I didn't start the game. Later on, I found out why. Some guy sent in a letter saying he was ex-military and was an excellent shot; if I was introduced before the game, he was going to shoot me.

I thought I put it all behind me when I went to Green Bay. Ha! New Orleans was the worst town we played in when we were there in the

1964 preseason. When we got there, all the white guys stayed at the Marriott. The black guys were bused across town to the black section. I remember the bus that took us from the airport dropped the white guys at the Marriott. The black players had to get off the bus, sit on the curb, and wait for taxis to take us to our hotel.

Apparently there was a mix-up about us not being able to stay to-gether. Somehow word didn't get to Coach Lombardi. He was furious. After that, we didn't stay at the Marriott again. Coach Lombardi had us stay all stay together in a hotel out by the airport. He also made Bourbon Street off-limits for the white players, since the black players weren't al-lowed down there. Max McGee ended up sneaking out after bed check, though, as he was known to do.

Despite some hesitancy on behalf of the pro football establishment, by the early 1960s, thanks to the efforts of some pro football owners and coaches, African American players started making strides toward equality when traveling down South. With the civil rights movement in full swing, the African American players themselves could finally stand up to Jim Crow without fear of reprisal. The battle for equality was heating up, and these brave players began to use their talents, status, and influence to join the fight for their rights.

8

FIGHTING BACK

Pro Players, Celebrities, and Entertainers
Make a Stand for Civil Rights

It was the 1960s, and the United States was changing. Thanks to the rise of the automobile and the passage of the Interstate Highway Act in 1956, Americans became more mobile. As people from all over the North and West ventured to the South for the first time, they began witnessing first-hand the injustices suffered by African Americans. People began to question segregation and the ways of the Jim Crow South.

In addition, the mass media, spurred on after World War II by the advent of television, brought the civil rights movement into America's living rooms. Heavy media coverage documented major civil rights events like *Brown v. Board of Education* in 1954; Emmett Till's murder, Rosa Parks's arrest, and the subsequent Montgomery Bus Boycott in 1955; the Little Rock Nine integrating Little Rock Central High School in 1957; the lunch counter protests inspired by North Carolina A&T students and the violence endured by the Freedom Riders in the early 1960s; and the March on Washington in 1963.

Before this upsurge in the civil rights movement, protesting against conditions in the South, such as inferior accommodations for African American players and segregated seating for black fans at southern stadiums, could get a player blackballed from the league. But as the movement gained steam and continued to inspire change, African American pro football players began standing up without fear of retaliation or blackballing. These brave players were joined by fellow athletes from other pro sports, in addition to prominent people in the entertainment industry.

One of the earliest protests in the world of pro sports occurred in basketball on January 16, 1959. Minneapolis Lakers rookie and future Hall of Famer Elgin Baylor took a large step forward to end discrimination in the South when he refused to play in a game against the Cincinnati Royals in Charleston, West Virginia, because the hotel the Lakers were to stay at would not accommodate the three African American players on the team. Although Baylor grew up in segregation in Washington, DC, he subsequently went to college in the more racially tolerant Pacific Northwest at the College of Idaho and then the University of Seattle. Baylor then went to Minneapolis, which was an integrated midwestern city. Although the team did find a black hotel that would take the whole team, the damage was done. Baylor refused to play. However, Ed Fleming and Boo Ellis, the other two African American Lakers, did play in the game.

Earlier in the season, the Lakers had played the Boston Celtics in Charlotte, North Carolina, and Baylor and his black teammates were not allowed to stay with their white teammates. The same scenario happened with the Celtics, as Bill Russell and the other black players were not allowed to stay with their white teammates. Baylor and Russell angrily complained after the Charlotte incident, and Lakers president Bob Short had assured Baylor that it would not happen again. When it did in Charleston, Baylor took a stand.

When Russell found out about Baylor's actions, he said,

> If Baylor had been fined or lost his year's salary for refusing to play, I would have shared my salary with him. Elgin didn't do what he did for himself alone. He did it for me and every other Negro player in the league. We're not pioneers, but fortunately we're in a position to do something about a thing like this, which we believe in so sincerely.

Professional wrestling, which combined sports and entertainment, had its own civil rights crusader in Tennessee in the late 1950s. In Memphis, where just a few years earlier Emlen Tunnell and Bob Jackson of the New York Giants were not allowed to play in an NFL exhibition game, there was an extremely popular professional wrestler by the name of Roscoe "Sputnik" Monroe. He received his nickname in 1957, shortly after the Soviet Union launched the Sputnik satellite, when a female fan in Mobile, Alabama, angry at the way Monroe was handling a wrestler she was rooting for, said during a television taping, "You're a communist—a damned Sputnik!" The nickname stuck. It was the height of the Cold War, and there was almost nothing worse you could call someone.

Monroe arrived in Memphis in 1958, and eventually matched Elvis Presley in popularity there. A mere three hundred people a night attended wrestling matches at Ellis Auditorium in Memphis before Monroe came along; due to his popularity, attendance and ticket sales skyrocketed.

At the time of Monroe's arrival, Memphis was not exactly a hotbed of racial harmony. White and black people in Memphis didn't mix, professionally or socially. Sputnik Monroe, however, chose to socialize with black people and fit in perfectly. In the black community in Memphis, there was no other white man as popular as Sputnik. He would frequent the black-only clubs on Beale Street, sporting a colorful suit and soaking up the attention of his adoring fans. While the white fans hated the loudmouth Sputnik, black fans loved him and his antiestablishment attitude. For white teenagers, Monroe became a rebellious idol, just like the rock-and-roll rebel Presley.

Monroe rose to prominence and began to fill the stands at Ellis Auditorium, with crowds of up to 7,000 fans per night. On August 17, 1959, a whopping 13,749 fans attended Monroe's match against Billy Wicks. That was more than Elvis Presley had attracted to Ellis Auditorium for his concerts. However, to Monroe's dismay, the venue was segregated. He vehemently opposed this and used his stature to enact change.

Monroe openly questioned the wrestling promoters' decision to seat black spectators only in the upper reaches of Ellis Auditorium. There were few seats in the upper balconies at Ellis, and as a result many black fans were turned away at the door, rather than being allowed to sit next to white patrons in the lower section. One night in 1959, Monroe took on Jim Crow and told the Memphis promoters that if black fans weren't allowed to sit in the lower section of the auditorium, he was done wrestling in Memphis. The promoters gave in, and the first recorded act of public integration in Memphis took place.

Although Monroe helped integrate the seating at Ellis Auditorium for professional wrestling, the venue still remained segregated for other events. The iconic R&B singer Sam Cooke found this out and took a similar stand as Monroe. Although there were potential legal and financial obstacles associated with canceling a concert, he decided he wasn't going to perform until the issue was rectified, canceling his concert scheduled for May 14, 1961. He then released a statement to the Negro press, declaring that it was "against his policy and the policy of his promoter to play to a forced segregated audience." Cooke added, "This is the first time that I have refused to perform at showtime simply because I have not been faced with a situation similar to this one." He went on to say to a representative of the NAACP, "I hope by refusing to play to a segregated audience, it will help to break down racial segregation here, and if I am ever booked here again, it won't be necessary to do a similar thing."

At the end of 1959, the world of professional tennis had an incident in Norfolk, Virginia. In December, African American tennis star Althea Gibson complained about segregated seating at one of her matches in Norfolk. Gibson had recently turned professional and was playing a match against Karol Fageros, a white player from Miami, before a Harlem Globetrotters game at the Norfolk City Arena. Before her match, Gibson proclaimed, "This is a sport, an international thing. And yet you have some people sitting here and some people sitting there. I don't like it. I didn't know this sort of thing still existed."

Gibson ended up playing her match as opposed to boycotting it. After the match, however, she publicly stated,

> There's only one difference between us—our color. Our eyes are the same; our mouths are the same. Do these people [the white spectators] think there is such a big difference that they have to sit by themselves? I don't want to skirt the law, but there must be something wrong with the law. Just think—adults acting like this.

The year 1960 was particularly important as far as protests in the South, with most of the protests dealing with the issue of segregated seating at events, both sporting and entertainment. The issue of segregated seating took on a whole new light when on February 1, 1960, black students from North Carolina A&T sat at a Walgreens lunch counter in Greensboro, North Carolina, and waited to be served. This incident led to the formation of the Student Nonviolent Coordinating Committee. SNCC played a role in the formation of the Freedom Riders down South, voter registration for blacks, and the March on Washington, where Dr. Martin Luther King Jr. made his famous "I Have a Dream" speech. Their actions led to other lunch counter sit-ins and demonstrations throughout the South.

In February 1960, just days after the North Carolina A&T students' protest, iconic African American actress and singer Lena Horne fought back against racism while she and her husband dined at the posh Luau Restaurant in Beverly Hills, California. A white patron at a nearby table, Harvey S. Vincent, allegedly said something about "not liking niggers," and Horne responded by throwing a hurricane lamp, dishes, and several ashtrays in Vincent's direction, while hollering at him, "This is America! You cannot insult people like that!" One of the ashtrays directly hit Vincent, leaving a gash on his forehead.

The police intervened, but Vincent declined to press charges. Horne admitted to the police, "I lost control." However, she refused the next day to apologize for her actions, saying, "My anger is directed against something that is wrong, not at something I have to apologize for. I really don't like to make scenes like that, but sometimes people push you too far."

Segregated seating protests appeared to pick up steam after the incident at Greensboro in 1960. Many of the protests that followed in the early 1960s dealt with the segregated seating issue, not just in pro football but in other sports and entertainment venues, like those previously mentioned.

In November 1960, when promoters were looking for a location for the third Floyd Patterson–Ingemar Johansson heavyweight title fight, Patterson, who was African American, made it known that he would not fight where the seating was segregated. The three cities competing for the fight were Los Angeles, New York, and Miami, the latter of which in the past had segregated seating for boxing matches. Patterson explained,

> The promotors of football games (the annual Orange Bowl Classic and the upcoming Professional Runner Up Bowl) have been selling integrated seats for some time with no unfavorable reaction. There's no reason why ticket sales for the fight should be different. It's something that's up to the people handling the bout.

The fight was held on March 13, 1961, at the Miami Beach Convention Hall. Fights between white and black boxers had been allowed in Miami for some fifteen years, but seating at those fights remained segregated. The City of Miami relented on the segregated seating issue, and the fight was on. It was the first title fight in Miami since 1934. Patterson retained his heavyweight crown with a sixth-round knockout of Johansson.

As mentioned previously, Houston was an important city in the fight against segregated seating, with African American newspaper columnist Lloyd Wells taking the Oilers to task over their segregated seating policy until the team finally implemented integrated seats in 1964. Also in Houston and again with the help of Wells, black participants in the annual Meet of Champions track competition boycotted the event because of segregated seating at Jeppesen Stadium, the first successful boycott by African Americans of a sporting event, on June 10, 1961. The athletes' refusal to participate in the Meet of Champions was a catalyst for later boycotts.

It wasn't just athletes and entertainers who joined together to fight against Jim Crow. The NBC television network also took a stand against segregated seating. The Blue–Gray Game was an all-star contest for college seniors that was played annually in Montgomery, Alabama. NBC refused to televise the game in 1963 because the local Lions Club did not allow African American players to participate and also implemented segregated seating throughout Cramton Stadium. The network came to this decision after consulting with the two major sponsors of the game, the Gillette Company and Chrysler Corporation. Promoters relented for the 1964 game, allowing African American players to participate; in addition, Cramton Stadium was desegregated. As a result, NBC signed the Blue–Gray Game to a ten-year contract and continued televising the contest.

NBC's Dan Blocker, best known as "Hoss" Cartwright on the popular western television show *Bonanza*, also joined the fight, canceling an appearance at the State Coliseum in Jackson, Mississippi, on February 1–2, 1964, because of segregated seating at the venue. He said, "I have long since been in sympathy with the Negro struggle for total citizenship; therefore, I would find an appearance before a segregated house completely incompatible with my moral concepts and indeed repugnant."

Just three weeks after Blocker refused to appear in Jackson, another person in the world of boxing joined the fray against de jure segregation. It was a few days before the much-anticipated Sonny Liston versus Cassius Clay heavyweight championship fight in Miami on February 25, 1964. Liston, the champion, protested the segregated seating in New Orleans theaters that were showing the fight on closed-circuit television. He said he would not permit the fight to be shown in places that were segregated. As a result, the Saenger and Loews theaters in New Orleans did not show the fight, while the New Orleans Municipal Auditorium, which had recently been desegregated by a federal court order, did show it.

With the backing of entertainers, other pro athletes, and even whole television networks, professional football players started fighting back against discrimination in the early 1960s. In one of the earliest recorded pro football protests, black and white teammates alike took a stand in solidarity against racism.

The Playoff Bowl, officially known as the Bert Bell Benefit Bowl, was a postseason game played in Miami from 1960 through 1969. Played a week after the NFL Championship Game, the Playoff Bowl provided more than a million dollars in pension revenue for players in its ten-year run. When the NFC and AFC were created after the merger of the NFL and AFL in 1970, the game was discontinued. It had been created to battle the rival AFL, adding another playoff game between the runners-up in the Eastern and Western Conferences.

The first Playoff Bowl game took place in Miami on January 7, 1961, with the Detroit Lions beating the Cleveland Browns, 17–16. Miami was drawn into a whirlwind of controversy in the days leading up to the game, with several Lions players, both black and white, protesting their segregated accommodations.

Prior to the Lions' actions in Miami, there seems to be no record of white pro footballers actively protesting racial inequality alongside their black teammates. None of the African American players interviewed mentioned white teammates protesting Jim Crow conditions. Some white players, like Alan Ameche, Raymond Berry, and Gino Marchetti of the Colts, commented to Lenny Moore and George Taliaferro that they wished they had taken action to defend their teammates, but none of them ultimately took the bold step to do so. Perhaps they did not want to risk losing their jobs.

Nevertheless, during the 1961 Playoff Bowl, several white players on the Lions took a stand. They were upset that Roger Brown and other African American players (Dick "Night Train" Lane being among them) had to stay in a "dinky" hotel away from their white teammates.

Brown recounted his trip to Miami in a 2017 interview:

> I believe pro football helped integrate every major city in the United States in the 1960s. After the 1960 season, we played in Miami in this new game called the Playoff Bowl. The black players, like Night Train Lane, Danny Lewis, and myself, were sent to the black part of town to stay in a dumpy old motel. We practiced at Dade Stadium in Miami.
>
> One day, the team bus picked up all of the white players at the Ivanhoe Hotel—a really nice place on Miami Beach—and then came over to our part of town to pick us up. Jim Gibbons, one of the white players, took a look at our motel and said, "What the hell are you guys doing here?" The word got out that blacks weren't allowed on Miami Beach. So later that day, Gibbons, Howard Cassidy, Nick Pietrosante, and Gail Cogdill went to head coach George Wilson to complain about our accommodations. They told him, "We want to stay as a team!" Wilson agreed, and we moved over to the Ivanhoe Hotel for the rest of our stay there in Miami. Thus, we integrated Miami Beach in 1960.
>
> After Miami Beach in 1960, we pretty much always stayed as a team, in New Orleans, Baltimore, Dallas, and so on. It got to a point by the early to mid-1960s in the NFL where teams said they were a team and they would stay together at a place or not stay at all. I eventually became best friends with Gail Cogdill, and we remained that way until he recently passed away. We first met at the 1960 College All-Star Game. We played the Colts on a Friday night and then went to Detroit together that Saturday for training camp. We eventually wanted to be roommates, but it never happened. That's the way it was back then. We just accepted it and remained friends. Teams were concerned that if

word of us rooming together got out, it might hurt ticket sales. That's
what teams cared about.

   That's like playing preseason games in the South. Do you think most
of the owners cared about how the black players would be treated?
Heck no. They were worried about ticket sales and making money.
The South wasn't the only place blacks had problems, either. It was
very difficult to find a house in the Detroit area. Cranbrook, Southfield,
Dearborn—I couldn't get a house in any of those areas. Discrimination
didn't automatically stop just because you were in the North as opposed
to the South.

While the Lions were staging their protest over inadequate accom-
modations for African American players, their opponents, the Cleveland
Browns, experienced an uprising of their own. According to Browns player
Bobby Mitchell,

> We went to Miami. The white players were taken to the white hotel,
> and all the black players, including Jim Brown, were left standing there.
> We were told we were going to our own hotel. Well, Jim Brown and
> Paul Brown didn't tolerate that. Jim wouldn't stand for staying in a
> rundown black hotel. Paul Brown then made sure we stayed together.
> Remember, he didn't schedule exhibition games in the South to avoid
> this kind of problem. He told the hotel, "We're the Cleveland Browns;
> we stay together as a team." The hotel gave in, and we got to stay in
> Miami Beach. However, we had to agree not to go out to the beach
> area. That was tough—not being able to go to the beach, looking out
> the hotel window watching everyone have fun.

Even after the Browns and Lions had successfully fought to stay together at the inaugural Playoff Bowl, there were still several instances where
pro football teams faced segregation. The Pittsburgh Steelers played in the
Playoff Bowl following the 1962 season, where they lost to the Lions,
17–10, on January 6, 1963. While the Lions stayed together as a team, the
Steelers did not.

   Not staying with his white counterparts did not appear to be a big
concern for the Steelers' Brady Keys. He recalled,

> When we went to Miami, there were six of us black players, like John
> Henry Johnson and "Big Daddy" Lipscomb. We all stayed in the black
> part of town. We were happy being together in the black part of town.
> We were free to do whatever we wanted. We didn't necessarily want to
> be with the white boys anyway. At that time, Miami was real cool. We

had our own bars and restaurants, and we stayed in black hotels. We had no curfew, as nobody would come check on us. As long as we showed up for practice and the game, we were cool. We encountered no problems because we stayed together and didn't mingle with the whites.

By the 1963 Playoff Bowl game, the lodging accommodations on Miami Beach were mostly integrated. Many of the participating teams stayed at the integrated Ivanhoe Hotel on Miami Beach, which was owned by St. Louis Cardinals baseball great Stan Musial.

Elsewhere, the fight for integration continued. When the Baltimore Colts took on the Steelers in Roanoke, Virginia, on August 12, 1961, a 24–20 Colts win, the NAACP stepped in to try to bring an end to segregated seating at Victory Stadium. The NAACP sent telegrams to four black Steelers (Eugene "Big Daddy" Lipscomb, John Henry Johnson, John Nisby, and Charles Scales) and four Colts (Lenny Moore, Joe Perry, Jim Parker, and Lenny Lyles). The telegram asked the players not to play "because we're engaged here in a fight for freedom, civil rights, and justice."

After a five-hour meeting involving team officials from the Steelers and Colts, the Roanoke Chamber of Commerce, and the Roanoke chapter of the NAACP, it was decided that the African American players on both squads would participate, in spite of the segregated seating, because of the money it would generate for local charities.

Although the protest was technically unsuccessful, as seating remained officially segregated at Victory Stadium for the game, the incident made the NFL aware of the conditions faced by African American players in the Jim Crow South. NFL commissioner Pete Rozelle said, "This situation has focused the attention of the NFL on the unhealthy condition existing in cities of this type. I am hopeful that in future seasons NFL teams will not play games for segregated audiences."

In the end, perhaps the NAACP and allied players were victorious after all, as the stands were *unofficially* integrated for the game. The *Pittsburgh Courier* stated in its August 19 edition, "As things turned out Negro ticket-holders were seated all over Victory Stadium, although such was not advertised because of the states' segregation laws."

Many years later, Lenny Moore recounted the event:

In Roanoke, we got involved with the NAACP. The president of the Roanoke NAACP, R. R. Wilkinson, sent myself and Joe Perry, who we had gotten in a trade with the 49ers, a telegram urging the black players on both teams to boycott the game because the seating at the stadium was to be segregated. The blacks had to sit in the end zone behind some chain link fence that blocked their view—just typical stuff for the South.

Even though at times we just wanted to play football and not get involved with this kind of stuff, we once again asked, "What would Jackie Robinson do?" I had met and spoken with Jackie in the past, and I knew he wouldn't back down from this challenge, so we decided that neither would we. Joe and I met with our general manager, Don Kellett, Carroll Rosenbloom, and Coach Ewbank and told them we were planning to boycott the game. They got the people in Roanoke to change the seating to first come, first served, regardless of race. Thus, we decided to play the game. However, when we took the field in pregame warmups, I looked in the stands and discovered the black fans were still seated together in certain areas. I thought, "How come the teams can be integrated but not the stands?"

Lenny Moore (24), Baltimore Colts, takes the handoff from John Unitas (19). *Robert Jacobus*

George Balthazar was a rookie with the Steelers in 1961. He recalled his trip to Roanoke:

> Staying with Roanoke with the Steelers in 1961 wasn't too bad. We did stay as a team in a small hotel that was on a hill overlooking the city. I do remember a little bit about the NAACP coming around our hotel, but I don't recall having an actual meeting with them about boycotting the game because of segregated seating. I really didn't give that much thought to the segregated seating in Roanoke. It wasn't the first time I had seen that. I'm from Houston, so I was used to segregated seating at my home stadium. The NAACP may very well have met with the black veterans on the Steelers. We had some guys who had been around for a while: Big Daddy Lipscomb, John Henry Johnson, Johnny Sample, and others. I was just a rookie trying to make the team. I really didn't pay that much attention to the protest, even though looking back I probably should have.

In the aftermath of Roanoke, the Steelers attempted to head off any further controversy a couple of weeks later. The Steelers traveled back to the South, and they played the St. Louis Cardinals in Jacksonville on August 26, a 24–14 Steeler win. According to a blurb in the *Pittsburgh Press* on the day of the game,

> While the Cards have been here for two days, today is a travel day for the Steelers. They left Pittsburgh this morning, will arrive early in the afternoon, spend the day at Jacksonville Naval Air Station, and return to Pittsburgh immediately after the game.
> Having learned a lesson at Roanoke, where the NAACP threatened to boycott a game to protest segregated seating, the Steelers decided to take no chance on a protest against segregated housing.

Balthazar said about the unusual arrangements,

> When the Steelers went to Jacksonville, we all stayed together at a military base in some barracks. I remember the white players complained because they had to stay there instead of some nice hotel downtown. It was hot there, with no air-conditioning; plus there was not a whole lot to do. I didn't realize we did this to prevent any potential problems like we had in Roanoke.

After Art Powell was cut from the Philadelphia Eagles in the 1960 preseason because of his refusal to play in a game in segregated Norfolk, he caught on with the New York Titans of the brand-new AFL. Powell became one of the early bright spots for the Titans and the AFL. In his first season, Powell caught 67 passes for 1,167 yards and 14 touchdowns. However, none of that prepared him for what was to come during an August 25 trip to Greenville, South Carolina, for a preseason game against the Houston Oilers.

"I had never been to a place with colored and white drinking fountains," Powell, a California native, said.

When the Titans arrived, Powell said General Manager Steve Sebo informed the approximately fifteen black players trying to make the Titans' final roster they would not accompany the white players to the team hotel. While the white players boarded a bus and left, black players were taken to the outskirts of town.

Powell said,

> They had these old things called jitneys—little bitty trucks with small seats. When we drove in, it was like something you'd see in an old movie. You go through a dirt road, past a bunch of trees, to this place they called a "colored only" resort.
>
> The swimming pool was like a swamp. There were no screens on the windows. There were mosquitoes and bugs as big as your fist. Of course, the air-conditioning doesn't work. So, it's a hundred degrees out, and you're just laying on your bed sweating like crazy.
>
> I told Steve Sebo I didn't think it was fair. You preach all year about team play, then you know darn well we're not going there as a team.

After the experience in Philadelphia, Powell did not attempt to get his African American teammates to join him. He suited up and sat by himself on the bench, listening to racial epithets from the bleachers behind him.

"I heard things I had never heard before and haven't heard since, and I can recall every word," Powell said. "People in those days were getting killed, and I was sitting there in the wide open. You just don't know what's going to happen next; I just wanted to get out alive."

According to Powell, several of his black teammates were angered by his actions. "They thought I was putting them out in front of a situation they didn't want to deal with. So I pretty much kept to myself. I didn't look for someone to side with me. I just made my choice, and in my gut I thought I made the right choice."

Moses Gray, a rookie offensive tackle out of Indiana University who briefly played with the Titans in 1961, was at Greenville. "It was difficult in Greenville," he said:

We couldn't stay at or eat in the white hotel. In fact, they wouldn't even let us dress at the stadium. Art Powell was my teammate for a short while. He was a real nice guy. We stayed at a colored motel. It was a different kind of experience. I really don't remember if Art sat that game out or not. I'm sure if he said it, he did. Things were still pretty rough in the South in the 1950s and 1960s. The All-Star boycott in New Orleans helped, but I really think it took until the 1970s until things got really better. Even in college in Indiana, we went to Baltimore as a special group to meet with some alumni sponsors. We tried to go into a restaurant and they told us, "We don't serve niggers in here!"

By the early 1960s, even civil rights icons attempted to enlist professional football players to help end the ways of the Jim Crow South. On August 11, 1962, the Pittsburgh Steelers traveled to Atlanta to play the Chicago Bears in a preseason game, which the Steelers won, 19–14. Once again, the Bears and Steelers squared up against segregated lodging and seating.

Joe Womack of the Steelers played his only NFL season in 1962. A halfback, Womack was leading all rookie NFL rushers in 1962, with 468 yards, until he was injured in his eleventh game of the season, effectively ending his career.

According to Womack,

When we played the Bears in Atlanta, that's when things started to change. The players went to the owners and said they didn't want to play if there was segregated seating or if we had to stay separate from our white teammates. Dr. Martin Luther King actually came and met with us and wanted us to march with him in Atlanta that weekend. We decided we wouldn't march, but we refused to play if we couldn't stay together or if there was segregated seating. We did accomplish both goals that weekend. You have to give Steelers owner Art Rooney credit. He helped make everything happen. When I think back, I was taking a big chance because I was a rookie. I had no leverage.

Two years after he sat out the exhibition game in Greenville as a member of the Titans, Art Powell, now a member of the Oakland Raiders, saw a potential problem when he looked at the preseason schedule. The Raiders were slated to play the New York Jets at Ladd Stadium in Mobile, Alabama, on August 23, 1963.

"We received word that we weren't going to stay together as a team," Powell said. "In addition, they were going to rope off a section for the colored fans to sit in, and the colored fans wouldn't be able to use the bathroom."

Powell decided once again to take a stand. This time, however, he had help—both from his African American teammates (most specifically Clem Daniels) and Raiders coach Al Davis. Powell regarded the situation as "my first big challenge with Al Davis, but it turned out it wasn't a challenge at all." Davis canceled the game and moved it to Oakland. Powell said, "Personally, I'd like to thank Al Davis for not once putting any pressure on the Negro players. We got full cooperation from the Raiders staff and the Oakland press."

After consulting with Powell, Bo Roberson, Clem Daniels, and Fred Williamson, Davis moved the game to Oakland. He said in a statement, "We are unhappy that it did not work out in Mobile, but the decision to cancel was the only one that could have been made under the circumstances. We were disappointed because we thought we had the problem licked. But these are our players and friends, and we are sticking by them."

In addition, Davis said, "When it was decided to play the game in Mobile, we were given assurances that the seating would be integrated. It's unfortunate that it worked out this way, because we would have taken a big step—a step that should have been taken a long time ago." He also added that the Raiders would no longer schedule games in segregated stadiums. "Al never put another game in the South during the time I was with the Raiders," Powell said.

Clem Daniels told his version of how the boycott came about:

> It was time to take a stand. By 1963 I was one of the premier running backs in the AFL, so now I could speak out—hopefully without fear of reprisal. A few days before we went to Mobile, a reporter for the *San Francisco Sun*, Sam Skinner, said, "I just talked to this guy in Mobile and he told me, 'We don't have a problem with our colored in Mobile. We've got a special section for our colored to sit in,' and that 'they're satisfied with the seating arrangements.'" Well, I called the guy in Mobile back, and he repeated the same thing to me. After I hung up, Skinner asked me, "Well, what are you going to do?" I told him I wasn't going. Skinner asked me, "Don't you have to talk to Al Davis about it first?" I told him no. They ended up moving the game to Oakland. Al Davis backed us up. He got on the phone and told AFL commissioner Joe Foss that we weren't going to play. That was the first time a group of players refused to play because of segregation. We were at the forefront.

Clem Daniels. *Prairie View A&M University*

The Raiders ended up playing the game at Frank Youell Field, their home stadium in Oakland, and they defeated the Jets, 43–16, in front of just 8,317 fans.

Daniels recalled,

You know, the more politically active and outspoken players like Art Powell and myself really kept up with the civil rights movement. The movement was really heating up by 1963. The March on Washington occurred just a few days after our boycott in Mobile. I had really wanted to go to that but I couldn't because of my commitment to the Raiders. I had no idea it would turn into the big event it became and that Martin Luther King would give his "I Have a Dream" speech there.

The civil rights movement helped give us the strength and courage to challenge Jim Crow conditions in the South. We kind of felt like somebody had our back through all of this. I think this feeling helped us when we had the later boycott in New Orleans. Medgar Evers was murdered just a few miles away a couple of months before in Mississippi. All of this helped us take a stand against what we thought was wrong. Al Davis backed us—that was important to us.

Apparently, the Raiders' boycott of their preseason game in Mobile led some teams to become more proactive rather than reactive when it came to dealing with separate accommodations and segregated seating in the South. Just days after the Raiders boycotted Mobile, there was talk of another potential boycott over segregated seating in Winston-Salem, North Carolina.

Just three days after Martin Luther King's "I Have a Dream" speech at the March on Washington, on August 31, 1963, the Denver Broncos played the Buffalo Bills in Winston-Salem, with the Bills taking a 21–14 victory.

A few days before the game, snippets started appearing in newspapers around the country in Associated Press clippings. On August 22, an AP wire story said in part,

> Coach Jack Faulkner, of the Denver Broncos of the American Football League, said Wednesday an exhibition game the Buffalo Bills at Winston-Salem, N.C., may be canceled or moved because of the segregation problem. The game is scheduled for August 31. Faulkner said he is awaiting word from officials of the Buffalo club and from Milt Woodward, assistant conference commissioner.

The next day, August 23, the same day as the Raiders boycott in Mobile, Buffalo informed the league that the game would in fact be played. The AFL league office also said they had received in writing assurances that there would be no segregation either in stadium seating or player accommodations.

Red Miller, who later became the Broncos head coach from 1977 to 1980—a stint that included an appearance in Super Bowl XII against the

Dallas Cowboys—was a Broncos assistant coach at the time. He explained the situation:

> I was an assistant to Coach Faulkner in Denver at the time. Unlike Mobile, there was no planned walkout by the players because of segregation. It was Faulkner and our general manager Dean Griffin being proactive in light of what happened in Mobile. Coach Faulkner made sure and found us a hotel that would take us all, and I believe Griffin got the segregated seating issue straightened out. Everybody was kind of on edge. The March on Washington, where Martin Luther King gave his "I Have a Dream" speech, had just happened, so you have to give everyone involved credit for having no problems in Winston-Salem.

On July 2, 1964, President Lyndon B. Johnson signed into law the landmark Civil Rights Act of 1964, which outlawed discrimination and segregation on the basis of race, religion, national origin, and gender in the workplace, schools, public accommodations, and federally assisted programs. Many hotels and other businesses in the Deep South, including restaurants, were still segregated before this act was passed. Now it was against federal law to discriminate or segregate. Although *Brown v. Board of Education* in 1954 had supposedly ended segregation in schools, there were only piecemeal efforts to do so. With the Civil Rights Act, schools now had to take actual steps like busing or redistricting to end segregation.

However, less than two months after the passage of the Civil Rights Act, most parts of the South were either slow or reluctant to follow federal law. This reluctance led to an incident involving the San Diego Chargers when they traveled to Atlanta to play the New York Jets in a preseason game on August 29.

The event in question took place at a pool hall across the street from the Atlanta Hilton, where the Chargers were staying (because the team's owner, Barron Hilton, also owned the hotel).

Tom Bass, who was a Chargers assistant coach at the time, recalled,

> We got into Atlanta and went and had a workout the night before our scheduled game. After the workout, some of the black guys went across the street to shoot pool. It was kind of all of our little guys. They came back across the street to say they were being hassled. The big black guys went over across the street, and things quickly quieted down.

African American offensive tackle Ernie Wright of the Chargers was more specific in his recollection of the encounter:

> We were playing in Atlanta, and next to the hotel we were staying at, they had a mall with a billiard parlor in it. The place was big; it had twenty or thirty tables in it. Of course, being competitive, we wanted to see who was the best pool shooter. So twelve of us went over there—half black, half white. We asked for the cues and balls and stuff to play, but the guy working there was on the phone. About fifteen minutes later, he came back and said, "Some of you guys can't come in here." We said, "What? What do you mean, 'some of you guys'?" He said, "Well, you colored. You colored boys, you colored guys can't stay here."
>
> So, we went back to Sid Gillman and said we weren't playing in the exhibition game the next day. We said, "If we can't be treated like human beings, we're not going to play a game." This was a Friday night, and the game was Saturday night. By Saturday morning, the governor of Georgia and the mayor of Atlanta were out there making all kinds of promises and so on and so forth. We did end up playing, but that episode became national news and in its own way contributed to the progress we see now.

Bob Hood was also in attendance during the Atlanta incident. At the time, Hood, who started his career with the Chargers as their water boy during the 1963 championship season, was just twenty years old. Hood eventually worked his way up to business manager by the 1970s. He just so happened to accompany the Chargers players to the pool hall. He recalled,

> I was there. We went to Atlanta to play an exhibition game against the Jets. The AFL and NFL played several exhibition games there during this time, because they were trying to get a franchise in Atlanta and they were trying to gauge interest in the area. I really had never dealt with a situation like this before. A couple of weeks before we went to Atlanta, we played the Oilers at Jeppesen Stadium in Houston. We got a taste of it there. One of Sid Gillman's rituals was to take all of the players to a movie the night before a game. In Houston, when we went to the theater, they wanted the black players to sit in the balcony. Sid ended up having the entire team sit up in the balcony so the black players wouldn't feel singled out.
>
> You know, Sid was the first coach to have black and white players room together on the road. He didn't make a big deal out of it. Sid figured if you had to play together, you could live together too.

Hood added,

> After Houston, we played the next week in Kansas City and then we
> went to Atlanta. Since Baron Hilton owned the Chargers, we stayed
> at the Hilton in Atlanta. It turns out there was a billiard hall across the
> street from the hotel. A lot of the guys liked to shoot pool, so a group of
> players, black and white, went over there. Lance Alworth, Tobin Rote,
> John Hadl, Ron Mix, Ernie Ladd, Earl Faison, and others were there.
> I also went because they invited me. Even though I was just the water
> boy, they included me. They considered me part of the team. Things
> were much more close-knit in those days.
>
> The manager went up to one of the white players—I don't remember
> who—and said, "The white guys are welcome to stay here and shoot
> pool, but the black players have to leave." Well, everyone decided to
> leave at that point. This was the first time I had ever dealt with anything
> like that. I had grown up in Southern California, and I didn't know
> prejudice existed. My dad had grown up in the South, and the reason
> we moved to California was because he didn't want me to grow up
> prejudiced.
>
> Apparently, after the black players got back to the hotel, they met
> and told Sid Gillman the next morning that they didn't want to play in
> the game that evening. The mayor of Atlanta came to the hotel to talk
> to the black players, trying to convince them to play. I wasn't there for
> any of these talks because I was just a kid. I think Ron Mix, who was
> going to law school at the time, helped persuade the black guys into
> playing that night. The game was played without a hitch. However, the
> Jets killed us. Just a few months later, Ron played the same role at the
> All-Star Game in New Orleans.

A blurb in *Sports Illustrated*'s September 7, 1964, issue claimed,

> Behind the surprising 34–6 defeat of the San Diego Chargers by the
> New York Jets last weekend was a racial incident that shattered the
> morale of the previously unbeaten Chargers. Staying at Atlanta's Hilton
> Inn, several of the Chargers, all Negroes, were asked to keep out of the
> plush poolroom. When some players protested, Head Coach Sid Gill-
> man asked his men to withdraw. They did, but the effect on team mo-
> rale was obvious. Even during the game several players said they were in
> no mood for football, and the team took what was only its second loss
> in the entire exhibition history of the Chargers.

A couple of weeks after the incident in Atlanta and about two months
after the Civil Rights Act was passed, the civil rights movement got one

more shot in the arm, not from pro football players, but from the most famous entertainers on the planet.

Jacksonville was another city in the South that was slow to end segregation. It was in this northeast Florida city that the Beatles got involved in the controversy over segregated seating. The Fab Four arrived in the United States for the first time from Liverpool, England, in February 1964. What followed was "Beatlemania" and a string of number-one hits like "I Want to Hold Your Hand," "Please Please Me," and "Twist and Shout."

In August, the Beatles went on their first concert tour of the United States. After starting in San Francisco and playing other western and northern cities, such as Las Vegas, Seattle, Philadelphia, Atlantic City, and Chicago, on September 11 the Beatles headed to Jacksonville for their first concert in the South.

The lads from Liverpool were to play at the Gator Bowl, with a seating capacity of sixty-two thousand. It was the first and only stadium the Beatles played in their inaugural 1964 tour.

When they found out that the seating was to be segregated, the Beatles refused to go on unless the situation was rectified. John Lennon said, "We never play to segregated audiences, and we're not going to start now. I'd sooner lose out on appearance money."

Larry Kane, a radio reporter from Miami, had covered the Beatles when they went there for their second appearance on *The Ed Sullivan Show*. He eventually became the only reporter to travel with the Beatles to every stop on their 1964 U.S. tour. Three weeks before their Jacksonville date, Kane found out about the segregated seating at the Gator Bowl in Jacksonville and informed the band. Paul McCartney said, "We're not going to play there." Lennon was more succinct. He said, "No fucking chance."

The Beatles sent out a press release that said simply, "We will not appear unless Negroes are allowed to sit anywhere." Finally, five hours before the Beatles were to perform, Gator Bowl and city officials relented on their segregation policy.

In the end, only twenty-three thousand fans attended—about nine thousand short of the number of tickets sold. Hurricane Dora had blown through northeast Florida the day before, and many who had bought tickets were unable to attend. But in the end, black and white fans could sit beside each other if they wished to.

Later, sometime after the concert, a couple of the Beatles reflected on their experience. Drummer Ringo Starr said, "We had never encountered anything like this before in England or at any of our American concerts.

We refused to go on. We were taking a chance at our careers, sure. We were young and we thought it was wrong, so we did it."

McCartney explained in 1966, "We never wanted to play South Africa or any places where blacks would be separated. It wasn't out of any goody-goody thing; we just thought, 'Why would you separate black people from white? That's stupid, isn't it?'"

After Jacksonville, the Beatles took more precautions. When they returned to the United States for their 1965 tour, they took no chances and had it written into their contracts that they would not play before segregated audiences.

Thus, through the collaborative efforts of entertainers, sports figures, and other celebrities, integration and equal rights started becoming a reality in the United States. These pioneer activists were assisted by such legislation as the Civil Rights Act of 1964, and fueled by the groundbreaking momentum of the civil rights movement, which reached a pinnacle with the March on Washington and Dr. Martin Luther King's "I Have a Dream" speech. In the world of pro football, one more incident that served to solidify the move toward equality in the league, both on and off the field: the January 1965 boycott of the All-Star Game in New Orleans.

9

BIG TROUBLE IN THE BIG EASY

The Boycott of the 1964 AFL All-Star Game

New Orleans was excited and looking forward to hosting the 1964 AFL All-Star Game, which was to be held on January 16, 1965. The city had high hopes of landing an NFL or AFL expansion team in the near future. A good showing of hospitality by the city could go a long way toward securing a franchise in the Crescent City. The city had made some advances and progress toward integration since 1949, when Wally Triplett, Bob Mann, and Mel Groomes of the Detroit Lions were held out of an exhibition game at City Park Stadium.

Several events in the 1950s and early 1960s led to a shift in policy in New Orleans and the state of Louisiana, allowing blacks to compete with whites on athletic fields and courts in addition to resolving the segregated seating controversy.

In 1955, African American boxer Joey Dorsey filed a suit in federal court asking for the removal of the Louisiana rule preventing white and black boxers from meeting in the ring. In 1958 the federal court in New Orleans ruled in Dorsey's favor, as they found Louisiana's law against inter-racial sporting events unconstitutional. Blacks and whites were now able to compete against each other in boxing rings in New Orleans and throughout the state of Louisiana.

The annual Sugar Bowl Basketball Tournament integrated in December 1955 when sophomore Al Avant of Marquette University took to the court.

What was also significant about the 1955 Sugar Bowl Basketball Tournament and Sugar Bowl football game on January 1, 1956, was the controversy created by the football matchup of Georgia Tech against Pittsburgh. The Panthers had an African American fullback and defensive back on their squad named Bobby Grier.

At first, Georgia Tech, an all-white institution, balked at facing Pittsburgh and Grier. Georgia state officials publicly shared their concern. The
Georgia Board of Regents eventually voted 10–1 to allow Georgia Tech
to play in the game, which the Yellow Jackets won, 6–0, thanks in part
to a controversial pass interference penalty against Grier. The game set a
precedent, and black and white players were now able to compete together
in athletic contests across Louisiana.

However, segregated seating still existed at sporting events in New
Orleans, and Louisiana as a whole, in the mid-1950s. Consequently, by the
late 1950s, the practice of segregated seating, like the segregation of athletic
contests, fell under severe criticism and scrutiny.

In 1957, Army was scheduled to play a collegiate football game in
New Orleans against Tulane University. Because Louisiana laws in 1957
still forbade integrated seating at sporting events, Army forced Tulane to
move the game to West Point.

It wasn't just integration at sporting events that concerned the people
of New Orleans. A 1962 article in the *Pittsburgh Courier* mentioned how
New Orleans merchants were stuck in the middle between segregation-
ists and antisegregationists. Groups like the White Citizens' Council were
threatening reprisals of businesses that integrated. On the other side, black
patrons were boycotting merchants for their segregationist practices. The
Association of Commerce in New Orleans seemed to be favorable toward
integration on the chance that it could lead to the NFL establishing a
franchise in New Orleans. It was said that New Orleans had lost out on a
baseball team because of segregated seating.

Segregated seating at sporting events in Louisiana was for the most part
eliminated on September 7, 1963, when New Orleans held an NFL exhibition doubleheader featuring the Detroit Lions taking on the Dallas Cowboys in the early game and the Baltimore Colts versus the Chicago Bears
in the nightcap. The practice of segregated seating at Tulane Stadium came
under scrutiny. African American fans were slow to buy tickets because of
Tulane's policies. This was a test for New Orleans, since the NFL and AFL
had recently developed a policy banning segregated seating at their events.
In 1962, NFL commissioner Pete Rozelle stated that no city maintaining
segregated seating would get an NFL franchise. Joe Foss, commissioner of
the AFL, took the same stance.

Dave Dixon, a forty-year-old real estate magnate in New Orleans,
was the man responsible for bringing the doubleheader to New Orleans.
Dixon knew that New Orleans didn't stand a chance to secure a pro football franchise if sporting events in New Orleans weren't integrated, and so

he set out to do that with his doubleheader at Tulane Stadium, a private venue. Dixon invited about twenty black leaders in New Orleans to meet and to ask them what it would take to file suit against the segregation laws. They told him that it would cost only $2,000. The man who led the fight was a thirty-four-year-old black attorney and NAACP field secretary named Ernest N. "Dutch" Morial, who later became the first black mayor of New Orleans. Morial filed suit in federal district court, and within three months, Louisiana's laws requiring segregated seating were declared unconstitutional.

Next Dixon had to get Tulane's board of directors to desegregate the stadium. A letter from William Ford, owner of the Detroit Lions, was key to the board's decision because Ford hinted at improved funding for Tulane from the Ford Foundation, a major source of grant money for Tulane. The board of directors balked a bit, but in the end they agreed to end segregated seating. The door was now open.

Dixon described how integrated seating went over with African Americans in New Orleans:

> When we put tickets on sale for our big doubleheader, I carefully instructed all personnel at the Tulane ticket office how to advise patrons of ticket availability. . . . The young ladies selling the tickets were to say, "Any unmarked seat is available. Everything is first come, first served."
>
> Finally, two weeks later our first African American football fan visited the Tulane ticket office . . . and our young lady handled the situation perfectly. She showed them the ticket chart and said, "First come, first served."
>
> At that moment our visitor asked, "You mean I can sit anywhere I want?"
>
> Our young lady answered affirmatively, at which point our "colored" football fan said, "Alleluia!"

On the night of the doubleheader, estimates were that more than 30 percent of the attendees were African American. A thunderstorm during the Colts/Bears game sent black and white fans running for cover. Dixon said later,

> I had a vision of blacks and whites hammering each other under that overhang, the media reports that would result, and the end of my dreams of an NFL franchise. . . . I was so scared I was shaking, and I rushed down from the press box to try and stop the carnage. But when

I got there, everyone was laughing. They were brought together by their discomfort.

Then, the following year, the landmark Civil Rights Act of 1964 was passed on July 2, outlawing discrimination based on race and segregation in public buildings. The AFL All-Star Game in 1965 would be the first big test of the new federal law. It appeared it would be smooth sailing heading into the game.

In fact, just five days before the start of the All-Star Game boycott, a UPI report from January 6, 1965, stated the AFL "will give New Orleans an extra hard look when they meet here next week." In addition, the article said, "Promoter Dave Dixon said Tuesday that the AFL has agreed to consider his proposal to play the league championship game here next December."

The AFL All-Star Game was scheduled for Saturday, January 16. The players for both squads arrived on January 10 for a week of practice.

A crowd of sixty thousand was expected for the contest. The proceeds from the game were slated to go into the players' pension accounts, so a good gate was crucial.

The West team, with twelve African American players on their roster, including Ernie Ladd, Clem Daniels, and Abner Haynes, were scheduled to stay at the Roosevelt Hotel, which had just been grudgingly integrated because of the Civil Rights Act of 1964. The East team, with nine African American players led by Buffalo Bills running back Cookie Gilchrist, were to stay at the Fontainebleau Hotel.

However, problems erupted almost as soon as the African American all-stars arrived. Numerous black all-stars told of the discrimination they faced when they arrived in New Orleans.

Kansas City Chiefs Hall of Fame linebacker Bobby Bell of the West team said,

I had been down in New Orleans prior to the All-Star Game for the Black America Beauty Pageant. There were some things that were different from Kansas City down in New Orleans. I had to stay in an all-black hotel on the other side of the tracks. All of the functions for the pageant were all-black. When the all-stars came to New Orleans in January 1965, the problems were supposedly worked out because New Orleans wanted a pro team. They guaranteed the black players could stay downtown and be able to go to the French Quarter, Bourbon Street, and anything else. We came into New Orleans—white and black players alike. The whites started grabbing cabs, and off they went to their hotels. The black players, when they went up to a white cab driver, were told, "No, can't go." After a couple of hours, a black porter came up to us and said we had to call a colored cab to come get us.

East squad member tight end Ernie Warlick of the Buffalo Bills added,

> The black players had been promised there wouldn't be any segregation in New Orleans. Actually, all the problems came as a complete surprise to us. We were led to believe that we could relax and enjoy ourselves in New Orleans just like other citizens. Maybe if we had been alerted to the fact that we wouldn't have the run of the town, we could have avoided this unpleasant situation. If they had told us this before, we'd have looked specifically for those cabs and sought out our entertainment in other places. They led us to believe everything was to be okay, and it wasn't.

Warlick said later that when he ordered his breakfast in the dining room of the Fontainebleau Hotel on the morning of January 10, "I lost my appetite when an older woman said loud enough for me to hear that she didn't want to eat in the same room as monkeys."

Later that evening, Warlick said,

> Two of my white Bills teammates, Mike Stratton and Jack Kemp, said, "C'mon, let's go to the French Quarter." So, we went to the French Quarter. We started to go into a place, and Mike and Jack went in first. As I started to go in, they said, "Naw, we don't serve your kind." Mike and Jack came back out to see what was going on, and I told them they wouldn't let me in. They said, "Let's try another place." We went to another place, and I was turned away there too. I finally told Mike and Jack, "You guys go ahead, I'm going back to the hotel. There's no point in you guys not being able to go have a good time." So I ended up taking a black taxi back to the hotel.

The West squad's Ernie Ladd of the Chargers, who had helped lead the protest at the Atlanta pool hall less than five months before, recalled,

> I flew into New Orleans and got a cab with Dick Westmoreland and Earl Faison, two of my Charger teammates. We even took a white cab with no problems. We went to the Roosevelt Hotel, where the West all-stars were staying. We then got ready to go down to the French Quarter, and the same cabdriver wouldn't pick us up and take us. We also couldn't get a cab to take us back to the Roosevelt Hotel from the French Quarter later. They told us we couldn't get in.

Faison was another member of the Chargers who was present in Atlanta, as well as New Orleans. "I remember checking into the hotel," Faison recalled, "and I heard some voices in the background saying, 'Is that Ernie Ladd?' And another guy said, 'No, Ernie Ladd is a bigger nigger than that. That Ladd is a big nigger.'"

Clem Daniels of the Raiders added,

> We were at the Hotel Roosevelt in the cafeteria. It had been raining, and Ernie Warlick went and hung his coat on the coat rack. A woman who was eating there in the restaurant got up, went over to the coat rack, and moved her coat away from Ernie's. That was the mentality of some people back in those days.

Defensive tackle Houston Antwine of the Boston Patriots recalled,

> I was staying at the Fontainebleau Hotel with the Eastern squad. Cookie Gilchrist and some of the other guys came in and said they wanted to go visit with some of the guys on the West team. We couldn't get cabs to take us over to the Roosevelt Hotel. The cabdrivers said, "We can't haul you guys. We're going to call some colored cabs for you." Cookie raised a whole bunch of noise about that. We eventually got over to the Roosevelt, and we started comparing notes with the other black players. We found out that we couldn't do this, we couldn't do that, we were insulted here, and so on.

Houston Oilers rookie running back Sid Blanks added, "I couldn't get any transportation to the hotel. I finally got a skycap to tell me, 'You need to get the right cab because you're colored.' I asked him what he meant. He said, 'They won't pick you up. It's a little different here. If you're colored, you have to ride in a colored cab.'"

Dick Westmoreland, of the San Diego Chargers and the West squad, recalled his experience riding an elevator at the Roosevelt Hotel:

> I thought I was pretty sharp. I had a nice brown suit on. And some cologne—Aqua Velva or whatever it was in those days. Anyway, there was an elderly white lady on the elevator with us. . . . She loudly asked as we were getting off the elevator, "What's that smell?" She was imply-ing that I smelled—I'm guessing because I was black.

Denver Broncos safety Austin "Goose" Gonsoulin, who was white, told of an encounter he and Clem Daniels had in a restaurant:

We walked into the restaurant, and Clem hung up his coat, and this little old lady came over and threw his coat on the ground. I told Clem not to worry about it—just go over and put it back on the hanger. The woman came back over and threw it down again. We finished breakfast, and we agreed it was too bad New Orleans hadn't come around to the times yet.

The Chiefs' Abner Haynes said,

At the All-Star Game it was time to stand up. How could I face my sons years later and tell them I chickened out? Things started as soon as I got off the plane. I was trying to get a cab with Dave Grayson and Clem Daniels, who had flown out to New Orleans with me. We waited in the cab line for thirty minutes, and no one would pick us up. They were avoiding us. Finally, we asked a black porter, "Hey, brother, help us get a cab!" He explained that we had to get a black cab. He got us one, and we went to the hotel. Then some people at the hotel were disrespectful to us. They called us monkeys. By the time I got to my room, I was ready to leave. I said to myself, "Why are we being subjected to this?" That's when we had our meeting.

Abner Haynes. *UNT Athletics*

Haynes also said, "Earl Faison and I were coming out of the hotel elevator and some whites said, 'It's a shame to see these niggers going and coming like they have a right to be here.'" Later, in the hotel dining room, Haynes encountered others who said, "'Look at them—they just jump around like monkeys in the zoo!' It was comments like these, on top of everything else, that led us to our decision to not play in New Orleans."

Haynes further reflected, "I ain't no punk, I ain't no boy, I ain't no Uncle Tom. I have dignity."

The final straw was when some of the players, mostly members of the Chargers, went down to Bourbon Street that evening and were refused entry into several clubs. When they arrived at one club, Earl Faison claimed, "A guy pulls out a gun and says, 'You are not coming in here. You niggers are not coming in here.'"

Dick Westmoreland added,

> We went to a club and we heard what sounded like some James Brown coming from inside. We said, "James Brown! Let's check it out!" We thought we had stumbled on a black club. We got to the doorway . . . and the guy at the door said, "Y'all can't come in here." My friend Earl Faison saw the gun, which I didn't see at the time.

Neither did Ernie Ladd, who, when he found out he was being denied entry into the club, said, "I'll snatch these doors off the hinges. What do you mean I can't come in?" No one knew if the doorman was taking Ladd seriously. But more words were exchanged.

Defensive back Dave Grayson, another one of the other black Chargers on the West squad, said, "The doorman had a gun in his waistband. He pointed it at Ernie and told him if he walked through the door, he was going to kill him."

"The doorman pulls out a gun, cocked it, and said, 'You are not coming in here. You niggers are not coming in here,'" recalled Faison. "We recoiled and jumped back. Ernie Ladd lunges forward. The guy points the gun at Ernie's nose and says, 'I *will* pull the trigger.'"

Somehow, in the end, no shots were fired and cooler heads prevailed. It was after this confrontation though that Ladd said, "I'm not going to play here under these conditions."

Garland Boyette, Ladd's uncle, said, "Ernie told me later he had a gun pulled on him in the French Quarter. He was very outspoken. If it was something that needed to be said, he would say it. I wouldn't put it past him that he would organize the boycott."

Garland Boyette (65) and Ernie Ladd (70). *Garland Boyette*

Ladd said,

Walt Sweeney, one of our white teammates with the Chargers, stopped
a cab for us to go back to the hotel. The cab driver wouldn't let us get
inside. Sweeney wanted to bust the guy's head, but I said, no, we would
walk back to the hotel. When we got back, Earl and I had a discussion,
and I told Earl I wasn't going to play in New Orleans under those conditions. Earl agreed and got in touch with Sherman Plunkett, and he got
us in touch with the black players from the East squad.

After running into continual problems, Ladd told Faison, his room-mate back at the Roosevelt Hotel, "I don't need to take this crap." West-moreland, another Charger on the West squad, said, "I'm taking my black ass back home. I'm not playing." Faison then said, "If you're not playing, I'm not playing."

Not surprisingly, the players leading the protests in New Orleans were the same ones who had protested other events in 1963 and 1964: Art Powell and Clem Daniels of the Raiders, who helped boycott the 1963 preseason game in Mobile because of segregated seating, and Ernie Ladd, Earl Faison, and Ernie Wright of the Chargers, who were part of the 1964 pool hall incident in Atlanta.

Marion Jackson, sportswriter for the black newspaper the *Birmingham World*, echoed the players' concerns, claiming in a January 16, 1965 col-umn, the "seeds of rebellion may have been planted."

Years later, Ladd recalled,

> I orchestrated the boycott. I waited for Earl; then I said I wasn't going to put up with this foolishness. I told him, "Let's get all of the black players together and get out." We had a similar experience earlier in the season at an exhibition game in Atlanta, and we had people there who lied to us and said things would be made right. We were not going to be taken in again.

Powell and Daniels also seemed to help organize the boycott. Since they had organized the boycott of the preseason game in Mobile the year before because of segregated seating, they were willing to help pull the trigger on the New Orleans boycott. Daniels said about his and Powell's roles in the proceedings,

> We came into New Orleans. I believe they were earmarked to get a franchise in the AFL. We registered at the Roosevelt Hotel. It seems like all the players I ran into had some type of racist experience. We decided to meet at noon the next day. We talked about our experi-ences with each other. The cream of the crop of AFL players was in that room. They eventually sent the city attorney and Dutch Morial, the head of the NAACP in New Orleans. He went on to become the mayor of New Orleans. They came to meet with us to try and convince us to play. They tried to tell us what we could accomplish if we did actually play the game. They didn't want to upset things. Finally, by about 3:30, I had had enough. I stood up and said, "I'm packing my bag." Art Powell, my Raiders teammate, said, "I'm coming too." If we

were going to do this, the biggest impact would be for us to leave New Orleans. We went to the airport and got on a plane back to Oakland.

A lot of people understood the problems we were having, but not too many wanted to do anything about it. They didn't have the intestinal fortitude. In terms of interracial relations, only a handful of players would take a leadership position. Two guys who really helped me were Jesse Owens and Jackie Robinson. I got to work with both of them, and they were adamant about racial problems and relenting on the racial issue. They encouraged me to go forward.

In addition, Ernie Warlick and Cookie Gilchrist of the Buffalo Bills also played a part in the boycott. Warlick recalled,

> The next morning Cookie called me up and said, "All the guys ran into some discrimination. We're having a meeting. We need to decide whether we're going to play." So we had a meeting. There were a couple of our white teammates there too. They couldn't believe it either.
>
> I had served four years in the military. Then I played five years in the Canadian Football League. I was outside my country, but I had no problem going anywhere in Canada. Then I came back to my country and couldn't do things because of the color of my skin. So we decided to take a stand.

Butch Byrd, Warlick and Gilchrist's teammate on the Bills and the East squad, said,

> We weren't out to correct anyone. We were just thinking, "They're showing us no respect. This is just pure hatred." We weren't thinking about making history, so to speak. We just knew we were treated badly, and we wanted to leave. Being from the north, in Albany, New York, I had never experienced racism in this way. The black guys from the South, they were scared to death.

Future U.S. congressman and Bills quarterback Jack Kemp added, "We eventually got in a room at the Roosevelt Hotel—East and West players both. I remember Cookie talking, Abner Haynes talking, Art Powell talking. I said, 'Well, we've got to do something. We can't just accept this. What do you think we should do?' We wanted the black guys to decide."

In room 990 of the Roosevelt Hotel, Dave Dixon, NAACP head Dutch Morial, and attorney Harry Kelleher, who had fought tirelessly in New Orleans for access to public accommodations for all people, met with the players to try and convince them to stay in New Orleans and play in the game.

Reporters who had gathered outside the door heard someone plead with the players,

> We're asking you men to cooperate with us. This would be a deadly blow to our community, and it would undo all of the good that has been done in this area. We have arranged for you men to have access to all of the better-class establishments—restaurants and nightclubs—in the French Quarter. Why penalize all these people because some discriminated against you?

In the end, the players ignored the pleas. "They were promising us cars," Houston Antwine recalled. "They were promising us everything, if we would just stay and play. But if we did, we would just be accepting the conditions. Everybody made plans to leave."

Ernie Warlick added, "They tried to convince us that all of this money had been spent. They said, 'Please! You've got to play the game. You can't walk out now!' Hey, they should have thought about that beforehand. We're not going to play."

"Sure enough, they brought in a black guy," Ernie Ladd recalled. "Then we agreed not to play. Earl and I were definitely not going to play. And Dick Westmoreland. Then all the white guys sided with us—Kemp and Mix and the others. They said, 'It's all or none.' We chose to go."

The twenty-one black players—more than a third of the two twenty-nine-player squads, voted 13–8 not to play. All the players in the room who had the most influence, including Cookie Gilchrist, Ernie Ladd, Abner Haynes, and Clem Daniels, voted to leave. And so they departed.

The All-Star Game boycott was yet another of many incidents where white players put their careers on the line by siding with their African American teammates. Although some did so grudgingly, many white all-stars stood in unison with the black players.

Abner Haynes recalled,

> Some of my white teammates were supportive. Jerry Mays and Mel Branch, who were with me on the Chiefs at the time, were at the All-Star Game. They came to me and asked if they could help—was there anything that they could do?
>
> One of the things the AFL needed was the unity of the white and black players for our new league. When the white players like Jack Kemp and my Chief teammate Jerry Mays heard what was happening,

them and most of our white all-star teammates stood behind us. They put their careers on the line for us. We were disrespected as men. We were not here because of color; we were here because of talent. Why should we go out and put our lives and careers on the line for people who didn't appreciate us? We were not appreciated in New Orleans. We had no leverage. We weren't playing for money; we were playing for progress. Football players took the lead. Places like Atlanta, New Orleans, and Miami were death holes for black players. Dave Grayson couldn't get a drink at the bar. Our white teammates were there for us. It was amazing the league moved the game. Stuff like that just didn't happen back then.

In an interview years later, Keith Lincoln of the San Diego Chargers, who was the MVP of the All-Star Game, said,

It was unbelievable to me. It was mind-boggling. I had never experienced anything like this. . . . I didn't know the difference between Chicano, Latino, African American, black, whatever. I had always been involved in sports, and it certainly was a rainbow coalition wherever I was and whenever I played sports. I know you can never sense what another person is feeling completely, but I mean I was just as shocked and offended and embarrassed and certainly felt sorry for them. How the hell can anyone be treated this way? Moving the All-Star Game out of there was absolutely the right thing to do, as far as I'm concerned.

Although the white players went along with the boycott, not all of them agreed with it. Patriots linebacker and future Pro Football Hall of Famer Nick Buoniconti was one of the more vocal white players, calling the walkout a "raw deal" that "hurt the league a great deal." He felt that the white players wanted to stay in New Orleans and play even after the black players walked out. He said, "As I see it, this hurt the league a great deal. I believe that this act set back any negotiations with the national league at least two years. It cost our pension fund $125,000 dollars, and it cost each of us money personally."

Buoniconti also felt that "most of the Negro players voted to walk out to protect the three or four players involved. They felt they had to back them up or let the three or four face trouble from their own teams later."

Abner Haynes said,

White boys like Nick Buoniconti were running their mouths. They hadn't gone through anything in their lives like we had gone through. They didn't feel anything like we had felt in our lives. They disrespected us. I wasn't much interested in playing football after what we had been through the past few days.

Many of the AFL players, white and black, were proud that they, the league, and the owners stood up for what was right. Some claim that wouldn't have happened in the older, more established NFL.

Ernie Ladd said,

The AFL owners like Lamar Hunt [Chiefs] and Bud Adams [Oilers] and Sonny Werblin [Jets] and Barron Hilton [Chargers] were the greatest men I've known over the years. Our owners understood us, they took a stand, and they helped make pro football. The NFL had great players, but they weren't real men. Whatever the owners told them, they did. The AFL gave birth to men who would stand up and fight. There were no yellow-bellied cowards in the AFL.

That afternoon Sid Gillman, coach of the West team, started calling roll on the team bus that would escort the players to practice. He was completely unaware of what had transpired at the Roosevelt Hotel. "Abner Haynes." No response. "Willie Lanier." No response. "Earl Faison." "Ernie Ladd, Buck Buchanan." Again, no response.

"None of the black players are here," said one player.

"Yeah, they're meeting and talking about boycotting the game," said another.

"Why?" asked Gillman. He was informed about the situation—that the black players faced racism and discrimination after they had arrived in New Orleans and were talking about boycotting the game.

Tom Bass, a Chargers assistant coach who was on the bus, added,

We got to New Orleans as a staff a day early. Things were calm. We stayed downtown. We slowly realized there was a problem. Finally, we were getting on a bus to ride over to the stadium and have a walk-through. There were only white guys on the bus. I found out that the African American players started having troubles when they couldn't get a cab from the airport to the hotel. The taxi drivers wouldn't pick them up. The next day, we didn't have practice. The talk was now whether we were going to play or not. I remember it was the day of the NFL All-Star Game. We had to wait around to see what the players had decided. Tobin Rote was in town, and he had rented a suite with a TV, so we watched the Pro Bowl and ate hot dogs and drank beer.

In Chicago, AFL commissioner Joe Foss had been attending a Chicago baseball writers dinner when he caught word of the boycott. At 8:30 p.m., the players notified Foss and the commissioner about their intention to boycott the game. Foss called a 10:30 a.m. press conference on January 11 and said, "I do not blame our Negro stars for doing what they did. I doubt that New Orleans is ready for the big league. If they can't treat big leaguers with the dignity and respect they deserve, then the city will have to suffer the consequences."

Foss added,

Dave Dixon assured me that New Orleans was ready was ready in all aspects for a game between racially mixed teams. Evidently, it isn't. They contacted as many businessmen as possible and got them to agree to treat the Negro players well. But they just couldn't get to everyone. Negro players run into problems in nearly every city. But I guess what went on in New Orleans was more than they could be expected to take. I can't say that I blame them.

Foss then made arrangements to have the game moved to Houston. Once it was announced that the game was being moved, everyone involved had to make arrangements to go there. In the meantime, there was a lot of speculation from those close to the situation and also those in the media as to why the boycott occurred.

Moon Landrieu, then a state senator and later mayor of New Orleans, speculated that sometimes it takes time for enforcement to catch up with legislation. The enforcement of the Civil Rights Act had not yet caught up with the legislation. It had only been six months since its passage. Landrieu cited an example: "I remember when the Supreme Court issued its ruling in *Brown v. Board of Education* in 1954. I excitedly told my law school classmate Norman Francis, 'It's over—those terrible days of segregation are gone!'" That was not the case. Years later throughout the South, schools were still segregated.

Landrieu also said,

We were trying to rid ourselves of some of the segregationist policies of Jimmie Davis, who was Louisiana governor in the early 1960s. I vaguely remember the All-Star Game boycott. Segregation was still choking our city back then, and New Orleans couldn't move forward until we looked at some of the issues. When I was part of city council in New Orleans in the late sixties, I got the Confederate flag removed from council chambers. Then, in 1969, I introduced an ordinance that prohibited segregation in all public places in New Orleans. The Civil Rights Act did outlaw a lot of that in 1964, but it left some things undone. Our ordinance included convention centers; places like that that weren't mentioned in the Civil Rights Act. It helped our city move forward and get past that terrible time in our history. It was a big factor in New Orleans taking a whole new look at the racial situation.

Norman Francis, Landrieu's law school classmate, who later became president of Xavier University in New Orleans, added,

I'm not going to say New Orleans is perfect in any way. We had—and have—problems. Some were pretty serious. But New Orleans at that time was probably not as bad as other Southern cities. It was more cosmopolitan, to an extent, more open. I remember being very surprised—and very disappointed—at the situation.

Dave Dixon said the loss of the All-Star Game was sad, but he could not blame the players for what they did. "It was just unfortunate to have occurred in New Orleans—a city renowned for its predominantly live-and-let-live attitudes," he said.

Other opinions about the boycott were varied. Mayor Victor Schiro provoked criticism by saying the black players should have just "rolled with the punches. . . . If these men played football only in cities where everybody loved them, they'd all be out of a job today."

Governor John McKeithen noted, somewhat jokingly, "There are some clubs down on Bourbon Street that won't even let our district attorney [Jim Garrison] in."

As expected, reaction to the player boycott and subsequent movement of the All-Star Game to Houston did not go over too well with Louisiana journalists. Bill Carter, sportswriter for the *Alexandria Daily Town Talk*, tried to lay the majority of the blame on the players. In a January 14 column, he wrote,

Some Negro players in New Orleans for the All-Star Game were making the rounds of dives in the French Quarter and were denied service. You might say they were looking for trouble and they found it. Then they called a meeting and voted to boycott the game.

The AFL officials showed their lack of authority by going along with the players, without making an investigation, and moved the game to Houston. New Orleans was left holding the bag—a bag full of pregame expenses. . . . This was proof that the AFL is still a "bush" league compared to the NFL. . . . I sincerely hope the project to move the All-Star Game to Houston is a complete flop.

Bill McIntyre, sports columnist for the *Shreveport Times*, cast blame on the players and the AFL leadership for the boycott. In his January 12, 1965, column, titled "Authority Is Absent in the AFL," he wrote,

> The decision by Commissioner Joe Foss and his subordinates of the American Football League to transfer that pro league's postseason All-Star Game from New Orleans to Houston—with less than a week's notice—because of an alleged "mutiny" among some 20 Negro players indicates that the AFL is still in its infancy. . . . The AFL, and Commissioner Foss, chose to take dictation from a minority group—and we couldn't care less if they were Negroes, Caucasians, or Monsters—which provides evidence that they have forfeited all pretenses of public trust and support.
>
> When a tire goes flat on your car, you don't ship the whole chassis off to the junkyard. The AFL did.
>
> When a quart of milk goes sour in your icebox, you don't condemn the nation's dairy farmers. The AFL did.
>
> And, one may ask, just why were the Negro football players in question so intent on living it up in the booze halls along Bourbon Street? We would have suspected that these were supposed to be athletes still in training on the eve of an All-Star Game.
>
> But to stage a walkout, or boycott, because several of the Negro players were unable to penetrate a nightspot or flag down a taxicab invites only contempt . . . and the decision by Commissioner Foss and his crowd to move the game at the last possible moment is even more deplorable. Dave Dixon in particular, a man who had been striving for four years to bring professional football to New Orleans, should sue for damages.
>
> The AFL's decision to take dictation from the 20 Negro players— and we will not dignify them by naming them here—reduces both the league and players to just one word apropos to sports: "Bush."

It wasn't just southern journalists who criticized the player boycott. Some journalists north of the Mason–Dixon Line also disapproved of what had transpired.

Dick Young, nationally syndicated sports columnist for the *New York Daily News*, wrote in his January 13 column,

> The deplorable part of the New Orleans incident, and all like it, is that the bigots aren't punished. It is the innocent bystander who is punished.

> It is Dave Dixon, who will blow a fortune, and it is the AFL, and it is
> the many fine people of New Orleans; they are the ones who suffer. . . .
> What I mean is, you don't judge an entire town by a slob cab driver,
> because there are lots of good cabbies, and you don't judge an entire city
> because some guy in some lousy gin mill insults you.

Young then took a backhanded swipe at the players for heading into the
French Quarter: "Come to think of it, what were they training for in New
Orleans, the AFL All-Star Game, or a drinking bout? When you walk in
there you're asking for trouble."

In the January 16, 1965, edition of the *Delaware County Daily Times* in
Chester, Pennsylvania, sports columnist Bob Franklin laid the blame on the
players and the AFL league office for being "gutless." He wrote,

> Those 21 Negro football players who refused to play in the AFL All-Star
> Game Saturday in New Orleans accomplished one thing: they caused
> their employer—the AFL—to lose at least $150,000.
>   Just what the sacrifice was made for is questionable. . . . They won't
> be welcome in Houston's top night spots either. There's little difference
> between Houston and New Orleans as far as segregation is concerned.
> Perhaps the players got some satisfaction out of letting New Orleans
> know they don't appreciate being treated as second class citizens. . . . In
> Houston, those players will go to the restaurants they choose to patron-
> ize and will be served with reluctance. Most taxis will take them where
> they wish to go, and if they happen to enter a night club which caters
> to white trade only, they will be refused, regardless of what the law says.
>   So, in the long run, they've accomplished little. All they've done is
> hurt the AFL, their bread and butter. In pulling out of New Orleans,
> these 21 players were being, in their own minds, gallant in defense of
> the Negro race. In going with them, the AFL was gutless.

Not be deterred, some of the assertions in Franklin's column were
challenged five days later in the editorial section of the *Daily Times* by
Enormal Clark, president of the Media Branch Chapter of the NAACP in
Swarthmore. In his letter, Clark stated in part,

> Mr. Franklin seeks to take to task the 21 Negro players who walked out
> of the AFL Pro Bowl game in New Orleans.
>   For Mr. Franklin's information those Negro players, in addition to
> being professional athletes, were American citizens, and as such had
> every right to be treated the same as any other American citizen, no
> matter what city they were in.

They had a right to refuse to perform in any city in which they were treated as anything but first-class citizens.

Mr. Franklin might as well get used to the idea; this is the year 1965. Negroes simply aren't going to accept the things and conditions of even a year ago. It is the now the Law of the Land that every American must be treated equally, and we are determined to see to it that this law is applied everywhere.

Mr. Franklin might as well get used to the idea: Negroes ain't acting like colored people anymore.

Players and coaches now had the task of getting to Houston, about 350 miles west of the Crescent City, to play the game on Saturday, January 16.

It was somewhat ironic that Houston was chosen as the new site for the game. It was well documented that Houston was dealing with its own civil rights issues in the early 1960s—especially segregated seating.

Ernie Ladd said,

It was interesting that the league chose to move the game to Houston. That city treated blacks pretty poorly for a time. They made the black spectators sit in the end zone. Lloyd Wells tried to get the black players on the Chargers to strike back in 1961, and I made the mistake of not listening to him. I'll never forget him saying, "Ernie Ladd, you're gutless like a worm. Stand up and show some guts." By then it was too late to do anything, but I'll never forget him saying, "Look at you, you big old gutless Ernie Ladd. You can run but you can't hide."

Tom Bass of the West coaching staff said,

It was finally announced we were going to Houston. The coaches' reaction was split. Some wanted to stay in New Orleans and play. Some of the coaches were very overt about it; they said it was wrong and they wanted to play. Overall, most of the coaches were happy we were going to Houston. We got to stay in the beautiful Shamrock Hilton. The whole thing did leave a bit of a bad taste in my mouth from the stance of "Why did we go to New Orleans in the first place if things like that were still going on there?" I knew things like this went on because I had been to the South before, scouting at the black colleges. Luckily the whole thing got smoothed over fairly quickly and the game came off smoothly in Houston.

East tight end Ernie Warlick recalled, "I got home to Buffalo and received a call either that night or the next morning: 'Get on a plane and go to Houston.'"

After he returned home to Buffalo, Bills defensive back Butch Byrd walked into his house and was told by his wife he needed to go to Houston: "I didn't even put my bags down; I walked right back out and to the airport and caught a flight to Houston."

The Raiders' Clem Daniels said,

> After my teammate Art and I got on the plane to take us back to Oakland, we ended up going from New Orleans to Denver to Chicago to Los Angeles and to San Francisco. When I finally walked into my apartment in Oakland, exhausted, Al Davis's secretary called me and said: "They moved the game to Houston. You need to catch the 4:00 p.m. flight there." I got to Houston and took a cab to the Shamrock Hilton Hotel. When I got there, TV reporters and the press were waiting. When I stepped out of the cab, Murray Olderman, a national columnist, asked me, "Why did you leave New Orleans?" I realized then the impact of what I had done. This was national news—a big story. When we got to Houston there was all types of dialogue. While I was there, I met with the president of Prairie View and my old coach Billy Nicks and got their advice about the possible repercussions of the boycott. They told me they and Prairie View were behind me 100 percent.

East defensive tackle Houston Antwine recounted

> A lot of the ballplayers were still ticked off when we got to Houston, and their attitude showed when we were practicing. I think the coaches couldn't get across some of the stuff they wanted. You had ballplayers with attitude. All they wanted to do was to get the game behind them. The incident didn't get the publicity I think it should have. We didn't feel it was properly addressed. Back in Boston, there was one little blip in the paper showing me with my bag, leaving the hotel. That was basically it. The hostility and the treatment we received in New Orleans was never, never really publicized. I've talked to Cookie, and he was really ticked off about it. Right now, if you ask somebody, "Do you remember the AFL All-Star Game that was supposed to be played in New Orleans?" nobody remembers what happened.

A couple of the white all-star players commented on the game being moved to Houston. Bob Talamini of the East team, a guard for the Houston Oilers, got to play the game in his home city. He said,

The AFL All-Star Game was supposed to be played in New Orleans. Back then a lot of towns were trying to promote football in the South. I know that we stayed in a nice hotel in New Orleans and the game was close to a sellout. It was going to put a lot of money in our pension. Some of the black players apparently had problems getting cabs, in addition to some other incidents. Next thing I know, they're moving the game to Houston. I thought, "There goes our pension money." It happened all of a sudden. So we just gathered our stuff and went to Houston, and we played at our home field at Jeppesen Stadium. I wouldn't say that we were that upset about it. I didn't have any real ax to grind with the black players. I went along with it. I was a little surprised and disappointed. I wasn't mad at anyone, though. I think New Orleans could have been a little more accommodating. That's the thing about athletics: If you're good enough, you're good enough. It doesn't matter what color you are. When I was on the New York Jets my last year in 1968, the year we won the Super Bowl, there were a lot of key black players on that team: Winston Hill, Emerson Boozer, Verlon Biggs, Matt Snell, Johnny Sample, and others.

Tommy Brooker of the Kansas City Chiefs and West team made his only all-star team in 1964. Brooker is best known for kicking the game-winning field goal in the second overtime of the 1962 AFL Championship Game, where the Dallas Texans defeated the Houston Oilers, 20–17. He said,

> I drove over to New Orleans for the game from Tuscaloosa, about a five-hour drive. Everybody else flew into New Orleans. When I found out the game was changed to Houston, I had no objections. Even though it was an all-star team, it was still a team. We just loaded up and went. I was not opposed to what happened. We were all-stars and we acted like all-stars. Really, the only big deal was when we went over to Houston, we all flew. I left my car in New Orleans. That meant after the game, I had to fly back to New Orleans, but then I had that five-hour drive to Tuscaloosa ahead of me. To me, that was a bigger pain than moving the game to Houston.

As far as the All-Star Game was concerned, the West squad blew open a close 17–14 lead at the half to rout the East team, 38–14. Keith Lincoln of the Chargers was the offensive MVP, with an 80-yard touchdown run and a 73-yard receiving touchdown on the first play from scrimmage. Willie Brown of the Broncos was the defensive MVP. The winning players on the West team each got $700, while the East squad players received $500 each.

Unfortunately, because of the short notice of the location change, only 15,446 fans came to Jeppesen Stadium. A mere $40,000 was put into the players' pension fund, as opposed to a potential $125,000 to $150,000 that would have been brought in if the game was played in New Orleans.

But some things are worth more than a packed house and big money.

In the end, the players who boycotted the All-Star Game in New Orleans were proud of what they had accomplished. The Bills' Ernie Warlick said, "I got hate mail and was invited to go back to Africa. But when I look back, it was one of the thrills of my life. We were a unified group. Every time we get together as a group, we talk about how unified we were. We hung together and got along. It's a great thrill that I've carried with me ever since."

Ernie Ladd added years later, "We did it because someone had to take a stand and stop the black players from being treated as second-class citizens. We didn't do it for publicity. We did it because of what was right and what was wrong."

So, after the passage of the Civil Rights Act of 1964 and the boycott of the AFL All-Star Game in New Orleans just a few months later in January 1965, the racial climate began to change in New Orleans and other cities in the South. Gradually, black patrons in New Orleans no longer were served in the kitchens of restaurants, were able to ride anywhere they pleased on public transportation, and could now shop at any store, or eat or drink at any restaurant or club in the French Quarter. The same rights were granted to African Americans in other southern cities as well. What remained to be seen, however, was whether the all-star boycott in New Orleans jeopardized the city's chance at a pro football franchise—along with other southern cities such as Atlanta, which were also vying for professional football teams.

10

THE ROAD TO
THE CLEVELAND SUMMIT

Southern Expansion and the
Final Exhibition Games in Dixie

After the January 1965 All-Star boycott in New Orleans, the question remained whether the AFL and NFL would continue their efforts to expand and establish franchises in New Orleans and other southern cities.

There were some lingering effects of the boycott immediately after the game, which lasted for a while thereafter. Some of the African American all-stars appeared to be punished for their role in the boycott. Less than a week after the All-Star Game, on January 20, Abner Haynes was traded by the Chiefs to the Denver Broncos for punter Jim Fraser and cash. In February the Bills sent Cookie Gilchrist, who was also seen as one of the organizers of the All-Star boycott, to the Broncos in exchange for fullback Billy Joe. The Broncos had now acquired the number one and number three all-time rushers in the AFL for next to nothing.

Haynes gave his take on the situation:

> Just a few days after the game, I was traded to Denver as punishment. Cookie Gilchrist, one of the other leaders, was traded there too. They were the worst team in the league. The owners would try to do things like this sometimes, to try and make you uncomfortable. It was a form of intimidation. This happened to a lot of the players, and many of them were out of the league in just a few years. Jack Steadman, the Chiefs GM, wrote me a two-page letter explaining that he thought I helped lead the boycott. He claimed it was not a football player's role to help out his people—his job was to play football and keep his mouth shut.
>
> I actually enjoyed Denver as much as anyplace. It was cool. I also had family up there, the Alexanders, which was my mom's side of the family. My parents, when I was growing up in Denton and Dallas, used to send me and my brothers and sisters to visit relatives for the summer in places that weren't segregated, so we could experience what it

was like to not face racism every day. I'm amazed my parents had the foresight and knowledge to do that. I also had a brother who had gone to college up there.

While white sportswriters both nationally and in Louisiana criticized the black players during and after the boycott for walking out, black sportswriters stood up to defend the players. The January 23, 1965, edition of the *Pittsburgh Courier* had three articles and columns devoted to the All-Star Game boycott.

Wendell Smith wrote in his column,

> New Orleans is a town not worthy of big league consideration. . . . The transfer of the game to Houston has, no doubt, killed whatever hopes New Orleans had for any kind of major league franchise . . . but the town has no chance whatsoever now. . . . The town hasn't grown up, it's not ready for major league attractions, and won't get them. Thus, New Orleans remains a tank town. It's even smaller than that fictitious hamlet known as Peyton Place.
>
> The entire sports world, as well as the nation, should bow low and long to the players who refused to tolerate New Orleans bigotry. We also owe Commissioner Foss and the American Football League a special salute because they did not hesitate to act when it was necessary to do so. They did not try to "smooth things" or pretend that what was happening in New Orleans was due to the sensitivity of the Negro players.

Bill Nunn Jr., sports editor for the *Courier*, offered his take on the situation in New Orleans in his column:

> The Negro athletes who refused to bow in the face of segregation in New Orleans last week are to be commended. While there have been scattered instances of Negro athletes taking firm steps against the injustices of Jim Crow before, never has such universal admiration for a group been so wide spread.
>
> To a man, the individuals who put principal [*sic*] above playing in a football game, have shown that courage can pay big dividends. When the 21 Negroes decided as a group that they would not perform in a city where they weren't accepted as citizens, they had no idea of the repercussions they might face. Despite this, they went ahead and made their move.

Nunn then made some interesting points at the end of his column:

> The decision to move the game to Houston was ironic in many ways. For three years Negroes in the Houston area boycotted the Houston Oilers' games because of their segregated seating pattern. Even today, Negro players in the league feel the Oilers aren't overly sincere in seeking tan talent. However, in recent years, the city of Houston has made tremendous strides in breaking down the pattern of racial discrimination. In the growing Texas metropolis, ball players are readily accepted in places of public accommodations. This is as it should be. And until cities like New Orleans learn to accept the status quo, they should be penalized for their shortcomings.

A third piece from the same issue of the *Courier* by Bill Curry, who was in attendance in New Orleans, placed the blame on the city and its residents. Titled "New Orleans Must Accept Blame for Negro Walkout," the article said in part,

> Close observation on the scene by the writer lays the blame directly on city officials in the much-publicized cancellation of the 1965 AFL All Star Game here last week. The 20 Negro players involved did meet racial incidents . . . but these incidents could have properly been taken care of with normal advance preparations by the city as well as the promoters.
>
> The game was well publicized weeks in advance, even with the help of the mayor, who appeared on local TV several times appealing for fans to support the attraction.
>
> But what the mayor and other city officials didn't do was properly orientate local businesses—entertainment places, transportation firms, etc.—on what was to be expected from them. I believe that had they been called in weeks before, or contacted long before, of what was expected to make this game a success, last Sunday's embarrassing incidents involving some unconcerned cabbies and cheap French Quarter nightclub doormen would not have occurred.
>
> Dave Dixon and his group, sincere as any group of persons can be in desiring the game and its integrated aspects, overlooked this important item—not intentionally, but accidentally—and their magnificent efforts went for naught because of a few unfortunate incidents that did not speak for the general citizenry of the town. It's tragic, but one must pay the price for a mistake. . . . It gave New Orleans another setback in its struggle to regain its once lofty national popularity.

Others who were not in the black media continued to criticize the All-Star Game boycott. Victor Schiro, then mayor of New Orleans, said in an interview in the January 26 edition of the *Shreveport Times* that he had received a "reef of letters from all over the country supporting New Orleans' position." He added that the image of the city was not damaged and "certainly won't affect our plans for a professional football team."

Schiro then went on to exclaim, "I think it was planned and organized. We were treated unfairly. The players went into dives and were treated the way you are in such places. If you look for trouble anywhere, you can find it."

Even as late as October 1965, the subject of the boycott came up at a meeting of the Shreveport Touchdown Club. Houston Oilers vice president John Breen was asked by reporters at the event how he would have handled the walkout. Breen replied, "I would have told Cookie Gilchrist and that bunch, 'You either play or you're out of football for life.' I would have said, 'I don't care what you do next year, but you play this game.'"

Breen went on to explain, "Why break a contract? All of the league officials were at the coaches' meeting. Why wasn't someone from the league there? You let them have their way, and pretty soon they'll walk all over you. You have to make them learn to honor a contract."

In spite of the setback of the All-Star Game boycott in New Orleans, Dave Dixon still had his sights set on getting a pro franchise in the Crescent City. Not to be denied, Dixon set out to right the wrong.

Dixon said NFL commissioner Pete Rozelle called him a few days after the boycott and told him the NFL was still interested in establishing a franchise there. Rozelle sent NFL representative Buddy Young to New Orleans to assess the situation. Dixon came up with the idea that a public display of him and Young eating at a New Orleans restaurant would go a long way to offset the bad publicity the boycott had caused. Dixon called Roy Alciatore, owner of the famous Antoine's, one of New Orleans' top restaurants.

"Restaurants had been sort of integrated by that time," Dixon recalled. "If whites and blacks wanted to have dinner together, they would do so in private rooms. So, I called Roy and said, 'Roy, here's my situation. I want to sit in the middle of the restaurant, and I'd like to have John Ketry [one of Antoine's longest-tenured employees] as my waiter.' He said, 'Let's do it.'"

Young and Dixon dined at Antoine's, and the dinner went a long way toward securing an NFL franchise for New Orleans in 1967. Geraldine Young, Buddy's widow, said, "Buddy was always very proud what he and

Dave Dixon accomplished in New Orleans. Buddy believed he had a role in the NFL putting a franchise in New Orleans."

That summer, Dixon was still courting AFL and NFL franchises to New Orleans. In an Associated Press article from July 1, 1965, Dixon said that he "had gotten an authentic feeler from the American Football League for a 1966 expansion franchise here." Dixon stated that just the day before he had received assurances of support from two NFL owners for an NFL franchise in New Orleans. Dixon also stated that renewed AFL interest in New Orleans "by no means infers that we have lost any interest in the National Football League, since New Orleans is the obvious companion city choice for Atlanta in the NFL."

By August, the All-Star Game boycott was becoming a memory. Although interest in New Orleans had sagged after the All-Star Game, it picked up steam again. One step New Orleans took to smooth things over was making sure the city's seventeen hundred taxis would operate on a nonsegregated basis. When the Colts and Cardinals came to New Orleans for an exhibition game on August 14, anticipation ran high. Seventy thousand fans were expected at Tulane Stadium. For weeks the people of New Orleans had been bombarded with the slogan "Let's Go Pro" on radio, TV, billboards, and newspapers. The tactics obviously drummed up interest and support for a team to be placed in New Orleans. Because of these efforts, coupled with those of Dave Dixon, the city of New Orleans was eventually awarded an NFL franchise, with play to begin in 1967.

However, before the Saints began play in 1967, the NFL and AFL decided to put franchises in southern cities for the 1966 season. Atlanta would be home to the NFL Falcons, while the AFL put the Dolphins in Miami.

Although de jure segregation had all but ended in southern cities, there were still challenges for African American players when they came to live in Atlanta and Miami.

A couple of the early African American Falcons were Texans Junior Coffey and Bill Harris. They differed in recalling their experiences in Atlanta.

After spending his rookie season with the 1965 NFL champion Green Bay Packers, Coffey was selected by the Atlanta Falcons in the 1966 Expansion Draft. His first two seasons, he was one of the bright spots for the expansion Falcons, rushing for 722 yards each year. He missed the entire 1968 and 1970 seasons with a knee injury, which severely limited his effectiveness for the rest of his career.

Coffey had positive memories of 1966 Atlanta:

Just to be honest, Atlanta was like an oasis. I felt the black population there was more educated. A lot owned their own businesses. About the only issue I had when I first got there was not being able to stay with the team the night before a game in a downtown hotel. It wasn't like Mississippi or New Orleans, for that matter. When I was in New Orleans, I was refused service in the restaurant bar of a place. They just ignored us until we got the hint and left. I think the old ways of the South lasted longer in New Orleans than in Atlanta.

Going to Atlanta, I didn't have a fear of the white people. I grew up in Texas, and I integrated my high school there. I had experience dealing with whites. I didn't actually "feel" the segregation in Atlanta. Once again, there were so many things to do in the black community, and they were highly educated. Eventually the coaches also checked out which hotels downtown would accommodate the black players. Another event that helped desegregation in Atlanta was when the Braves moved there from Milwaukee. Hank Aaron came to Atlanta, and I think he laid the groundwork for the rest of us—we just moved into the situation.

Harris was a running back from the University of Colorado via Galveston, Texas. As a senior at still-segregated Galveston Central High School, Harris led the Bearcats to the 1963 state title in the Prairie View Interscholastic League, the league for African Americans. He went to Colorado because white colleges in Texas were just beginning the desegregation process.

The rookie Harris had a good training camp in 1968, but just before the regular season began, he suffered a severely bruised thigh that sent him to the hospital for a week. He was finally activated for the last six games of the season.

Harris did not carry the same positive feelings for Atlanta that Junior Coffey had. He said,

I went to training camp with the Falcons my rookie year in 1968 in Johnson City, Tennessee. After we broke camp, we had to drive to Atlanta and try and find housing. There were about a half-dozen black players, and we were looking for apartments. There were some brand-new apartments not far from the practice facility. Some of the white players went there and found an apartment. When we went there, we were told it was full. I went back to our coaches and said, "This is not going to work." Then, my car was stolen. The cops basically did nothing about it. I said to myself, "This is not going to fly." Well, one day I was interviewed live for one of the Atlanta TV stations. The reporter asked me, "How do you like Atlanta?" I proceeded to tell them how I couldn't find housing and how my car was stolen. Well, their switchboard lit up! And you know what? The next thing you know, I had an apartment.

Well, in Atlanta there was racial stuff in the locker room and I didn't care for it, and I asked my coach Norm Van Brocklin to be traded. He said no. The next year I left training camp because of racial stuff. I was ready to call a press conference to make it public, but Pete Rozelle stepped in and got me traded to Minnesota. That worked well—I liked it there. I got to go to the Super Bowl after the 1969 season. In the end, I didn't care much for Atlanta.

As far as the Dolphins, several former players, black and white, reminisced about the expansion team. Two players who were taken by the Dolphins in the 1966 Expansion Draft were Gene Mingo and Willie West. Mingo and West had been teammates with the 1964 Denver Broncos, but an incident on a road trip to Oakland during the season led them to eventually end up in Miami. Mingo and West were traded (but not blackballed like earlier black players) when it was found they had two white women up in their room before a game. The two all-stars were immediately traded— Mingo to Oakland and West to New York. After the 1965 season, both players were left unprotected by their respective teams and eventually went to the Dolphins in the Expansion Draft.

Mingo described the event that led to his demise with the Broncos:

We were caught in our hotel rooms with two Caucasian girls. Cal Kunz, our team president, said it was "conduct detrimental to the team." They wanted to claim they were prostitutes. They were just girls. My wife had a good friend in Oakland, her name was Edna, where we were going to be playing. Willie West and I had some dinner, and this Edna invited two of her coworker friends. When the dinner was over, we were going to be late getting back to the hotel, and these two girls who were at the dinner with us offered to take us back in their VW. We said okay, and they dropped us off.

I guess they made a lot of noise pulling into the parking lot of the hotel, because two of our white teammates, Ray Jacobs and Tom Nomina, looked out of their hotel window and saw it was a couple of white girls dropping us off. We said goodnight to the ladies. Well, they snuck up to our rooms. I asked Willie, "Did you invite them up?" Willie said no. They were good looking, but I had just gotten married six months before. We knew one of our assistant coaches, Red Miller, would be coming by for a curfew check. We panicked and had the girls hide in the room. One hid in the shower, and another hid in the closet. Red came by and checked on us, didn't find the girls, and he went on his way. Well, the women stayed for another hour or so. Nothing happened, but then there was a knock on the door. It was Red Miller again, and he says, "I hear you've got two white women in your room." Red said Cal Kunz, the team president, was mad. He said they had gotten a complaint from the front desk saying we were too loud.

We were told to report to Broncos GM Dean Griffing the next morning. I begged Dean the next morning to not do anything. He said it was "conduct detrimental to the team." We were put on a plane back to Denver. The next thing you knew, Willie and I were traded. I went to Oakland, and Willie went to New York. Then, in 1966, we were both picked up by the Dolphins. Hey, it was the sixties—things were still prejudiced. I had white teammates who had been caught with women in their rooms and nothing happened to them.

Mingo's career and marriage floundered after that. He ended up in Miami for 1966.

West and Mingo also discussed what it was like to be African American in Miami in 1966. West said,

Miami was quasi-desegregated when I went there in 1966. There was still a lot of discrimination. There were certain areas where I couldn't rent a house. There were some other problems, but Miami was going through the process of integration. Even to this day they're still trying to desegregate some areas. Miami was a little different than some other places in the South, like Mississippi or Alabama. Miami was a tourist area, and they had a lot of conventions. Things were a little more relaxed. People came from all over.

To tell the truth, I was treated better in Miami than in Phoenix or Las Vegas. Even in San Diego, where I was from, things were unwritten there. There were places blacks could go and places they couldn't. Phoenix was more or less segregated in 1960. I was out there to play in a now-defunct all-star game called the Copper Bowl. We were not allowed to go in restaurants in Phoenix. We didn't know it was going to be that way until we got there. I remember we sat there for a while and we were ignored at first. No one would bring us menus. Finally, someone from the restaurant came over and said, "We can't serve you. You have to go around back."

Then, the coaches decided to take the team up to Las Vegas to have some fun. We went to one of the larger casinos—I think it was the MGM Grand. The team got inside the casino and I knew something was wrong. The guards that were in there were a good fifty feet away from us, and they just started staring down the black players. We got the message. The coaches gathered up all of the black players and took us up front. We were told by the casino that we couldn't stay there. The coaches asked us if they wanted us to take the rest of the players back to Phoenix too. We said, "No, it's not their fault. Let them stay here and have some fun."

Mingo had a slightly different view of Miami.

I felt Miami was very prejudiced. It was very hard for the black players to get housing. Nobody wanted to rent to the black players. We were getting ready to leave Miami, but our coach, George Wilson, talked Dolphins owner Joe Robbie into doing something about it. When I came into Miami with my wife and baby, we went to a hotel on Biscayne Boulevard. It said "Vacancy" on the sign. When we got out of the car and they saw us, the "No Vacancy" sign went on. We went to another hotel down the street, and I went inside and walked into the lobby to see if there were any rooms. Mind you, I could see all kinds of room keys in the boxes behind the counter. When I was told there were no rooms available, I lost my cool with the manager. I said, "I'm with the Dolphins, and if I have my way you will not have an AFL team in Miami!" The manager perked up and said, "Oh, you're with the Dolphins? What do you know, a room just became available!"

Then it became time to find an apartment. My wife went looking for an apartment with the wife of a black teammate of mine, Wendell Hayes. They went to an apartment complex that advertised there were apartments available, but when they got there, the lady working there apologized to them and said they had rented the apartment already. We ended up with an apartment in the black area of town.

Once we got settled in, and the people of Miami found out I played for the Dolphins and was their field goal kicker, I was treated well. Two of the team dentists would take us fishing. There's a main street in Miami—I can't remember the name of it—but they had restaurants, stores, and shops there. Once they found out I was a Dolphin, I was welcomed there. If I hadn't been on the team, I couldn't have gone anywhere near those places.

Bob Petrich, along with Earl Faison, were two former San Diego Chargers who made their way to the 1966 expansion Dolphins. Petrich explained,

Things were more open in California. I wound up in Miami with Earl Faison, my old teammate from San Diego. We almost got killed there.

We had no idea it was like that. Hey, it was the South. We trained in Boca Raton. It was out in the country back then. Attitudes toward blacks were different there than in Miami, which was a little more open, more metropolitan.

I went to go eat lunch one day with Earl. Where we went, it was mixed. I went to go sit with Earl, which was at a table with all blacks. Earl told me, "You can't sit here." I really didn't care what anyone said or thought. Earl then said, "If you sit with me, it could cause a problem. Not for you, but for me." For Earl's sake, I didn't sit with him. That would have never happened in San Diego. We also heard through the grapevine that one of George Wilson's assistants, Les Bingaman, had said that he "didn't want any blacks on his defensive line." That meant Earl, who was black. We never would have heard that in San Diego either. Sid Gillman would have never tolerated that.

Billy Joe spoke about the repercussions some of the African American Dolphins faced when they complained about the de facto segregation still present in Miami. Joe said,

I was the first player chosen by the Dolphins in the Expansion Draft. Miami wasn't good. If you stayed within the confines of the team, it was okay. A lot of restaurants and hotels were still segregated. At training camp in 1967, several of us black players complained to Coach George Wilson: me, Al Dotson, Bo Roberson, and Dick Westmoreland. We were all cut from the team.

I actually lived in Miami Beach for a short time in 1967 before I got cut. I may have been the first black to do that. Even though I lived there, there were certain places I couldn't go into, like the Fontaine-bleau Hotel. The Fontainebleau was a little like the Las Vegas casinos. Stars like Lena Horne and Harry Belafonte were allowed to perform there, but when their show was over, they weren't allowed to stay at the hotel.

When New Orleans was finally awarded the Saints franchise by the NFL, set to begin play in 1967, a couple of their black players spoke about if and how anything had changed there since the All-Star Game in 1965.

Walt "Flea" Roberts is forever remembered by Saints fans, because on November 5, 1967, he returned an opening kickoff against the Philadelphia Eagles for a 91-yard touchdown to help lead the Saints to a 31–24 win—the first in team history. Roberts spoke about heading to New Orleans to play for the expansion Saints:

New Orleans was very difficult. It was like two worlds. I had never lived in the South. When I told my mom I was going to New Orleans, she was very concerned. My wife and I flew down to New Orleans to sign my contract. Getting a taxi was no problem from the airport to the Fontainebleau Hotel, where we were supposed to be staying. I was going to meet Al Tabor, a black scout and assistant coach with the Saints, to discuss and sign my contract. However, when I went up to the front desk and told them I had a reservation for Roberts, they said, "Oh no you don't." I knew right then what they meant. Luckily, Mr. Tabor with the Saints got it straightened out. I guess since I was a Saint it was okay to be black and stay there.

Finding a place to live in New Orleans was challenging too. A lot of the black players lived in Algiers, which is a mostly black part of New Orleans. Myself and some of the other black players moved to Gretna, just outside of New Orleans, to a place called the Bridge Plaza Condos. As soon as the players moved in, the whites moved out. It became a ghost town.

Another incident I remember was when there were about four or five Saints and we were looking for a place to eat in town. I was the only black guy in the group. When we got to this one place, there was a "Whites Only" sign on the door. My white teammates were not happy; in fact, they wanted to fight. I told them, "That's okay. You guys don't understand. I have to live for another day." Most of the time, the racism and discrimination was not overt like that. It was covert—like what happened at the Fontainebleau Hotel or those condos in Gretna.

Roberts concluded,

One other observation: After the stigma of the AFL All-Star Game being moved a couple years earlier from New Orleans, the city and the Saints were trying to change the image of the city. I remember Buddy Young with the NFL came to New Orleans to try and make the Saints' transition smooth. I also felt the Saints kept a larger number of black players on their roster than other NFL teams to help overcome New Orleans's image.

Defensive back George Youngblood also came to the Saints during the 1967 season. He played for them in 1968, went to the Bears in 1969, and returned to New Orleans in 1970. He said,

New Orleans was much different from California, where I was from. I had to find out what was allowed and what was not. That's not why I was in New Orleans at that time, though. I was there to play football—

not to challenge anything. There were places in New Orleans I could and couldn't go. This was new to me, being from California. Housing was difficult. We were not welcome in certain parts of the city. Eventually some of us had to find a place in Mississippi to stay.

Now, when I returned to New Orleans in 1970, things had changed a lot. Things were a little more open. Blacks could go anywhere just about. An ordinance had been passed that enabled blacks to be able to go to restaurants, clubs, hotels, and other places. I think part of the reason it was passed was the Super Bowl between the Chiefs and Vikings was to be played there and they wanted to avoid any problems with people coming in from out of town. It helped the city move forward.

Bill Harris didn't appear to share Youngblood's opinion that New Orleans had changed by 1970. After being traded from Atlanta to the Vikings for their Super Bowl IV run in 1969, Harris ended up in New Orleans. He explained,

> After two seasons in Minnesota, Vikings general manager Jim Finks ends up in New Orleans, and guess where I end up? It ticked me off. I refused to go at first. New Orleans was worse than Atlanta. We trained in Hattiesburg, Mississippi. The Klan was keeping an eye on us. The last straw for me was when we were by some railroad tracks one evening and there was a sign posted by them that read, "Nigger, if you're reading this sign, you've been here too long." I left camp that night and went back to Colorado. Pete Rozelle got involved again. The NFL didn't want any kind of discussion on race. New Orleans was still a pretty new franchise, and they didn't want any bad publicity. Eventually I went back to camp, but I didn't last long. I played in our second game of the season against the 49ers, and that was it. I guess they didn't want any troublemakers.

Problems with African American players finding adequate housing, among other issues, were not limited to south of the Mason–Dixon Line. There was still de facto discrimination going on in the North.

Dave Robinson of the Green Bay Packers talked about the difficulties of being African American and trying to find housing in Green Bay, Wisconsin:

> What happened in Green Bay a few times was when we needed an apartment, we would have Lionel Aldridge call and ask if there were any available because he sounded like a white guy. However, whenever we

would get there, they would say, "I'm sorry, it's rented." It wasn't easy by any means being black in Green Bay in the 1960s.

Just one state to the west and 275 miles from Green Bay were the Twin Cities of Minneapolis and St. Paul, home of the Minnesota Vikings. It was there where Vikings rookie wide receiver Gene Washington also encountered discrimination when he tried to find housing for himself and his new bride, Claudith.

Washington came to the club in 1967 as a first-round draft pick from Michigan State. He was originally from LaPorte, Texas, and attended Michigan State because Texas colleges were still segregated in the early 1960s. Washington and his wife got a taste of discrimination up in the Twin Cities.

He recalled,

> 1967 was my rookie year with the Vikings. I got married to my wife, Claudith, in San Francisco. She was living with her sister out there. I played in a couple of all-star games that summer, and then Claudith and I had to go to Minneapolis in July to try and find an apartment. There

Gene Washington, Minnesota Vikings. *Michigan State University Athletics*

were some nice complexes near Lake Nokomis, which was near the airport, and Met Stadium, where we played. It was a very nice area. We went to a local real estate office, and we went in and told the man there we were looking for an apartment. The guy was very nice, but he informed us there was nothing in the area. We didn't think too much of it, so Claudith and I started to leave.

As we were walking out, there was another guy who worked there who noticed us and said, "You're Gene Washington of the Vikings! You must be looking for a place to live—this is a great place." Claudith and I looked at each other dumbfounded. We asked ourselves, "Why would that guy do that?" Just because I was a Viking, we were treated different. In other words, if you happen to be a Viking and you're black, it's okay. If not, tough luck. And it was all just because he recognized me. We told him no thanks.

By 1966, more changes were occurring in the South and professional football. With new franchises being placed in Atlanta and Miami that year, followed by New Orleans in 1967, the Washington Redskins lost their status as the "Team of the South." Undoubtedly, another factor in the Redskins losing their following in the South was that owner George Preston Marshall had to relinquish power of the Redskins because of illness.

Marshall had a stroke in the summer of 1963. Earlier, in January 1963, Marshall was one of seventeen men to be inducted into the inaugural class of the Pro Football Hall of Fame, along with football legends like Jim Thorpe, Red Grange, Don Hutson, Bronko Nagurski, Sammy Baugh, and George Halas. Marshall was the only living inductee unable to attend the ceremony. By December, Marshall was bedridden with arteriosclerosis, diabetes, a stomach aneurism, emphysema, and a weakened heart, requiring around-the-clock care.

Edward Bennett Williams, a high-powered Washington attorney who was a minority stockholder in the Redskins, took over day-to-day operations of the Redskins from Marshall in 1965. Jack Kent Cooke, the majority stockholder of the Redskins, was based in California and tended to running his other professional team, the Los Angeles Lakers. It was Williams who lured Vince Lombardi out of retirement to coach the Redskins in 1969. In retrospect it was somewhat ironic that what had been the most racist organization in professional football ended up hiring Lombardi, considered to be the least racist man in the sport. Marshall died on August 9, 1969, just as Lombardi's Redskins were getting ready to take the field for the first time.

As late as 1965, Redskins played three of their six preseason games in the South. With Marshall no longer running the Redskins, they started playing fewer games in the South. Washington just played one in the South in each preseason from 1966 to 1970, and after that ceased playing preseason games in the South.

The Falcons, Dolphins, and Saints joining the rank of professional teams undoubtedly had an effect on the Redskins and other professional football franchises playing preseason games in the South. The new franchises sprouting up in the South meant the beginning of the end of neutral-site preseason games in the South. As late as 1962, there were a record number of exhibition games played by the NFL and AFL—seven in each league. After the 1964 season and the AFL All-Star Game boycott in early 1965, fewer and fewer preseason games were played in the South. There were several factors behind this. One was the previously mentioned decline of George Preston Marshall and the number of Redskins exhibition games in the South. Additionally, professional teams got to where they didn't want to give up the revenue a home preseason game would bring. Finally, as more franchises were added in the South, southern cities no longer had the need to try to lure pro football teams to their cities in hope of someday securing a franchise. The only neutral-site exhibition game played anymore is the Pro Football Hall of Fame game at Fawcett Stadium in Canton, which coincides with the Hall of Fame induction the last week of July.

All of the factors mentioned herein meant that fewer and fewer neutral-site preseason games were played in the South. In 1971, for the first time since the end of World War II, no neutral-site exhibition games were played in the South. Only a smattering of neutral-site preseason games were played in the South by the mid-1970s, and by the time the NFL went to a sixteen-game schedule in 1978, the practice ended.

Finally, the boycott of the AFL All-Star Game in New Orleans in January 1965, coupled with mid-1960s civil rights legislation like the Voting Rights Act of 1965 (which eliminated poll taxes and literacy tests as a prerequisite to vote in southern states, thus opening the door for African Americans to vote), helped lead up to the most well-known protest by African American athletes—the Cleveland Summit of 1967. The protest, which was the brainchild of Jim Brown, probably the most famous African American athlete in the mid-1960s, was in fact organized by a couple of former Browns teammates, John Wooten and Walter Beach, who themselves had faced discrimination and blackballing during their professional football careers. The Cleveland Summit included the most famous black athletes of the day, including Bill Russell, Lew Alcindor (now Kareem

Abdul-Jabbar), Willie Davis, and Bobby Mitchell. The meeting was held to show support for boxer Muhammad Ali, whose 1967 decision to not serve in the U.S. Army during the Vietnam War era because of his religious beliefs cost him his heavyweight crown.

The Cleveland Summit had its roots in Miami three years earlier. In January 1964, the Cleveland Browns played the Packers in the Playoff Bowl. Much of Miami was still segregated then, but the Browns were able to stay together in the same hotel on Miami Beach. After practice, African American players on both the Browns and Packers would gather at a famous black night spot called Sir John's Club. It was in the Overtown district of the city, just northwest of downtown. Overtown (originally called Colored Town) was the black part of Miami. Through the years, many famous entertainers, including Count Basie, Louis Armstrong, Ella Fitzgerald, and Billie Holliday, played in clubs there. Unable to spend the night after they played a gig at a Miami Beach hotel, the black performers had to stay "over town" in their black hotels because of segregation laws, thus giving Overtown its name.

As chance would have it, the boxer then known as Cassius Clay, who was in Miami training for his first championship bout with Sonny Liston, frequented Sir John's Club with his entourage. Clay struck up a friendship with the Browns and Packers players—especially Jim Brown. This chance encounter eventually led to the Cleveland Summit three years later. John Wooten later admitted, "The summit in Cleveland to support Ali never would have happened if we hadn't met him at the Sir John's Club in Miami."

Wooten elaborated,

Let me give you some background about how we came to support Ali. Ali was a strong supporter of the Negro Industrial Economic Union [NIEU] that had been founded by Jim Brown. He and some other players put it together, and there were chapters in Cleveland, where the headquarters were; Washington, DC; Harlem; Oakland; Los Angeles; and Kansas City. Ali, besides morally supporting the organization, also supported it very generously financially.

When we played the Packers in Miami after the 1963 season, we met Ali at the Sir John Hotel and Club, a popular spot for blacks in Miami. Ali was training there to fight Sonny Liston. We all hung out at the Sir John's Club, along with black doctors, lawyers, teachers, and other professionals. Three or so years later when Ali refused to step forward in Houston to be inducted into the army, we already had a relationship with him and also knew him because he had supported the Black Eco-

nomic Union [BEU, with its name changed from the NEIU in 1966].
As you know, they stripped him of his title and they were possibly going
to put him in jail for being a draft dodger.

That's when Jim Brown came to Ali's aid. Jim called me and said,
"We gotta stand by the Champ." We decided we were going to meet
in Cleveland. I started calling people, and everyone who I called, who
are in the famous photograph, came without hesitation. No one asked,
"Who's gonna pay?" They all said, "When do you want me to come?"

Now when Ali came to Cleveland, we all met with him first to make
sure he was sincere and serious before we went public. Ali explained to
us that he was an ordained black minister of Islam and that he did not
believe in war or in killing people. That was good enough for us. We
sided with him. Once we got behind the Champ, we also didn't worry
about any repercussions. It was never discussed among us.

Walter Beach, who had been friends with Brown as well as his teammate on the Browns, was also at the Cleveland Summit. Five years earlier,
Beach had been blackballed by the AFL for leading a protest by African
American Boston Patriots players against accommodations when they went
to New Orleans. He recalled,

1967 Cleveland Summit. *John Wooten*

Jim and I stayed close. In fact, in June 1967, I got a call from Jim. He wanted me to be part of a group of black athletes who would consider backing Muhammad Ali's refusal to be drafted into the army. That's where the famous picture comes from, and that's why I'm in it.

That's the first time, and I think the only time, that many prominent black athletes got together to support one of their own. We were unified in our support of Ali. I was working for Cleveland mayor Carl B. Stokes at the time, who was the first black mayor of Cleveland and I believe of any major American city. It was a special moment—it was one of the most important events of my life. We came together as black men, not as pro athletes. Ali had the courage to take a stand and we stood beside him.

★ ★ ★

Through adversity came unity, and through trial came strength.

When black athletes from all walks rallied to defend one of their own at the Cleveland Summit, it was a groundbreaking moment for professional sports in America. Everything had led up to that very instant—where arm in arm, a solid front line had formed to defend the right to religious freedom of the most popular and beloved boxer in the world. Here was a powerful African American athlete standing strong to protest injustice. He did not stand alone, voicing his opinion with his fellow competitors from all disciplines by his side.

For pro football, the era of exhibition games in the Deep South had ended. Franchises were established throughout the South—and in those stands, black and white fans alike learned to cheer on and celebrate the feats of both black and white players, perhaps with dwindling regard for discriminatory practices and the politics of race as time moved forward beyond the forties through the sixties, into the seventies and on to the present day.

The civil rights movement had made incredible strides for all people in the United States. And professional sports would never be the same. Through the concerted efforts of players, owners, and at times even fans, the chain of cause and effect became blurred. The game that came to be known as America's favorite sport marched along the same road of progress as the great nation that birthed it. Players became protestors and progressive leaders. Activists became fans and football enthusiasts. Both were one and the same. And through many trials over the course of many years, these brave, progressive figures contributed to protect and uplift a sacred bond and ritual as old as humanity itself—the art of play.

What is it about the practice of play that seems to touch the core of who we are as human beings? Perhaps it is because we are called to return to our youthful innocence when we engage in a game. Martin Luther King Jr. had a dream that "little black boys and black girls will be able to join hands with little white boys and white girls as sisters and brothers." Some could say that sports invites us to play again like children and rediscover that innocence. No matter how big the budget or the crowd, it is the core component of teamwork that keeps the ball moving down the field. Teamwork requires unity. And through unity comes strength.

The road to the Cleveland Summit was a steep and treacherous incline without a peak or ending point. That uphill road continues on as the legacy of protest in professional sports and entertainment pushes our society further along in the quest for equality, even today. Continuing along that road will require increased endurance and training as we travel and refine the path first carved out by those who came before us, that their stories be known, remembered, and upheld with due respect and honor, earning their rightful place in both sports history and American history. They remain as pioneers and founders of America's favorite sport, but also pillars of strength in the push for a better world—those who dared to live and play in Dixie.

BIBLIOGRAPHY

BOOKS

Atwood, Gretchen. *Lost Champions: Four Men, Two Teams, and the Breaking of Pro Football's Color Line*. New York: Bloomsbury, 2016.

Beach, Walter. *Consider This*. Rock Hill, SC: New World Media, 2014.

Boyles, Royce, and Dave Robinson. *The Lombardi Impact: Twenty People Who Were Brushed by Greatness*. Rock Springs, WI: Rock Springs Publishers, 2011.

———. *The Lombardi Legacy: Thirty People Who Were Touched by Greatness*. Louisville, KY: Goose Creek Publishers, 2009.

Boyles, Royce, and Herb Adderley. *Lombardi's Left Side*. Olathe, KS: Ascend Books, 2012.

Brown, Paul, and Jack Clary. *PB: The Paul Brown Story*. New York: Atheneum, 1979.

Cantor, George. *Paul Brown: The Man Who Invented Modern Football*. Chicago: Triumph, 2008.

Carroll, Kevin. *Houston Oilers: The Early Years*. Fort Worth, TX: Eakin Press, 2001.

Davis, Willie, with Jim Martyka and Andrea Erickson Davis. *Closing the Gap: Lombardi, the Packers Dynasty, and the Pursuit of Excellence*. Chicago: Triumph, 2012.

Dixon, Dave. *The Saints, the Superdome, and the Scandal: An Insider's Perspective*. Gretna, LA: Pelican, 2008.

Eisenberg, John. *Cotton Bowl Days: Growing Up with Dallas and the Cowboys in the 1960s*. New York: Simon and Schuster, 1997.

———. *Ten Gallon War: The NFL's Cowboys, the AFL's Texans, and the Feud for Dallas's Pro Football Future*. Boston: Houghton Mifflin Harcourt, 2012.

Golenbock, Peter. *Landry's Boys: An Oral History of a Team and an Era*. Chicago: Triumph, 1997.

Herskowitz, Mickey. *The Golden Age of Pro Football: NFL Football in the 1950s*. Dallas, TX: Taylor, 1974.

Jacobs, Proverb. *Autobiography of an Unknown Football Player.* Bloomington, IN: AuthorHouse, 2014.

Klobuchar, Jim. *True Hearts and Purple Heads: An Unauthorized Biography of a Football Team.* Minneapolis, MN: Ross and Haines, 1970.

Knight, Dawn. *Taliaferro: Breaking Barriers from the NFL Draft to the Ivory Tower.* Bloomington: Indiana University Press, 2007.

Levy, Alan. *Tackling Jim Crow: Racial Segregation in Professional Football.* Jefferson, NC: McFarland, 2003.

Maraniss, David. *When Pride Still Mattered: A Life of Vince Lombardi.* New York: Simon and Schuster, 1999.

Miller, Jeff. *Going Long: The Wild 10-Year Saga of the Renegade American Football League in the Words of Those Who Lived It.* New York: McGraw-Hill, 2003.

Moore, Lenny, with Jeffrey Jay Ellish. *All Things Being Equal: The Autobiography of Lenny Moore.* Champaign, IL: Sports Publishing, 2005.

O'Toole, Andrew. *Paul Brown: The Rise and Fall and Rise Again of Football's Most Innovative Coach.* Cincinnati, OH: Clerisy, 2008.

Patrick, Latrina. *The Brady Keys Jr. Story: Overcoming Adversity by Staying within the Blessing.* Albany, NY: Keys Group, 1999.

Piascik, Andy. *The Best Show in Football: The 1946–1955 Cleveland Browns.* New York: Taylor Trade, 2007.

———. *Gridiron Gauntlet: The Story of the Men Who Integrated Pro Football in Their Own Words.* New York: Taylor Trade, 2009.

Rappoport, Ken. *The Little League That Could: A History of the American Football League.* New York: Taylor Trade, 2010.

Ross, Charles. *Mavericks, Money, and Men: The AFL, Black Players, and the Evolution of Modern Football.* Philadelphia, PA: Temple University Press, 2016.

———. *Outside the Lines: African Americans and the Integration of the National Football League.* New York: New York University Press, 1999.

Ryczek, William. *Crash of the Titans: The Early Years of the New York Jets and the AFL.* Kingston, NY: Total Sports, 2000.

Smith, Thomas G. *Showdown: JFK and the Integration of the Washington Redskins.* Boston: Beacon, 2011.

Webster, Gary. *The League That Didn't Exist: A History of the All-America Football Conference, 1946–1949.* Jefferson, NC: McFarland, 2019.

NEWSPAPERS

Aberdeen Daily World
Abilene Reporter News
Adrian Daily Telegram
Akron Beacon Journal
Albuquerque Journal

Alexandria Town Talk
Ames Daily Tribune
Anniston Star
Appleton Post-Crescent
Arizona Republic
Ashville Citizen Times
Atlanta Constitution
Baltimore Sun
Battle Creek Enquirer
Baytown Sun
Berkshire Eagle
Binghamton Press and Sun Bulletin
Brownsville Herald
Brownwood Bulletin
Bryan Eagle
Chicago Daily Tribune
Cincinnati Enquirer
Clarion Ledger
Connellsville Daily Courier
Corpus Christi Caller Times
Corsicana Daily Sun
Corvallis Gazette-Times
Cumberland News
Delaware County Daily Times
Detroit Free Press
East Liverpool Review
Eureka Humboldt Standard
Farmington Daily Times
Fort Lauderdale News
Fresno Bee
Galveston Daily News
Greeley Daily Tribune
Green Bay Press Gazette
Greenwood Commonwealth
Hampton Roads Daily Press
Hartford Courant
Hazleton Plain Speaker
Houston Forward Times
Houston Informer
Jackson Clarion Ledger
Kerrville Mountain Sun
Kingsport Times-News
La Crosse Review Tribune

Lake Charles American Press
Lansing State Journal
Lincoln Evening Journal
Long Beach Independent
Los Angeles Times
Louisville Courier Journal
Lubbock Avalanche Journal
Lubbock Evening Journal
Lubbock Morning Avalanche
McKinney Courier-Gazette
Miami News
Minneapolis Star Tribune
Minnesota Spokesman-Recorder
Montgomery Advertiser
Muncie Star Press
Nashville Tennessean
New York Age
Newark Advocate
Oakland Tribune
Odessa American
Oshkosh Northwestern
Palm Beach Post
Pampa Daily News
Paris News
Pasadena Independent-Star News
Pensacola News Journal
Philadelphia Daily News
Philadelphia Inquirer
Pittsburgh Courier
Pittsburgh Post-Gazette
Pittsburgh Press
Pocono Record
Racine Journal Times
Raleigh Register
Richmond Palladium-Item
Salem Statesman Journal
Salina Journal
San Saba News
Sandusky Register
Santa Barbara Independent
Santa Fe New Mexican
Shreveport Times
Sioux Falls Argus Leader

Somerset Daily American
South Jersey Courier-Post
Tallahassee Democrat
Terre Haute Tribune
Traverse City Record Eagle
Tucson Daily Citizen
USA Today
Valley Morning Star
Waco News Tribune
Waco Tribune Herald
Warren County Observer
Weirton Daily Times
Windsor Star

INTERVIEWS

Arbanas, Fred, April 11, 2017
Balthazar, George, July 12, 2017
Barnett, Tom, March 2, 2017
Bates, Ted, March 23, 2017, April 26, 2017
Beach, Walter, April 12, 2017
Boyette, Garland, May 17, 2015, May 23, 2017
Bradley, Harold, August 1, 2017
Brooker, Tommy, May 10, 2017
Brown, Robert, May 20, 2018
Brown, Roger, March 4, 2017
Bullocks, Amos, April 14, 2017
Burford, Chris, April 26, 2017
Caleb, Jamie, March 11, 2017
Clarke, Frank, May 26, 2015, February 26, 2017
Coffey, Junior, July 24, 2016, March 5, 2017
Cole, Emerson, April 11, 2017
Colo, Don, February 22, 2017
Cronin, Gene, February 4, 2019
Daniels, Clem, July 6, 2015, February 22, 2017, March 24, 2017, April 26, 2018
Davidson, Cotton, April 26, 2017
Denson, Al, June 30, 2017
Disch, Jimmy, May 6, 2017
Donahue, Oscar, May 1, 2017
Dotson, Alphonse, September 8, 2015
Dowler, Boyd, June 9, 2015
Ferguson, Charles, April 14, 2017

Fleming, Marv, August 17, 2015, March 27, 2017
Flores, Tom, April 11, 2017
Ford, Henry, March 20, 2017
Ford, Rochelle, March 20, 2017
Garron, Larry, February 28, 2017
Gilliam, Frank, July 19, 2016, November 2, 2017
Gilliam, Jon, July 1, 2017
Granderson, Rufus, July 6, 2015
Granger, Charles, July 10, 2017
Grant, Bud, February 15, 2017
Gray, Moses, April 21, 2018
Green, Cornell, April 17, 2017
Green, Credell, April 22, 2018
Groman, Bill, April 10, 2015, April 2, 2017
Harris Bill, August 5, 2015
Haynes, Abner, July 23, 2016, April 8, 2017, April 29, 2017
Hennigan, Charlie, April 10, 2015
Hollis, Wilburn, April 17, 2017
Holmes, Charles, May 12, 2017
Hood, Bob, February 6, 2019
Howard, Sherman, April 7, 2016, March 21, 2017, April 15, 2017
Irvin, Willie, March 12, 2017
Jamison, Al, April 17, 2017
Joe, Billy, June 30, 2017
Jones, Dub, April 5, 2017
Kercher, Dick, February 6, 2019
Keys, Brady, February 28, 2017
Kramer, Jerry, March 28, 2017
Landrieu, Moon, May 10, 2017
Lanphear, Dan, April 25, 2017
Lundgren, Hal, March 12, 2015
Macon, Eddie, January 12, 2015
Macon-Gayles, Marilyn, December 5, 2017
Marchetti, Gino, April 3, 2016, March 24, 2017
Martin, Blanche, May 9, 2017
McClairen, Jack, March 3, 2017
McMillan, Ernie, February 27, 2017
Mestnik, Frank, March 31, 2017
Miller, Red, June 30, 2017
Mingo, Gene, February 26, 2017, March 5, 2017, June 28, 2017
Mitchell, Bobby, March 11, 2017
Moore, Lenny, February 27, 2017, March 27, 2017
Ortmann, Chuck, March 21, 2017

Perry, Maxine, April 26, 2018
Petrich, Bob, January 16, 2019
Powell, Preston, November 15, 2016
Reed, Bobby, April 20, 2017
Reid, Joseph, April 3, 2016
Renfro, Mel, August 17, 2015
Roberts, C. R., March 8, 2017
Roberts, Walt, August 17, 2015, March 5, 2017
Robinson, Dave, April 4, 2017, April 15, 2017
Sanders, Lonnie, April 5, 2017
Switzer, Veryl, March 10, 2017
Talamini, Bob, April 17, 2017
Taliaferro, George, April 5, 2016, March 22, 2017
Taliaferro, Viola, April 5, 2016
Taylor, Lionel, February 26, 2017, June 29, 2017
Thomas, John, April 5, 2017
Toburen, Nelson, April 3, 2017
Toth, Zollie, April 3, 2016
Triplett, Leonore, April 5, 2016
Triplett, Wally, April 5, 2016
Washington, Gene, April 30, 2015, May 5, 2015
Watkins, Bobby, March 10, 2017
West, Willie, March 3, 2017, June 29, 2017
Williams, Robert, April 8, 2019
Williams, Sid, December 8, 2017
Witcher, Al, April 19, 2017
Womack, Joe, April 12, 2017
Wooten, John, May 21, 2015, February 9, 2017, September 6, 2017
Young, Geraldine, April 4, 2016
Youngblood, George, March 5, 2017
Zatkoff, Roger, February 4, 2019

INDEX

Page numbers in *italics* refer to images and photos.